Strategic
Alignment

Woodslane Press Pty Ltd
7/5 Vuko Place, Warriewood, NSW 2102
Email: info@woodslane.com.au
Website: www.woodslane.com.au

First edition published in 2004 by Richmond Ventures
This second edition published in 2010 by Woodslane Press

This edition © 2010 Woodslane Press, text © 2004 and 2010 Dr Norman Chorn and Terry Hunter

This work is copyright. All rights reserved. Apart from any fair dealing for the purposes of study, research or review, as permitted under Australian copyright law, no part of this publication may be reproduced, distributed, or transmitted in any other form or by any means, including photocopying, recording, or other electronic or mechanical methods, without the prior written permission of the publisher. For permission requests, write to the publisher, addressed "Attention: Permissions Coordinator", at the address above. Every effort has been made to obtain permissions relating to information reproduced in this publication. The information in this publication is based upon the current state of commercial and industry practice and the general circumstances as at the date of publication. No person shall rely on any of the contents of this publication and the publisher and the author expressly exclude all liability for direct and indirect loss suffered by any person resulting in any way from the use or reliance on this publication or any part of it. Any opinions and advice are offered solely in pursuance of the author's and publisher's intention to provide information, and have not been specifically sought.

National Library of Australia Cataloguing-in-Publication entry

Author:	Chorn, Norman.
Title:	Strategic alignment: How to align the organisation with its current and future environment / Norman Chorn.
Edition:	2nd ed.
ISBN:	9781921606311 (pbk.)
Note:	Includes index
Subjects:	Strategic planning.
	Management.
	Organizational change.
Dewey Number:	658.4012

Design and layout by Alexandra Berthold and Vanessa Wilton
Printed in China

Strategic Alignment

How to align the organisation with its current and future environment

2ND EDITION

Norman Chorn
with Terri Hunter

Strategic Alignment

Contents

FOREWORD TO THE SECOND EDITION..vii

ACKNOWLEDGMENTS ix

INTRODUCTION: HOW I GOT HERE xi

CHAPTER 1: Creating organisational effectiveness.............................1

CHAPTER 2: Describing environment, strategy, culture and leadership by considering behaviour.........................19

CHAPTER 3: Understanding your operating environment.................35

CHAPTER 4: Developing a winning strategy......................................71

CHAPTER 5: Developing an appropriate culture................................79

CHAPTER 6: Leading the organisation to strategic alignment........133

CHAPTER 7: Designing your organisation for strategic alignment.....153

CHAPTER 8: Inducing change to create strategic alignment...........195

CHAPTER 9: Aligning with the new normal......................................221

APPENDIX 1: Theoretical basis of strategic alignment.....................235

APPENDIX 2: PADI ideal types...243

APPENDIX 3: Strategic alignment diagnostic...................................249

REFERENCES 255

INDEX 259

ABOUT THE AUTHORS 264

Strategic Alignment

Foreword
to the second edition

Since the first edition was published in 2004, much has happened to change the way we think about organisations and the environments in which they operate.

The global financial crisis (GFC) has been significant to this change. The breakdown in confidence within the global financial system and the deep recession it pre-empted, has provided an extremely difficult set of conditions for organisations, both in developing and developed economies. While the history of the GFC is still being written and interpreted, we know that many organisations failed, or had to make painful adjustments during these difficult economic conditions.

Some speculate that our current ways of thinking about management and organisations are outmoded and that they no longer fit the requirements of the communities they serve. Analysts point to questionable practices by leaders that may have contributed to the high number of corporate failures. But many organisations, without excessive or "high-flying" practices, also failed or had to make painful adjustments in order to survive.

What can we learn from this difficult period from which we are now beginning to emerge? Are there practices and processes that can improve our ability to survive these environmental shocks? Some may argue that the jolt from the GFC was so profound that little could have been done to anticipate and survive it.

This may be true, but we have observed some interesting characteristics from organisations that display high levels of durability during times of change and crisis. While this may not be the whole answer to the issue of long-term survival, these so-called "resilient" organisations offer useful insights into practices that promote longer-term prosperity.

As a consequence of this period of turbulence and intense reflection, I have thought long and hard about the approach of **Strategic Alignment** outlined in this book. The so-called conditions of "new normal" – where discontinuity, uncertainty and change have become the norm – have prompted me to re-examine certain aspects of organisations and their strategies as they cope with these conditions. The issues of new organisational capabilities and alternative organisation designs have also required some attention.

I believe that the essential tenets of **Strategic Alignment** are still valid under the conditions of the "new normal", but I have added an additional chapter to deal with some of the additional complexities in aligning the organisation with these conditions. Chapter 9, *Aligning with the New Normal,* examines how leaders can create some of the capabilities and approaches that are necessary for coping and thriving in the post GFC environment.

Dr Norman Chorn
norman.chorn@centstrat.com
www.centstrat.com

Acknowledgments

The ideas for this book were initially conceived while completing my doctoral research in South Africa during the early 1980's. When I moved to Australia, I had the opportunity to develop them further in my consulting, research and teaching.

Since them, my colleagues and I have been using the frameworks and models in a range of different applications. They have been referred to and applied in research papers, articles and consulting assignments. The feedback I have received from these applications has been invaluable in refining and further developing the concepts.

In a sense then, this book is an attempt to capture all my experiences and views on the concept of Strategic Alignment. But I am clear that this would not have been possible save for the efforts of a number of people.

My colleagues at Centre for Corporate Strategy deserve special mention. Ivan Nurick, Nandi Herholdt, Tom Hannemann and others played an important role in giving me feedback and helping to develop certain aspects of the models. To them, I am very grateful. Indeed, a number of my associates have embraced and used the Strategic Alignment concepts in their own consulting models – I guess that imitation is the highest compliment I could receive!

Over the years, my clients have used and embraced the frameworks with enthusiasm and have helped me to see how they may be applied in the understanding of organisations and their effectiveness. Some of them are mentioned in the book. Others have contributed to the insights I have gained along the way. I thank you for the opportunity of working with you and affording me the "live" case studies.

The Strategic Alignment framework has also been the subject of many programs at universities in Australia, New Zealand, South Africa and the United Kingdom. Many of these students have used the frameworks in their research assignments and given me material to use in my teaching and consulting.

I am grateful to Andrew Swaffer at Woodslane Publishing for the guidance and encouragement while preparing the second edition. Alex Berthold did a wonderful job of layout, editing and generally improving the look and feel of the book.

Finally, none of his would have been possible without the unstinting support and expert contribution made by my wife Terri. It was she who persuaded me to write the book in the first instance, and then proceeded to support me in every way while I worked my way through it.

Moreover, Terri contributed to the cases and examples referred to in the book. She also provides the important psychological viewpoint I relied on so heavily to develop and refine some of the concepts in the first place. To you, Terri, I owe a special gratitude.

Introduction

How I got here

"Another bloody management book?"

This was the reaction from a number of managers and executives when I told them what I had been doing for the last months. And I can understand their scepticism and disbelief that yet another book might be written that purported to tell them how to add value to their customers; how to focus their strategy or how to re-engineer their organisation.

Most organisations I know are involved in so many different simultaneous initiatives that their management has difficulty in knowing where to allocate their time and effort. All too often, the new initiative is the result of some "breakthrough" approach in the latest management text.

Often, when conducting a strategy session with a client, I am asked questions like:

➤ So where does this fit in with the new performance management program we began last year?

➤ Is the restructure still going ahead?

➤ And what happened to the change management program we started three years ago?

Managers don't need another "breakthrough" initiative. They don't need another management text suggesting new ways of improving the performance of their organisation. They are too busy sorting out how to manage with all the existing approaches and initiatives!

So why have I written this book? What value am I hoping to add to the already overcrowded sections of management texts available in bookstores and lining the shelves of manager's offices?

The most common requests I have from managers and executives relate to how they can make sense of it all:

> How can we respond to all these customer requests without getting the staff offside?

> How can I keep the board and shareholders happy while dealing with our competitors?

> Where should I be spending my time to maximise my impact?

> How can we improve our performance now while still investing for the future?

> What do my staff really want – how do I motivate them and improve the enthusiasm in this organisation?

It seems to me that managers are looking for ways of navigating through the complexities of customers, strategy, organisational culture and leadership. They want some clarity in how to deal with competing demands for their time. And they want to know how they can improve the performance of their organisation and people now and into the future.

I have written this book in the hope that the insights herein will provide some guidance as to how to make sense of it all. I have tried to distil some of the lessons learned through my 25 years of experience in industry, consulting and research.

My colleagues and I have observed and worked with successful and unsuccessful management teams. We have researched the change management and performance improvement practices of some 320 medium-large Australian and multi-national organisations. And I have interviewed over 200 senior and general managers in order to understand the challenges and complexities of leading both private and public sector organisations.

Through all of this, I have learned some things about organisational effectiveness that I hope can be of some use to you. I have also learned a great deal about myself and my own behaviour. I hope that this, too, can be of some value as we consider our own journeys through organisations.

What this book is about

The book, in some way, mirrors the journey of learning I have taken in my career. Unbeknown to me at the time, my early research quest in South Africa, trying to understand organisations and their effectiveness, was leading me in a direction that would bring understanding of my own behaviour.

As I carried out my research and worked with organisations, the woman who was to become my wife was on her own quest to understand individual and team behaviours in organisations. Terri Hunter and I started from quite different perspectives, but these two focuses were eventually to bring us together.

My early concerns in my management, teaching and consulting career were about making the organisation more effective within its current and emerging environment. Consequently, I focused on understanding and meeting customer needs; achieving competitive advantage and managing cultural change through effective leadership. It was a very systems-oriented perspective and addressed people and their learning as mere "elements" within the overall system.

My work fitted loosely with what theorists today call the "positioning" school of strategic management, and is best represented by the various contributions of Harvard's Michael Porter and others (eg, Porter (1980, 1985), Mintzberg

(1978, 1979). The focus of this school of thought is to ensure that the organisation adapts to the demands of the competitive environment and customer needs. Accordingly, the approach addresses how well the various parts of the organisation "fit" the demands of the environment and customer needs.

Terri's work, on the other hand, was concerned with the contribution made by individuals and teams to organisational effectiveness. It emphasised the issues of learning and development in people and teams, and the resultant impact on organisations. She helped me to understand that there are other very valid perspectives to adopt when seeking to understand effectiveness in organisations. I learned that it was possible to synthesise the "hard" approaches of competitive advantage and strategic positioning with the "soft" approach of learning and cultural development.

As a consequence, my attention shifted beyond the current market and competitive environment towards a study of the future and the development of new organisational capabilities – how organisations *can* develop strategy and capabilities in the face of increasing uncertainty and change. I focused on scenario planning and organisational learning as ways of understanding and managing the future competitive environment of the organisation.

This approach may be termed the "learning" school of thought, and was popularised by the works of Schwartz & Davis (1981), Van der Heijden et al (2002) and de Geus (1988). The approach seeks to study and understand the nature of alternative futures that may be faced by the organisation, and then to equip the organisation to deal with these. It also assists the organisation to select a "preferred" future and to pursue a course of action to maximise the chances of achieving it.

The two approaches are compared in the table overleaf:

	Positioning	Learning
Underlying basis of strategy	A fit between the organisation and market opportunities	Developing the capabilities necessary for current and future opportunities
Competitive advantage achieved through…	Good positioning and differentiation of product / service offering	Out-thinking and out-planning the competition
Survival of small players through…	Finding and defending a niche in the market	Flexibility through studying and understanding the evolution of the market
Risk reduced through…	Developing a portfolio of products or businesses	Developing a range of capabilities for alternative conditions and markets
Centre invests in….	Strategies of the various business units	Learning and development, strategic planning

These two approaches are quite different in their philosophies, research and even consulting/planning tools. They may even be described as somewhat contradictory, because they start from such different premises. While the positioning school begins from the "outside" and works in, the learning approach starts within the organisation and works out.

Accordingly, one has to be careful in using both approaches simultaneously as they are based on different assumptions about the way that success is achieved. However, if applied appropriately, both can be used to provide useful insights for improving performance and moving the organisation forward.

This book is about how we might use both of these perspectives to make our organisations more effective. It demonstrates that there are ways to create sense out of confusion by using two seemingly contradictory approaches in an holistic way.

What you could gain from reading this book

- ► You will understand how the **Strategic Alignment** framework can assist you in understanding and diagnosing your organisation within its operating environment.

- ► You will be able to take steps to ensure that your operating environment, strategy, culture and leadership are working together, rather than at odds with each other, in order to improve the effectiveness of your organisation.

- ► You will understand the role of leadership in producing organisational effectiveness and designing organisations that are relevant to their environments.

Outline of the book

The first chapter addresses the issue of organisational effectiveness and introduces us to contingency theory – a key assumption underpinning the views expressed in the book. It also outlines the Strategic Alignment framework and demonstrates the linkages with organisational effectiveness.

Chapter 2 explores Strategic Alignment in more detail and outlines a Jungian-based model that is used to operationalise the concept. This "PADI" model is used throughout the book to explore the areas of environment, strategy, culture and leadership.

Chapter 3 examines the Operating Environment and its major elements. There is a particular focus on *customers* and the need to align with their needs in order for the organisation to be effective and relevant.

Chapter 4 deals with the development of an appropriate *strategy* to meet customers' needs. It also explores the issues of balance, focus and competitive advantage in more detail.

Chapter 5 focuses on the issue of *culture* in organisations. It deals with the description, classification and measurement of culture, and also outlines the different approaches to align it with strategy and the organisation's needs. Shaping organisational culture is also discussed in some detail.

Leadership and its role in producing strategic alignment and organisational effectiveness is covered in Chapter 6. The significant leverage of leadership in shaping the culture is also discussed.

Chapter 7 deals with the difficult issue of *organisation design and structure*. The key dimensions and principles of organisation design are outlined, and a summary checklist is included to assist the manager.

Chapter 8 outlines a series of practical steps that can be taken to bring about strategic alignment in your organisation and deals with aspects of strategic and organisational change.

Finally Chapter 9 considers some of the more recent challenges brought on by the post GFC conditions, where environments display characteristics of undue discontinuity, uncertainty and change, the so-called "new normal". New approaches to designing organisations and strategy are considered in order to equip the organisation for the future.

Strategic Alignment

Chapter 1
Creating organisational effectiveness

Effective organisations

From the very beginning of my working career, I was interested in how to make organisations more effective. As a customer in a retail store or as a student working in a restaurant, I had a fascination with the different ways organisations seem to function.

Some organisations seemed to work so smoothly and efficiently, while others failed to meet the expectations of customers – no matter how hard the staff tried. There seemed to be so many different factors at work in making it effective or ineffective, that trying to understand this became something of a quest for me.

I was acutely interested in the different theories of organisation effectiveness and tried to read them all. But there were so many, and they often contradicted each other. And so, by default, I arrived at my own understanding of how organisations become effective – by eliminating those theories that didn't make sense to me or that failed to provide insight.

In the end, every theory or model has some value to add. Theories are like windows to the world – they offer you different perspectives that are valid to different degrees. From my research experience I learned that the ultimate test of a good theory does not necessarily depend on how closely it resembles reality, but rather, on the quality of the insights that it affords you.

In Search of Excellence in an organisation

The consulting and research work of Peters and Waterman (1982) in their best-seller *In Search of Excellence* did much to popularise the notion that there are certain attributes which highly effective organisations share. While it is true that the book and their popularity spawned a raft of "excellence" research and many books with "excellence" in the title, their work forms part of a larger body of knowledge that might be termed "trait" or "attribute" theory.

In the view of the trait and attribute theorists, effective organisations share a set of common attributes that make them effective. In order to develop effectiveness, therefore, organisations have to develop attributes such as:

- Tight focus on customers and markets;
- Flat structures;
- Decentralised controls;
- Empowered staff;
- A concentration on core activities;
- Controls that are both loose and tight;
- Team structures;
- Consultative decision-making.

These approaches have highlighted how various strategies, structures and processes may be used to drive the effectiveness of an organisation. But their limitation is that they do not adequately distinguish between different organisations in different contexts.

They do not explain, for example, how two organisations with completely different strategies, cultures, leadership styles and structures can both be highly effective and successful. Consider the example on the previous page of

	Advertising agency	Gold mine
Primary focus	Customers and market	Production processes
Structure	Flat	Relatively hierarchical
Controls	Decentralised	Relatively centralised
Decision-making	Consultative	Analytical, relatively centralised

an advertising agency and a gold mine. They would have little in common with respect to their focus, structures, controls or decision-making.

I recognise how artificial this comparison is, but it does illustrate an important point – the attributes that define an effective organisation are not universal. They depend on many factors such as:

- Market conditions;
- Customer expectations;
- Management preferences;
- Staff needs and capabilities;
- Technology availability.

Perhaps this is why many of the organisations held up as examples of excellence by Peters and Waterman (1982) were in decline some two years later (see the article "Whoops!" in *Business Week*). The problem with a number of these organisations is that they had failed to *remain relevant* to their markets, available technology and so on.

It would seem, therefore, that the attributes of effectiveness are contingent upon other factors in the environment and within the organisation. So the important contribution of these theories is that they highlight some of the factors that can be used to drive effectiveness, but they *do not represent universally desirable attributes in an organisation.*

Because of this, we need to be careful of attempting to create effectiveness in one organisation by simply emulating the "excellent" attributes found in another.

A contingency approach

In contrast to the trait theories, the contingency approach recognises that the requirements for effectiveness depend on the prevailing conditions, such as the market, technology and existing capabilities. Like the trait theories, there is a long list of contributors to this school of thought.

Alfred Chandler (1962) made a major contribution to our understanding of effectiveness in different contexts when he undertook a longitudinal study of some 20 major US organisations. He found that the form of the organisation should shift in response to changes in environmental conditions and that certain organisational forms were suited to particular environmental conditions.

Chandler argued that the strategy of the organisation (in response to environmental conditions) would give rise to a specific organisational form. When this strategy produced a "fit" with the environment, and the organisational form produced a "fit" with the strategy, the organisation enjoyed higher levels of economic return. In other words, when the particular strategy was associated with a particular environment and particular organisational form, the combination produced higher levels of effectiveness.

This is the essence of contingency theory: the nature of the effectiveness depends on the context. The effective strategy depends on the environment, and the effective organisational form (structure) depends on the strategy. Chandler defined the terms of the so-called *Strategy – Structure* debate, and his work gave rise to many similar studies to research the contingency relationships that define effectiveness (Rumelt (1972, 1979), Channon (1973), Dyas (1972) Kono (1984)).

4 player.

Parallel to this is the contribution of those who have studied the relationships between environment and organisation form. Burns & Stalker (1961), Lawrence & Lorsch (1967) and Emory & Trist (1965) have demonstrated that the nature of an effective organisation is dependent upon the conditions in the environment.

As a result, contingency theory demonstrates that effectiveness is indeed driven by the presence of a number of desirable attributes, but the nature of these attributes depends upon the context. So, a flat structure (as in the case of an advertising agency) may be effective in certain conditions, but completely ineffective in another.

A lesson from the psychologists

In my discussion on this point with Terri, I learned that psychologists have had a similar raging debate for over one hundred years in their quest to explain human behaviour – the trait theorists versus the contingency/situational theorists!

It seems that a wise approach is to accept that both approaches have something of value to offer. The trait theories have identified the important dimensions and qualities that describe behaviour, while the contingency approach outlines how these apply in different circumstances and contexts.

Again, both theories offer windows to the world – but neither offers the door to the full truth!

I believe that we can learn from the psychologists and attempt to adopt a more holistic perspective that uses both approaches.

Looking at effectiveness in a holistic way

So far we know that that effectiveness can be driven by certain attributes, but the desirability of a particular attribute depends on the context of the situation. But this leads to several questions:

- Which attributes work in which context?

- When does a flat structure produce effectiveness? Or when do the conditions favour a more traditional hierarchical structure?

- When is it appropriate to have the production process rather than the customer as the primary focus?

- And when is it appropriate to have a consensus/consultative culture instead of one that emphasises empowerment and autonomy?

I believe that we can go some way to answering these questions if we consider the issue of effectiveness more holistically. In my PhD research conducted in South Africa, I found that it was useful to look at organisational effectiveness at four levels:

By considering each of the four areas, we can begin to examine the various combinations that produce effectiveness.

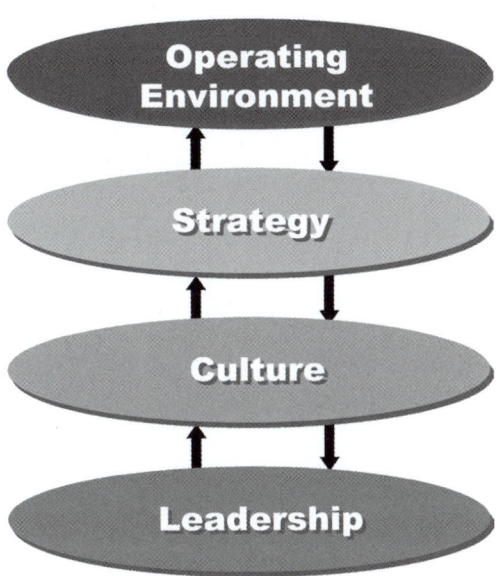

In short, we will show that organisational effectiveness can be explained and defined in terms of the particular combinations of environment, strategy, culture and leadership. In other words:

- Certain strategy types are best suited to certain environmental conditions;
- Specific cultural forms support specific strategies;
- Certain leadership styles are appropriate for certain cultures.

The specific nature of these relationships will be further discussed in the next chapter. But first, we will briefly consider each of the four areas in the *Strategic Alignment* framework.

1. The operating environment

The operating environment includes all the external constraints and possibilities that are placed on the organisation as it seeks to go about its business. This includes customers, shareholders, competitors, legislative requirements, technology and the like.

It is useful to think of the operating environment as *"the rules of the game"*, in that it determines the criteria by which organisations may be measured.

Strategic Alignment

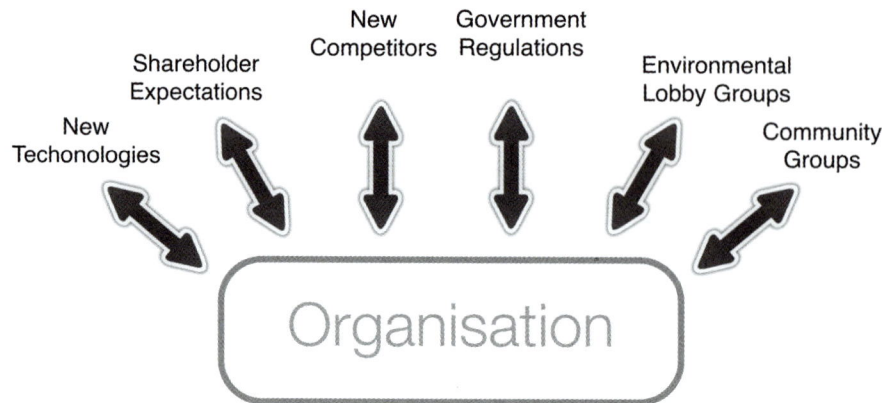

> If we consider the mobile phone company, Vodafone Australia, we could describe their operating environment ("rules of the game") as follows:
>
> ➤ Their customers have an expectation of good and reliable coverage, together with easy to understand, value-for-money call plans
>
> ➤ Management have to choose a strategic position with regard to the new G3 technologies that offer better data compression and faster download times
>
> ➤ Vodafone shareholders have an expectation that the company will earn an acceptable return on the large investment made in transmission infrastructure and retail stores
>
> ➤ New competitors like Orange and Virgin are entering the market with different positioning strategies
>
> ➤ Environmental lobby groups are becoming increasingly vocal about the electro-magnetic radiation (EMR) being emitted from the transmission towers and are resisting the installation of new towers in built-up areas

Chapter 1

> ➤ *Community groups are becoming more forceful in demanding better protection from the EMR emitted by handsets and are demanding more research and safeguards*

In many cases, the "rules" are not obvious or explicit. They usually need to be identified by *conscious enquiry and research*. In the next chapter I will discuss how we can describe and characterise these "rules", but for now it is important to recognise that the risk to the organisation will increase as soon as it breaks the rules or attempts to set new ones. (By the same token, this increased risk is often rewarded by greater returns in the future).

Ultimately, an organisation will choose whether it wishes to play by the rules (respond to customers' needs) or attempt to change the market by setting up new rules. Apple Computers set up new rules for the computing market when they launched their version of the personal computer – "Apple Macintosh". In their case, the risk of breaking the rules was well rewarded once the new product became successful and was accepted by the market.

Note that this definition of the operating environment is taken *at a point in time,* that is, the rules will change over time.

2. Strategy

Strategy is about choice. It is about assessing trade-offs and deciding to jump one way rather than another. Strategy is choosing which market, products, businesses and activities to engage in and how you will do it.

In this sense, it is useful to think of strategy as *"the way you play the game"*.

For the purpose of discussing organisational effectiveness, I have used the distinction made by Mintzberg between "intended strategy" and "realised strategy".

Strategic Alignment

While intended strategy represents the aims and intentions of the organisation, *realised strategy* refers to the actual patterns of behaviour displayed by the organisation in its operating environment. In other words, the *realised strategy* describes *what the organisation actually does*.

> In our example of Vodafone Australia, the business has a strategy of aggressively pursuing the domestic market, particularly the youth and "younger lifestyle" segments. This is evidenced by their heavy retail presence and the image they create with their television and print advertising.

Strategy is choosing which games to play and how you will play them

Culture is the capabilities needed to play the game

3. Culture

I have come across many definitions of organisational culture, but the one that seems to make the most sense is *"the way we do things around here"*. This refers to the patterns of behaviour that take place inside the organisation as it goes about its business. It would include the way that:

- Communication occurs through the organisation;
- Decisions are made;
- Rules, procedure and policies are implemented;
- Change is managed;
- The organisation responds to external influences and opportunities;
- Work tasks are allocated and rewarded;
- Performance is managed and rewarded.

Culture and strategy are opposite sides of the same coin. Strategy refers to the pattern of behaviours and actions that occur in the operating environment, while culture refers to the behaviour and actions that occur within the organisation. Because of this, *it is rare for an organisation to successfully change its strategy (outside) without altering its culture (inside).*

> *I have worked with the SPL Group for many years. They are Australia's largest and most successful wholesale distributor of hand-tools and hardware. They began business as a small wholesaler that focused on the needs of independent "mom and pop" hardware stores.*

In the 1970s, the independent hardware stores had great difficulty stocking smaller items such as nails, screws and small hand-tools, as these were all supplied loose by the wholesalers. This made merchandising, stock control and shrinkage a nightmare for the storekeepers. Zenith Hardware, as they were known in those days, revolutionised the industry by developing convenient, customer-friendly packaging for all the small, difficult-to-handle items of merchandise.

They built a strong business that was based on servicing the needs of the independent hardware store. As a result, their business grew and they became a leading player in the industry.

However, the industry began to change in the late 1980s with the entry and growth of the major chains into the market (BBC, Mitre 10, John Danks and others). As their market share grew, Zenith began to view these chains and "majors" as competitors, since they were taking business away from Zenith's traditional customer base (the independent, "mom and pop" stores). In addition, the culture and style of Zenith was not well aligned with the more sophisticated approach of the majors, who liked to develop national campaigns supported by large marketing programs.

In the late 1980s, Zenith merged with Siddons Ramset (manufacturers of tools and fasteners), and the resultant business ultimately became known as the SPL Group. Management recognised that one of the key challenges they faced was to build a business relationship with the majors, since they were rapidly gaining market share at the expense of the independents.

We quickly worked out that the culture of the SPL Group was not well suited to the purchasing and business style of the majors. In particular, we realised that the culture of the organisation had to change in order to allow the firm to pursue a strategy of sophisticated marketing and strategic partnering with the majors.

> *While the intended strategy of partnership with the majors was easy to develop, the ability to successfully implement this strategy was dependent on a change in culture within the organisation.*
>
> *The new culture was one that recognised the importance of the majors in the market and engaged in strategic partnerships for the development of more sophisticated marketing programs. The culture change took place over some 20 months with the active involvement of senior management in a range of initiatives. This included:*
>
> - *A change in the job descriptions and performance targets of the sales force;*
>
> - *Training in relationship and account management;*
>
> - *A series of "road shows" as management engaged in workshop discussions with the staff;*
>
> - *New performance appraisal approaches for staff.*
>
> *It took some three years until the cultural transformation was complete. While the business made progress in their strategy with the majors right from the outset, the full implementation of the new strategy only occurred once the cultural transformation was complete*

As the example above illustrates, we may describe culture as the *"organisation's ability to play the game"*.

Strategic Alignment

4. Leadership

Leadership shapes' the organisation's capabilities to play the game

Leaders craft the organisation's strategic direction and shape the culture to ensure that it is on course. Leadership *"shapes the organisation's capabilities to play the game"*.

We will discuss leadership in more depth in a later chapter, but for the present it is important to note that leadership is a multiple concept – there are many leaders within the organisation. When referring to leadership, we are usually referring to the so-called dominant coalition – the group that have the ability to shape the culture and strategic direction of the organisational unit under question.

We know from many other studies that there isn't one correct leadership style. In fact, it is more useful to speak of the most *appropriate leadership style* than the correct/best leadership style.

But how do we know which is the most appropriate leadership style? For that matter, how do we know which is the most appropriate culture for a particular strategy? Or operating environment? In other words, how do we develop an effective organisation?

Contingency theory tells us that the most appropriate strategy, culture or leadership approach depends on the context of the operating environment. But it does not always give us a clear indication of how to select the best combination of strategy, culture and leadership for a particular set of conditions in the operating environment. For that, we need to look at the *Strategic Alignment* framework.

Strategic Alignment as an indicator of effectiveness

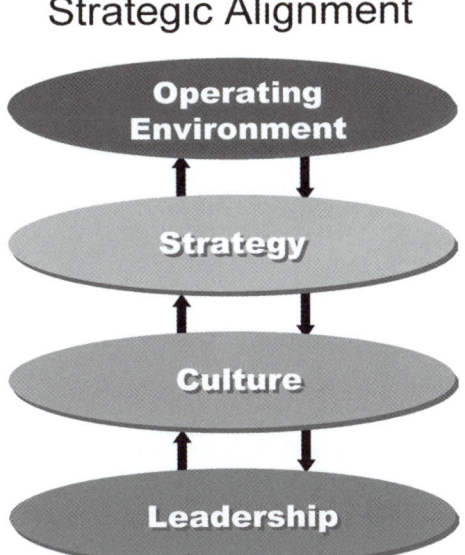

The important principle that we have established is that there is an appropriate culture for each strategy, an appropriate strategy for each environment, and so on. Another way of saying that is *organisational effectiveness depends on the degree of fit (alignment)* between the various elements.

> *In the example of the SPL Group we saw that a shift occurred within the operating environment. Where once the hardware market had been dominated by independent, "mom and pop" stores who relied heavily on the merchandising assistance provided by the SPL Group, the market was changing. The majors were beginning to take over the market. Their needs and expectations from hardware suppliers were quite different.*
>
> *Accordingly, the SPL Group had to develop a new strategy that emphasised strategic partnering and more sophisticated marketing programs. The new strategy could not be successfully implemented until the culture of the organisation was changed. This change in culture was not a natural consequence of the shift in strategy – it had to be planned and launched as a conscious initiative by management.*
>
> *And finally, the cultural change was made possible by an active involvement of the organisation's leadership. They knew that they had a major role to play in shaping the capabilities of the SPL Group to play by the new rules of the game.*

So, as we change the operating environment, each of the other areas has to change in order to maintain the overall alignment. This, in turn, should assist the organisation in maintaining or even enhancing its effectiveness.

More alignment leads to more effectiveness

My PhD research examined the organisational effectiveness of 53 organisations, exploring the relationship between organisational strategy and culture. I showed that the "goodness of fit" is related to the level of organisation effectiveness. In other words, the greater the level of *alignment* between the various areas of environment, strategy, culture and leadership, the more effective the organisation is likely to be.

By studying this theory in my initial sample, I found that the better the degree of fit, the more likely the organisation was to earn good economic returns:

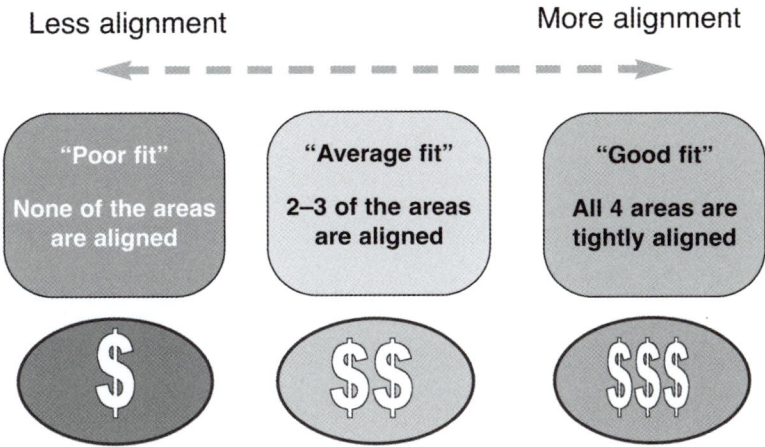

Economic returns and profitability are by no means the only measures of effectiveness in organisations. I also measured the effectiveness using other criteria such as customer satisfaction and stakeholder satisfaction.

However, as a generalisation, we may say that *organisational effectiveness is associated with increasing levels of strategic alignment*. This is an important principle that we will rely on as we continue our discussion of organisational effectiveness.

But now we need to turn our attention to the issue of describing different types of operating environments, strategies, cultures and leadership styles. Once we have done this, we are in a position to assess the degree of alignment in an organisation. Moreover, we can then begin increasing the effectiveness of our own organisations by developing appropriate strategy, culture and leadership that are in alignment with their operating environments.

Chapter 1

Chapter 2
Describing environment, strategy, culture and leadership by considering behaviour

The previous chapter discussed behaviours – or more accurately, patterns of behaviour:

➤ Strategy is the pattern of behaviour and actions taken by the organisation in its operating environment; *[handwritten: Choices in response to operating environment]*

➤ Culture is the patterns of behaviour within the organisation; and *[handwritten: Choices in response to internal environment]*

➤ Leadership is the behaviours and actions required to craft the strategic direction and culture of the organisation.

Further:

➤ The operating environment may be understood as the patterns of behaviour displayed by customers, competitors, stakeholders and the like.

In order to use the *Strategic Alignment* framework to measure and describe organisational effectiveness, we need to be able to measure and describe each of the four elements in a *common* way. I have found it useful to use *patterns of behaviour* as a means of describing these various areas.

The work of Carl Jung is particularly useful for understanding patterns of behaviour in individuals. Jung, a Swiss psychologist, worked closely with Sigmund Freud during the earlier part of his career, and is best known for his contribution to the understanding of personality types and what he termed archetypes.

While the broader aspects of Jung's work on psychological type are beyond the scope of this text, a number of observations made by Jung and some of the trait theorists are particularly useful for our analysis (Jung C, (1968, 1971), Cattell (1946, 1973), Costa & McCrae (1988, 1993)) and show such patterns of behaviour are robust and observable (Hunter 1998).

Understanding patterns of behaviour

> Behaviour is rarely random — it usually conforms to an overall pattern

Jung identified that most people, over the course of their lives, behave according to a pattern. Except in rare cases, the behaviour is not random, and adheres broadly to a given pattern. In this way, there is some predictability about the behaviour of people, such that their past behaviour is usually a good approximation of how they will behave in the future.

Where people get together in groups – for example, a work group – the group behaviour becomes quite pronounced over time and the patterns become fairly robust. This is what we term an organisational culture – where the pattern of behaviour describes the nature of the interaction and collaboration between the group members. As we know from our own experience, once the culture has formed, it is difficult to change and is often quite difficult even to verbalise.

> Although we are all unique — we differ from each other in similar ways

This phenomenon is sometimes called the "uniqueness paradox" (Miller (1984)). Although individuals all have unique personalities and attributes, the points of difference are always similar. In other words, people may be described by way of a number of common personality and behavioural dimensions. Although we may each have different combinations or amounts of these attributes, the attributes are always the same.

For example, each individual member of a group of dentists is unique. But the group, as a whole, manifests quite different behaviours from a group of wrestlers. This means that *we can use the same dimensions of behaviour to describe both the dentists and the wrestlers – but the two groups would display very different patterns of behaviour along these dimensions.*

We can detect these *patterns* in the behaviour of individuals, teams, organisations, industries, communities and countries. Jung called these patters of behaviour *archetypes* (Jung (1971)). Many researchers have drawn on Jung's work to conclude that these enduring patters of behaviour can be detected in all aspects of organisational behaviour (Handy (1994), Harrison (1972)).

In my research (Chorn (1986)) we have found that these patterns can be described by four discrete types – what we have termed "logics".

I have chosen the term "logics" to describe these types of patterns since I wanted to distinguish this work from that of other researchers – for example, the "Myers-Briggs" *Type* Indicator (MBTI). These frameworks refer primarily to behavioural types in individuals, while we have applied the concept at a group or organisational level. In addition, I have found that the term "logics" has "harder", more business-like connotations, and is more readily understood and accepted in the organisational environment.

These logics are thought to create characteristic forces that explain behaviour in organisations and organisational settings. They may be understood as an imperative or a need to behave in a certain way, or focus on a particular thing. Appendix 1 contains a short article discussing the theoretical underpinnings of the model.

The model below demonstrates how these four logics can be used to describe different patterns of behaviour in organisations:

Strategic Alignment

Four different "logics" in patterns of behaviour

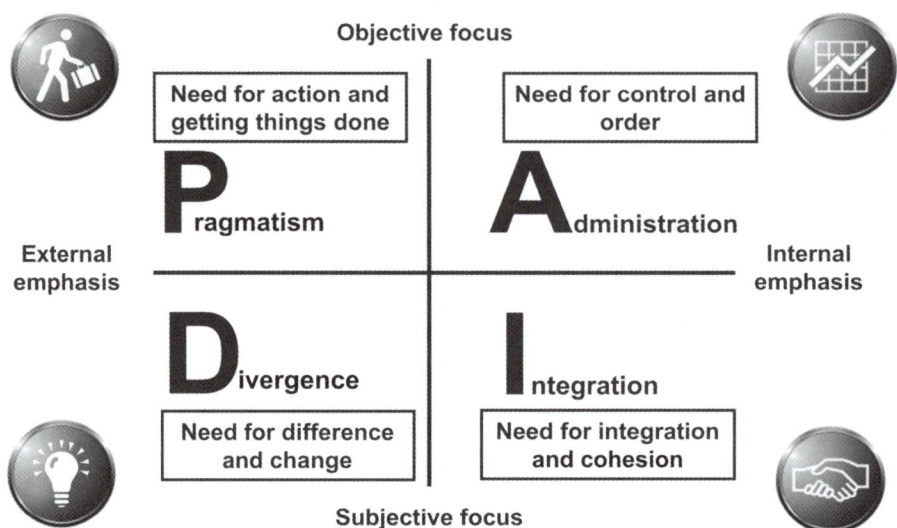

- ➤ **Pragmatism** (P) Logic: a force or need for speed, energy and getting things done, that is, the *need for completion* is the prime motivator;

- ➤ **Administration** (A) Logic: a force or need for stability, control and continuity of the present, beyond anything else, that is, the *need for order* is the prime motivator;

- ➤ **Divergence** (D) Logic: a force or need for high levels of difference, innovation and quantum shifts in the way things are, that is, the *need for change* is the prime motivator;

- ➤ **Integration** (I) Logic: a force or need for cooperation and harmony, that is, the *need for good relations* is the prime motivator.

By taking the letters of each of the logics, we get the so-called PADI model of ***Strategic Alignment***.

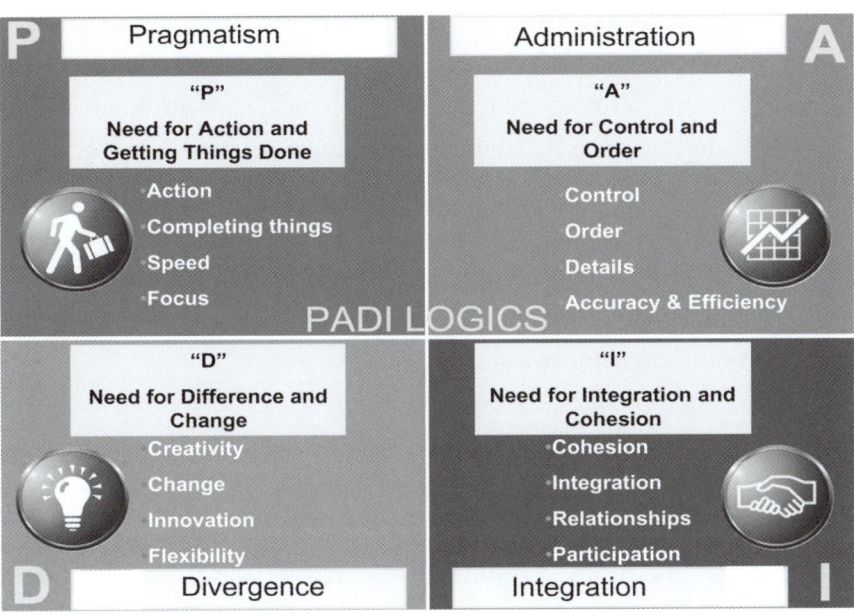

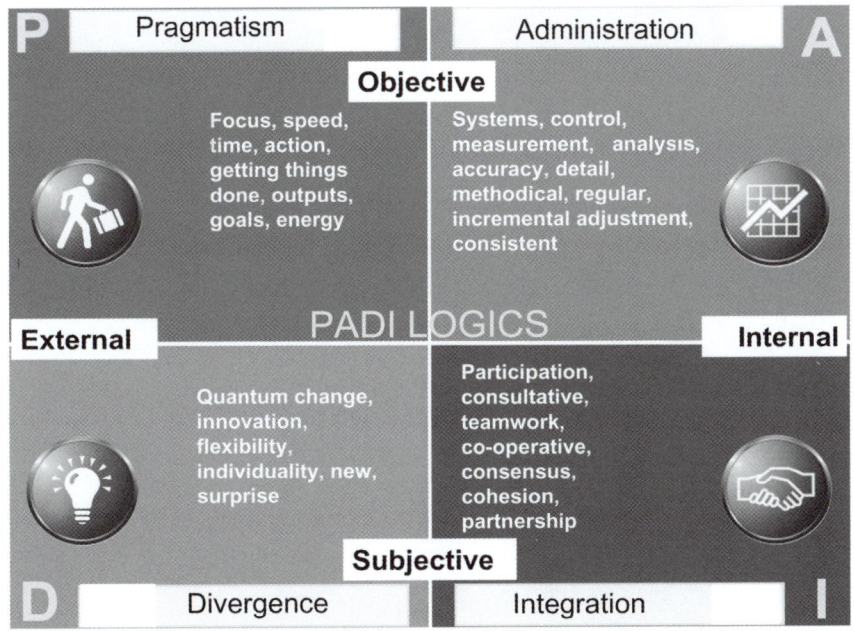

The idea of a dominant logic

The four logics or forces exist in all environments, strategies, cultures and leadership styles – but to varying degrees. Usually, one or two logics dominate to give an essence or defining character to a particular, environment, strategy, culture or leadership approach. For example, some patterns may contain more "I" than "P", "D" or "A".

- A "P" organisation might be a SWAT team in a police force. Their primary focus is to operate quickly, directly and with high energy in order to achieve a stated goal.

- An "A" organisation might be an auditing firm that operates under very firm standards, controls and systems.

- A "D" organisation could be a research and development laboratory where the emphasis is on the development of new and creative solutions to disease.

- An "I" organisation might be a country club where the emphasis is on creating an environment of belonging through involving everyone in participative decision-making.

In practice, however, we find that most organisations or strategies are rarely a *"pure"* "P", "A", "D" or "I". Logics usually occur in combinations. For example, two logics may occur in an equal combination (eg, 'PA'), or one may be dominant with the support of another (eg, "Pa" or "Id"). *When logics occur in combination, they are almost always adjacent to one another in the PADI quadrant:*

Chapter 2

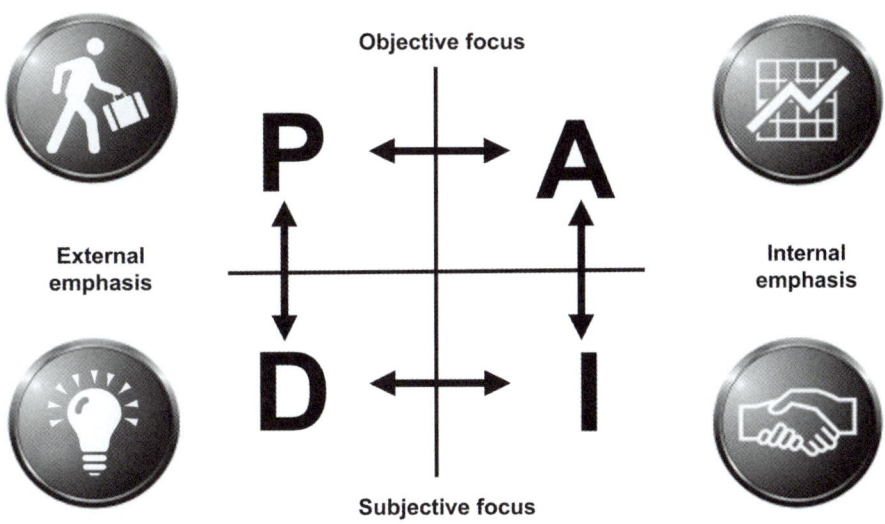

PADI combinations are usually adjacent

Our convention is to use the dominant logic before the secondary logic, for example, "Pa", "Id" or "Ai".

Accordingly, we find the following combinations possible in describing the logics of environments, strategies, cultures and leadership styles:

More detailed examples of organisations with different combined logics may be found in Appendix 2.

The logics in practice

Although all four logics do occur at any point in time within a strategy, a work group or an individual, one or two "compatible" logics will tend to dominate. The others – although present – will tend to be less important.

So, for example, we may say that a work group has a "Pa" logic. This suggests that the group has an emphasis on *high-energy, driving behaviour* with a focus on *getting things done as speedily as possible*. The group will also be concerned (but less so) with the need for doing things in a *systematic and orderly way*. The group will be least concerned with being different/creative and achieving a cohesive partnering style.

Sales Team – a "Pa" work group

A good example of a "Pa" work group might be a sales team who are primarily concerned with the achievement of their individual sales targets for their respective territories. Their dominant approach will be a "pushing", driving style that emphasises getting things done quickly in an action-oriented fashion.

Although important, they are less concerned with ensuring that their sales reports are completed accurately and systematically. Administration is clearly of secondary importance to them. However, they realise that their bonuses and expense refunds are dependent on getting their "paper work" done properly, so they will allocated the necessary time to get it done.

Finally, they are not very concerned with group cohesion or developing participate approaches with their colleagues. They find this too time consuming and it does not assist them in achieving their primary goal — individual sales targets.

What's the problem with diagonals?

Why do we say that the PADI logics rarely occur in a diagonal combination?

- ➤ Why can't we have a strategy or a work group that emphasises speed and integration at the same time?

- ➤ What about customers who want everything all at the same time – fast response, accuracy, innovation and close partnerships?

- ➤ Why can't a culture focus on flexibility and control at the same time?

We will discuss these issues in more detail in Chapters 3 and 4, but for the present, let's consider the following:

In a "P" strategy or group, the emphasis is on speed and getting things done as directly as possible. This means that the team develops a particular style of working, that is, action-oriented with high levels of individual autonomy and empowerment. Think of the SWAT team.

In an "I" strategy or group, the emphasis is on spending time and developing a close partnering approach so that things are done in a consensus way. This emphasises doing things slowly and carefully so that all opinions are catered for. This is not likely to suit the SWAT team, as it is too time consuming and does not allow for taking more risky options.

Similarly, a customer that seeks fast response is typically not interested in spending lots of time with the supplier. They seek an "arms-length" approach, while a customer who wants a relationship is keen to spend the time to do things "together" with you.

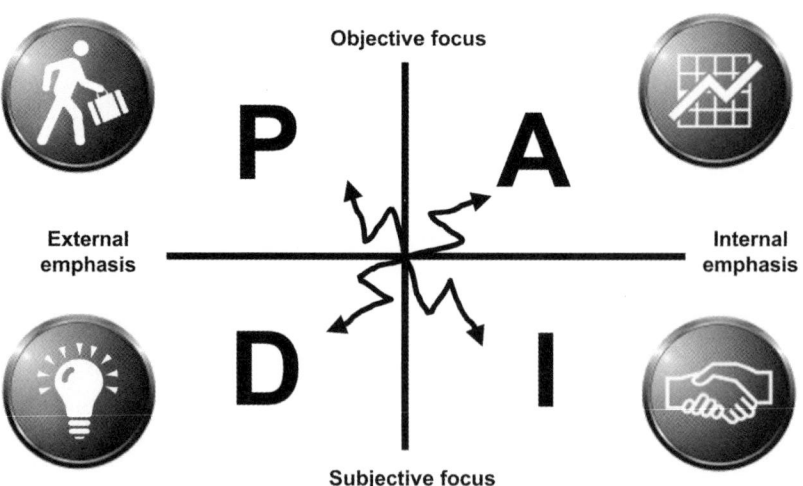

Diagonal combinations are difficult

As we will see in the following chapters, the diagonal logics set up powerful contradictory forces within the organisation that do not coexist readily. However, there are ways of dealing with these contradictions and we shall explore them in due course.

PADI and the Strategic Alignment model

PADI allows us to characterise each element of the *Strategic Alignment* model – and to describe your whole organisation in context with its operating environment. By determining the dominant logic of your strategy, culture and leadership style, you are able to determine whether they are appropriate for the organisation and also pinpoint problem areas.

In order to improve the overall effectiveness of the organisation, your task is then to shape the various areas according to the appropriate logic. As previously discussed, the research suggests that your organisation will perform at its best when the strategy, culture and leadership approach are all internally consistent and aligned with the requirements of the operating environment:

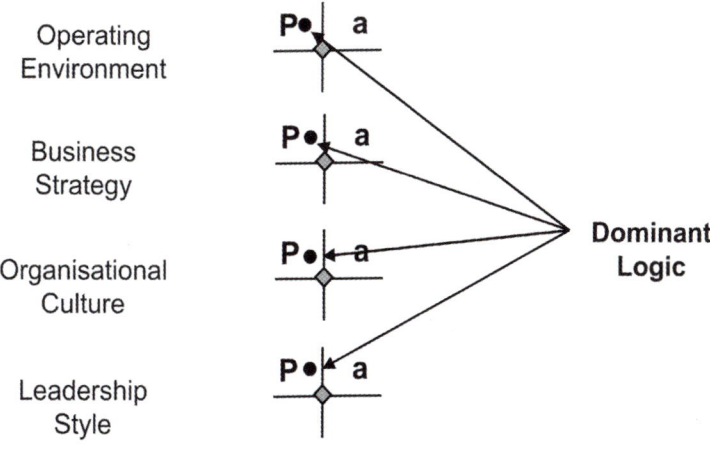

Strategic Alignment

In the example of our earlier sales team, we see that they are working in a "Pa" environment. Accordingly, they have adopted a "Pa" strategy, "Pa" culture and are lead by way of a "Pa" leadership style. As the diagram suggests, this particular work group is effective because they are in perfect *Strategic Alignment*. If the conditions in the environment were altered, then a different strategy, culture and leadership style would be appropriate. Case 2: The hospitality industry

CASE 1: THE RACING CAR TEAM

Consider the example of the racing car team. Their task is to win by being the fastest car to cross the finish line on the day. On race day they are operating within a "P" environment. Their strategy will be to examine every aspect of their system to maximise the speed of the car.

The driver will be mentally and physically fit and will be able to negotiate the vehicle at speeds of 260-300 km per hour for up to ten hours. Fast reflexes enable the driver to respond to cars, unexpected objects that cross their path, or a blown tyre.

The car will be built for speed. It won't be equipped with a CD player for easy listening. It won't be equipped with a tow bar in case the driver needs to pull a trailer. It will be low to the ground to improve cornering and would lose its muffler if it were ever taken off road. The team in the pits will be geared to get their jobs done quickly. As they change tyres there won't be time for them to ensure that everyone has been consulted and that everyone is feeling good about the decisions that are being made. They will be empowered to make quick decisions if something goes wrong. Throughout the race, the leader of the team will need to create a sense of energy and focus within the team. To achieve success all elements will need to be working together but on their individual tasks.

Similarly, if you are servicing a "P" market, all elements should be geared to deliver to this market. Your strategy will be to develop faster, less bureaucratic and more direct ways of accomplishing results. Your culture will be characterised by action and energy. Decision-making will be de-centralised. You will have systems that facilitate rapid collection of information on your current performance relative to your competitors.

Strategy will be crafted as circumstances unfold. Internal communication methods will facilitate quick answers via email or phone and will probably be impersonal. Effective leaders will set unambiguous, challenging targets and will provide an environment where people are unencumbered by procedures. They will demand action and have a low tolerance for ambiguity, precedent or personal feelings.

CASE 2: THE HOSPITALITY INDUSTRY

In our consulting work, my colleagues and I worked with a number of major Australian and multi-national organisations. My partner, Ivan Nurick, worked extensively with Accor Asia Pacific. Accor is the largest hospitality management group in Australia, New Zealand and New Caledonia, operating under the Sofitel, Novotel, Mercure, Ibis and Formula One brands.

Our research showed subtle differences in customer needs according to whether the guests' stay was for leisure or business purposes. This information helped one hotel manager to solve a perplexing riddle. He noticed that during the week his customers appeared to be very satisfied. By the end of the week he had received very few complaints and staff reported few difficulties. Over the weekend periods, however, customers appeared quite dissatisfied and by Monday mornings his in-tray was full of complaints.

Strategic Alignment

His staff assured him that they were not doing anything differently on the weekends compared to weekdays. Research showed that business guests, who predominantly stayed in the hotel on weekdays, had a stronger P requirement for service. They needed service to be fast and efficient. They needed fast response rather than warm feelings. Checking in and out needed to be completed without delay so they could get to their next meeting or catch their next plane. Their requests needed to be met quickly as there was work to be done.

Leisure guests, however, showed a greater need for an "I" component to their service. For them, the experience of staying in the hotel was part of their holiday and not just a place to make some phone calls and sleep at the end of the day. Ambience was important and while they didn't expect the service to be slow, they had more time to exchange pleasantries with staff. The hotel general manager set about overhauling the orientation of his weekend service delivery.

By 5 o'clock on Friday afternoons the flavour of service delivery was completely different. Staff uniforms were more casual, ambient music was changed and staff were trained to focus more on the customer's pleasant experience of the hotel. The result after just a few weeks of implementing the new approach was a dramatic reduction in customer complaints.

At the Sydney Convention and Exhibition Centre (the Centre), misalignment between the approach of the Executive and the approach of the next layer of management was discovered. The middle management believed that the Executive were undisciplined and unable to make decisions. They believed that the Executive seemed to value the wrong things. The Executive thought that account managers should be innovative, creative people (D) who were able to surprise their customers with new ideas.

A study of the Executive showed that the group was "DP". They valued ideas, innovation, creativity and results. The management team, however, was "PA". They wanted closure on decisions and a structured approach. Customer research showed that what customers predominantly wanted from the Centre was an event that ran according to plan – everything provided on time, according to their event order and within budget (A). If a problem was to arise during the event, such as an audio-visual failure, or if equipment had been left at the office, they would then require fast responses and flexibility (P). Overall, their service requirement was "PA".

The Centre went about re-aligning its business to "PA" values. The Executive team built mechanisms into their relationships with staff to create a more systematic approach. They ensured that closure was reached on decisions. They developed internal processes for the business rather than just dictating what results they wanted to see.

At the level of the operating environment, the Centre set about further systematising their customer service delivery approaches according to "PA" values. A new event management function was set up in the organisation with a member on the Executive team. This function would develop the processes to integrate operations so that a highly systematic, responsive service was provided according to a "PA" logic.

So, what does this all mean?

The *Strategic Alignment* framework is a diagnostic tool that can help us understand how the organisation is working, and, perhaps more importantly, how to improve the overall effectiveness of the organisation by increasing the level of alignment.

So far, however, we have considered fairly simple examples. In some cases, organisations will face a number of different markets, each with different operating conditions. Or the organisation may have different business units, each with different strategies and focus.

We need to consider some of these issues and also how to apply the PADI model in more specific circumstances. We will do this as we explore the following chapters on the different areas of *Strategic Alignment*.

Chapter 3
Understanding your operating environment

A logical place to start

In many of the conversations I have with senior managers, "*Where do I begin?*" is a question I am asked regularly.

I have found that a good place to begin is the operating environment. "*Let's start by understanding your operating environment – and in particular, your customer needs*", I reply.

My reason for saying this is based on the *Strategic Alignment* framework. If we can understand the needs of their customers within the operating environment, we can then begin to explore the options for strategy. Once a strategy has been chosen, the appropriate culture and leadership style can be identified:

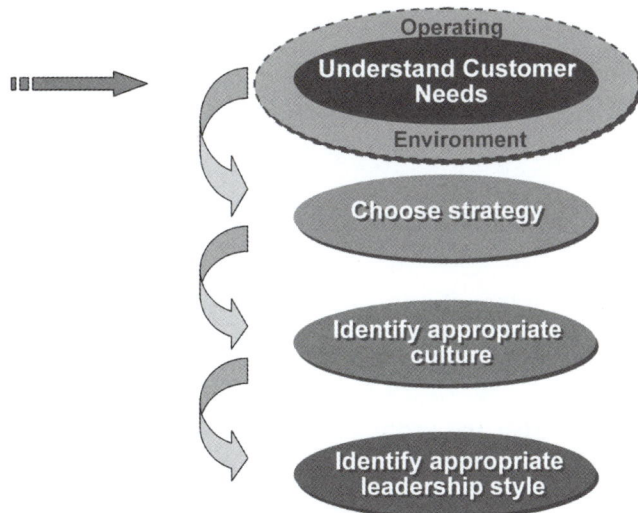

Because the operating environment has been defined as *the rules of the game*, it seems sensible to begin by exploring this as the starting point. Whether you position your organisation as rule taker, rule breaker or rule maker, it is useful to at least understand the current rules as a starting point.

This may seem like an obvious point, but I have observed so many client organisations charge ahead with strategy development, culture change or leadership programs without having a good understanding of the operating environment to guide their efforts. They steam right ahead without checking if they are heading in the right direction!

> *In the case of the SPL Group, management first spent time studying and understanding the new operating environment.*
>
> *They analysed the needs of the new customers – the major chains. They spoke to their buyers and studied their strategies in the market. They also considered the impact that this new retailing force would have on the hardware market.*
>
> *Only when they fully understood the needs of this new environment, did they begin developing options for strategy.*

As you may have noticed, I am particularly keen on understanding the *customer needs* in the environment as the starting point. Why is this?

From a philosophical point of view, the primary *purpose of the organisation is to meet the needs of its customers*. This seems to hold good for both profit and non-profit organisations. There are many who will argue that this is not so – and that the purpose of the organisation is to make a profit for its shareholders.

My view is that the profit earned by the organisation is simply the *result* of doing a good job in meeting the customer's needs – it is but one measure of effectiveness. As we know, there are other measures of effectiveness – such as customer satisfaction and long-term survival.

In any event, we could argue that the argument is purely one of semantics, but it seems that an important *raison d' etre* of an organisation is its ability to meet customer needs, because without satisfying the needs of its customers, the organisation's long-term future does not appear to be too secure. Therefore, we start by understanding the customer needs.

Another reason for starting here is a practical issue. As we know, the operating environment is made up of a number of factors such as competitors, legislation, technology and the like.

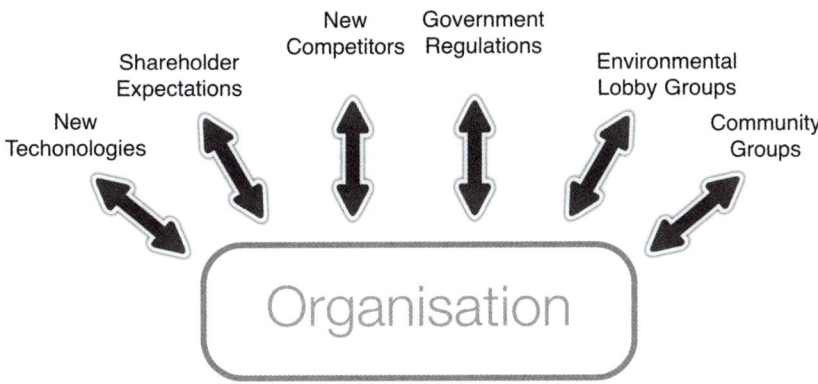

I have found that it is useful to start with an understanding and analysis of the customer's needs, and then to consider what effect the other factors (in the operating environment) will have on meeting and satisfying those needs.

In other words, while those other factors may change the customer's needs (or your ability to meet those needs) over time, the organisation still has to find a way of meeting them. The organisation cannot survive for very long if it does not meet the needs of its customers!

When we focus on customer needs, we will seek to answer four questions:

1. Who is the customer?

2. How can we examine the needs of customers?

3. How can we describe customers' needs and segment the markets we operate in?

4. How can we account for the other factors in the operating environment that might affect customers' needs in the future?

Question 1: Who is the customer?

I begin many of my strategy sessions by asking who the customers are. Without clarity on this matter, it is difficult to achieve clarity in your strategy, or indeed to achieve alignment (and effectiveness) in the organisation.

This is not always as easy as it seems. Many organisations confuse their customers with their other stakeholders and partners. This is often the case in not-for-profit organisations.

So, before moving on, it may be useful to provide a few definitions.

Customer
A customer is someone who *benefits directly* from and/or *receives* the product or service you provide. They usually pay for it directly, although this in itself is not a defining characteristic. (Often, in the case of public services, the customer pays for the services indirectly though taxes).

Chapter 3

The term "customer" is used interchangeably with "client" or "consumer". Although I recognise there are subtle differences in these terms, it is useful to have a common term when presenting our theories.

Stakeholder
A stakeholder is someone who has a vested interest in how well you meet the needs of the customer and a vested interest in your long-term future.

Stakeholders include shareholders, boards of directors, unions or the tax office, for example.

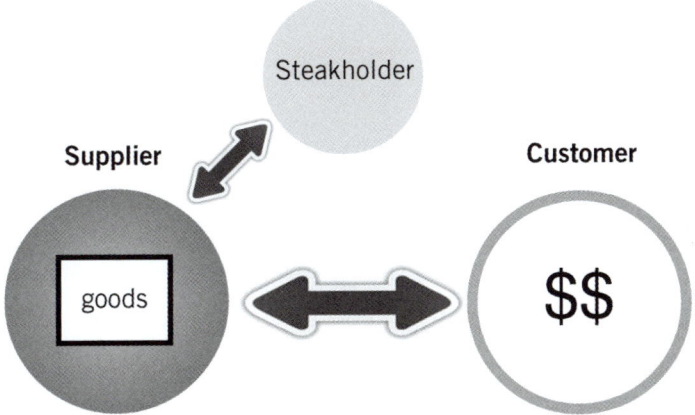

Partner
A partner is someone with whom you collaborate in order to meet the needs of your customer.

An example might be an associate company or another division with whom you are collaborating to produce a product or service for the customer.

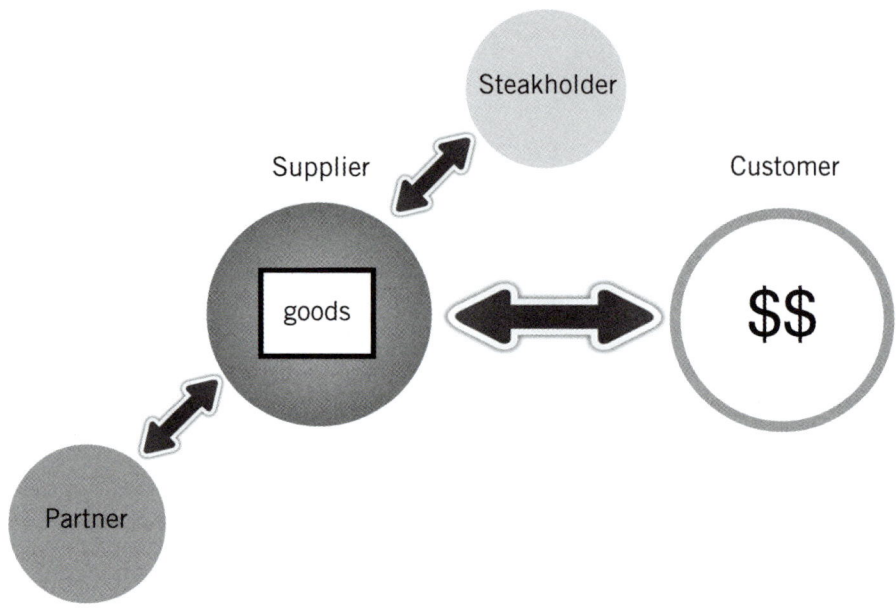

Some common errors in defining your customer

In my consulting activities, I have seen two common errors in defining customers.

Trap 1: Mistaking a stakeholder as a customer

This problem is common, but not confined, to public sector organisations. An organisation may define a stakeholder (such as a Chairperson or Minister) as a customer and then seek to meet their needs as they would do a regular customer.

Chapter 3

Why is this a problem? Surely it's a good thing to serve and meet the needs of your stakeholders? Of course it is, but the problem is the way in which this *defocuses* the organisation from its real purpose.

> *Let's consider the example of the Inspector-General division in the Australian Defence Force (ADF) – the equivalent of the internal auditor of the military organisation.*
>
> *The role of the Inspector General's division is to ensure that managers in the ADF use public funds with integrity and efficiency. In other words, the effectiveness of the division is measured in terms of how well ADF funds are used.*
>
> *When the Inspector General's division defined its customer as the Chief of the Defence Force (who they report to, and is, therefore, a stakeholder), their focus was to demonstrate good service to this "customer". Prior to 1996, this approach led to a "gotcha" culture that sought to "catch" the ADF managers using funds inappropriately. The measure of effectiveness was the number of fraud cases and offenders identified to the Chief of the Defence Force. In effect, the number of offenders and fraud cases uncovered was regarded by the staff as a means of indicating to their stakeholder (Chief of the Defence Force) that they were performing effectively.*
>
> *Unfortunately, this had a number of negative consequences. First, it led to mistrust and suspicion of the Inspector General's division, and a general lack of cooperation. Secondly, in much the same way as a lack of disease does not imply good health; the number of fraud cases did not necessarily imply effective use of ADF funds.*
>
> *Following the appointment of a new Inspector General, the division examined its overall strategic purpose and focus. The senior managers recognised*

Understanding your operating environment

Strategic Alignment

> *that the criterion of success (the effective use of ADF funds by ADF managers) was best achieved by working collaboratively with these ADF managers and improving their overall financial and resource management capabilities.*
>
> *In order to affect this shift in orientation and style by the Inspector General's staff, the definition of the customer was changed. The ADF managers were recognised as the customers of the Inspector General's division. As a consequence, they became the prime focus and raison d' etre of the organisation. This would eventually contribute to a more effective and cooperative relationship between the Inspector General's division and ADF managers.*

Trap 2: Defining another internal business unit as a customer

I have found great difficulty in understanding the philosophy or logic in the concept of "internal customers". I realise that it has had benefits in assisting organisations to become more responsive and to develop a better service orientation, but there are a number of less obvious shortfalls in this approach:

1. In a normal "customer-service provider" relationship there is an underlying "power" imbalance, whereby the customer specifies their needs and the supplier attempts to meet these. In addition, the customer has the ability to choose an alternative supplier if unhappy with the quality or level of service.

   Consider the case where an operating business unit is "buying" a specialist service like human resources or marketing from an internal supplier (for example, a human resources or marketing business unit). In these cases, the specialist expert should be supplying a service that he or she considers best for the organisation as a whole, rather than simply meeting the needs of the operating business unit.

2. The power imbalance means that, in many cases, the specialist unit sub-optimises its contribution to the organisation by simply responding to the specified needs of the operating unit. In addition, the performance and contribution of the specialist unit is judged by operating managers who don't necessarily have the required expertise to do so.

In organisations that have adopted the internal customer perspective, there is often a complex web of internal relationships. Sometimes these are supplemented by internal Service Level Agreements (SLAs) to ensure that the internal service providers are meeting the needs of the operating business units.

My experience is that an undue level of attention and focus is then given to meeting all these internally-generated service standards. In effect, large parts of the organisation are concerned about servicing each other! This can dilute the level of attention and focus given to the *real* customer, that is, the one that actually buys a service or product on the outside and pays with *real* dollars.

A good case in point was a Melbourne-based national retailer that I worked with some years ago. They had an elaborate system of internal SLAs designed to ensure that all the internal service providers were meeting the needs of their internal customers.

The merchandising division was servA good case in point was a Melbourne-based national retailer that I worked with some years ago. They had an

Strategic Alignment

> *elaborate system of internal SLAs designed to ensure that all the internal service providers were meeting the needs of their internal customers. The merchandising division was servicing the needs of the retail division; the finance division was servicing the needs of the merchandising and retail divisions and so on.*
>
> *Staff surveys suggested that the requirements to maintain the system of internal SLAs were very time consuming and diverted resources from servicing the external customers in the store. In addition, we found that some of the internal divisions had lost sight of the "real" customer (the shoppers in the stores) in their attempt to meet the needs of their internal customers.*
>
> *This was becoming a major issue for the organisation as the market had recently seen the entry of a new Japanese-owned department store in the city and some of the traditional competitors had begun to increase their level of customer service as a key competitive strategy. Customer satisfaction research commissioned by my client confirmed that their satisfaction levels (external) had declined, and that shoppers had noted that store assistants often "seemed busy doing paper work and other things".*

My experience has shown that it is often better to define only the *external* customer as your *customer*. In this way, other internal divisions become your *partners* which all collaborate in meeting the needs of the customer. This has the following advantages:

➤ The whole organisation can focus on meeting the needs of the real customer

➤ Internal divisions and business units can collaborate equally as partners and jointly discover the optimal way to meet customer needs. (If divisions are unable to resolve internal disputes, the problem may well be related to an inappropriate organisation design or performance measures. We discuss this further in Chapter 7).

Key points in summary

The key points in defining your customer may be summarised as:

- ➤ Customers should be a major focus of the organisation's purpose.

- ➤ It is important to distinguish between customers, stakeholder and partners.

- ➤ Be wary of defining your stakeholders as customers, as this can defocus the organisation.

- ➤ Customers are usually external to the organisation – focusing on internal customers can dilute the overall effort in meeting the external customers' needs.

Question 2:
How can we examine customers' needs?

I find that defining your customer is like a good spring-cleaning – it highlights what really has to be done. Once we have defined who the customer is, the question of understanding their needs becomes easier to answer.

"*The customer is king*" but like a real king they may not always understand the deeper implications of what they want!

Strategic Alignment

Often, even customers themselves do not always have the ability to tell you what they want – they don't always understand what really drives their own buying behaviour. This may sound hard to believe, so I would like to share two examples with you:

> *The advertising agency*
>
> *In my earlier working career, I had a short (and unsuccessful) stint as a client service manager of a medium-sized advertising agency in Johannesburg, South Africa. It was during the apartheid era in South Africa, when most state and para-statal organisations were run by government appointees.*
>
> *I accepted an advertising brief from an old friend I had known at university. He was employed as the communications manager with the state-owned electricity commission.*
>
> *As I understood the brief from my friend, the electricity commission was keen to "modernise" its public image as a progressive organisation that employed modern technology to expand the electricity grid in South Africa. (At the time, many of the living areas set aside for occupation by "non-white" citizens had no electricity).*
>
> *Our creative team went to work and, encouraged by the brief I had presented to them, developed an innovative and provocative advertising campaign. The theme of the campaign was the notion of a progressive organisation expanding the availability of electricity throughout South Africa.*
>
> *When the campaign was presented to the conservative, government-appointed management committee, it fell like the proverbial lead balloon!*
>
> *The by-line of the campaign? "What South Africa needs is a little more power sharing!" Needless to say, management was unimpressed and we did not win the business!*

> ### The banking organisation
>
> *In my consulting in Australia, I came upon a Western Australian banking organisation that had been suffering market share losses to nationally-based rival organisations.*
>
> *In an attempt to develop a counter-strategy, they decided to conduct a broad-based polling of their customers' views. Since their management team was generally suspicious of consultants, they elected to do it themselves.*
>
> *Their middle and senior level managers visited a broad cross-section of customers and asked them a series of pre-determined questions designed to find out what customers really wanted. The bank believed that they could develop an effective competitive strategy to win back market share by incorporating their customer needs into the strategy. Nothing revolutionary here, so far!*
>
> *They were successful in achieving a high rate of completed interviews – customers were keen to talk and to share their views with the representatives of the bank. A large volume of data was collected and they set about trying to interpret and making sense of it all. And this is where they ran into trouble and were compelled to seek professional assistance.*
>
> *Although the data told them much about the various operational difficulties that customers had been experiencing, management was unable to make much sense of what customer really wanted. In broad terms, what the data revealed was that customers wanted "interest-free loans over indefinite periods of time." We could have told them that for nothing!*

So, what issues do these case studies illustrate? I have identified three issues that may be useful as you consider the needs of your customers:

Strategic Alignment

1. Drilling down to understand customer needs

It is not always informative to accept what customers say *at face value*. In the same way as the Western Australian bank found that customers want "everything" (interest-free loans over indefinite periods of time), buyers of motor vehicles want "performance", "economy", "safety", "reliability" and "value for money".

Customers do not always reveal their real purchase drivers or needs. I don't suggest they are attempting to deceive – but rather that they are not always aware of the factors they use to select one supplier over another. Accordingly, they will often offer the "rational" and sensible requirements such as "value-for-money", "good service" and the like.

Unfortunately, understanding these needs do not necessarily help us achieve a better competitive strategy, as the WA bank example proves. In addition, as my experience in the advertising industry suggested, taking these needs at face value (ie, that the electricity commission wanted to portray a progressive, innovative image) can sometimes get you into real trouble!

So, the real message is that one has to drill down beyond what is expressed by the customer. Whether intentional or not, the initial needs expressed by the customer may be concealing a very different set of needs that could result in a very different strategy. "Drilling down" may include:

- ➤ understanding the *context* of the customer;

- ➤ recognising the *trade-offs* that are implied in the way needs are expressed.

2. Understanding the context of the customer

The advertising agency case shows the danger of ignoring the context in which customer needs are expressed. I accepted a brief from an old university friend of similar age and outlook on life. I took at face value his description of the commission's needs and then used this to brief the creative team. Accordingly, we created our "strategy" (advertising campaign) based on these expressed needs.

However, had I considered the context of the situation, I would have known that:

- the organisation was known for its low-risk approach to most business dealings;

- the management committee was populated by middle-aged men of a conservative nature;

- the management had been appointed by a right-wing government with clearly-expressed reactionary views.

The references to "power-sharing" could not have been further off the mark!

The message here is that one has to account for the context of the customer to fully understand the needs. Often, simply looking at the *behaviour patterns* of the customer allows good insight into their needs. A customer that demonstrates low-risk behaviour in their market is unlikely to respond to *your* definition of "innovative" or "progressive".

However, they may believe that they are innovative and progressive *in their own terms*. So, the challenge is to understand the real meaning of the needs that customers express. And this can only be done once we have considered their context and/or past patterns of behaviour.

Perhaps my advertising career may have been extended had I recognised that something as simple as a new font on the logo or the use of a different colour would be interpreted as an "innovative and progressive" image by the electricity commission's management team!

Strategic Alignment

3. Recognising the importance of need "trade-offs"

The third insight from the examples above relates to the fact that customers do not always recognise the priorities they give to their different needs.

Both my PhD research, and that conducted by my consultancy, the Centre for Corporate Strategy, reveals that there are distinct patterns that can be identified when we examine customer needs.

When we *examine* customer needs (as opposed to simply asking the customer what they want), we notice that these needs do not appear as a wish list of apparently unrelated product and service attributes (eg, "interest-free loans over indefinite periods of time"). Instead, the needs are expressed in clear patterns that reflect the priorities and specific trade-offs that customers make.

For example, customers know that fast service in a restaurant will come at the expense of having a detailed discussion with the waiter about way the food is prepared. And that a cheap meal means that one has to accept some limitations in the scope of the menu.

Or in the case of the WA bank, an examination of needs would have demonstrated that customers trade-off personal service in favour of lower interest rates (prices), particularly where they purchase or use standard or simple products and services. This would have been more useful information than trying to interpret the wish list of needs customers asked for.

So, if we examine the *patterns* of behaviour that customers display in their purchasing *behaviour*, we see that there are clear priorities expressed and trade-offs made. Understanding this is very useful in interpreting customer needs and using the information to set strategy.

Key points in summary

The key points in examining customer's needs are:

- ➤ We have to drill down beyond what customers say in order to interpret their needs – we can't always accept it at face value.

- ➤ The customer's context is important in understanding their needs – their patterns of behaviour reveal much of their real needs.

- ➤ Customers' behaviour expresses clear priorities and trade-offs that they make.

Question 3:
How can we describe customers' needs?

Using archetypes to describe customer needs

In discussing customers' needs with clients, I find that it is often easier to describe these in some form of stereotypical example or archetype. For example, we have all used the term "*just like a bloody Volvo driver!*" We all know that this stereotype conjures up images of a conservative, usually over-cautious driver that seems to have little awareness of who else is on the road!

(Incidentally, Volvo is working hard on changing this image with their new range of vehicles, and their current advertising plays strongly on this imagery making the buyer *wish* to be "a bloody Volvo driver").

There are a number of benefits of using these *archetypes* to describe customer needs and behaviour:

- ➤ They produce a "complete picture" of the customer and their needs – this makes it easier to understand and remember.

Strategic Alignment

> ➤ The archetype also reflects the priorities that have been expressed and the trade-offs that have been made.

So, we know that the "traditional" Volvo driver (previous to the new positioning Volvo are attempting) has safety and long vehicle life as the key priorities. We also know that they have, therefore, traded-off the attributes of high speed, performance and sporty looks in favour of these priorities.

I have found it very useful to use these archetypes to express customer needs as it summarises vast quantities of information and presents real choices when it comes to setting strategy.

PADI as a customer archetype

Our research has shown that we can use the PADI model as a way of summarising and presenting customer needs and preferences: It allows us to recognise the patterns that exist in our customers' behaviours. It reduces the complexity of having to interpret long wish lists.

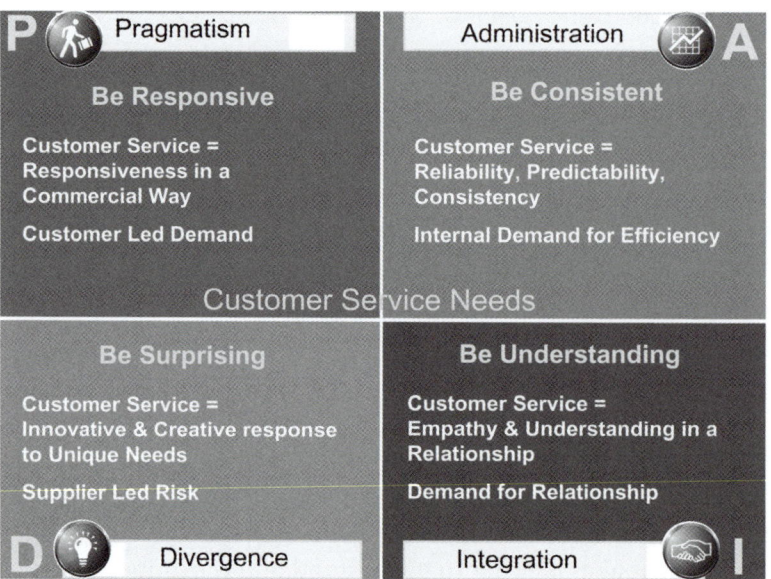

Importantly, the model describes a customer's behaviour and needs with respect to a particular purchase situation. For example, I might display "P" needs when having my motor vehicle serviced ("I want the car ready at 5:00 pm — no excuses!"), but have strong "I" preferences in dealing with my medical doctor ("Please see if you can help me with this pain in my back").

So, we are not suggesting that the PADI model describes who the person is — but rather that it describes his or her behaviour in a particular purchase situation.

The model suggests that customer behaviour (and therefore needs) may be represented by a dominant logic, as the analysis in the last chapter outlined

Examples of customer needs in PADI terms

The "P" environment
- Same day express distribution of standard articles – eg, a daily newspaper
- Lunchtime diners in a business/commercial centre
- Fire Fighting Services
- Courier services

Characteristics
A drive for speed, action, rapid response and value

The "A" environment
- Utilities (eg, water, electricity, gas)
- ATM banking services
- MacDonald's restaurants
- Steel mills

Characteristics
A drive for consistency, reliability, standardisation and low cost

The "D" environment
- Fashion, music and entertainment industries
- Kid's computer games
- Research and development laboratories
- Emerging technologies and services

Characteristics
A drive for rapid change, creativity, low sensitivity to price, and novel approaches

The "I" environment
- Loyalty programs (Frequent flyer, "privilege" cards)
- Family restaurants
- The local greengrocer or butcher
- Social workers

Characteristics
A drive for empathy, relationships, understanding, and loyalty

Strategic Alignment

We know from our research that customers whose behaviour is driven by a particular logic are making trade-offs. It's not that customers driven by the "P" logic will not value empathy or other aspects of the "I" logic, but rather they will not value it as much as quick, responsive service.

While you are waiting for your sandwich to be made during your 15-minute break between appointments, no doubt you will appreciate it if the deli assistant is pleasant and friendly. But you will probably be annoyed if this chatting about the weather and the latest sports results slows the process.

Customers generally know that if they want fast service, they will trade-off spending time with the service provider. They know if they buy a Porsche, they will be trading-off low price and luggage space for status and performance. If they choose to stay at a backpacker hotel, they will trade-off a bedside phone and valet parking in favour of a low price.

The PADI model helps us to understand the priorities and trade-offs customers are prepared to make. This information is very useful when we have to set our strategy to meet their dominant needs.

> *McDonalds discovered a long time ago what was driving their fast food market. What people bought when they came to McDonalds was low-priced food of consistent quality and style. Clearly this market is an "A" type market. The success of McDonalds lies in the fact that a customer could walk into any store in the country and receive the same standard of food and service.*
>
> *This is reflected again in their recent "back-to-basics" strategy where they announced a move away from specials and one-off menu offerings as this only "confused the customer".*
>
> *At McDonalds, customer service is highly systematised so that consistent*

> *products are delivered in a consistent manner. Customer service staff know that developing deep understanding with customers is unimportant, as is providing new and unusual serving suggestions. McDonalds' systems allow them to provide food relatively quickly, but they are not quick when a customer has a unique request such as a Big Mac without "special sauce".*
>
> *In this sense their speed is not the responsiveness of the "P" type. But what they provide is outstanding "A" service as they have aligned their organisation to deliver to this market.*

In Appendix 3, I have included a short "diagnostic" questionnaire that can assist you in determining the dominant logic of your market or customer group. Please exercise care in using it, as it provides an indicative result only. *I always recommend more rigorous research and analysis before you make major strategic decisions.*

Using PADI to build understanding of customer needs through the organisation

I have found great success in using the PADI concept to share our understanding of a customer segment with staff in the organisation. In particular, it can be quite powerful in an organisation when the underlying logic in a market segment is clearly understood by staff at the customer interface.

For example, if those servicing an "A" market know that, above all, what the customer wants is a consistent product/service experience, they do not need all the details of the latest customer research. PADI can create a common, short-hand language at the customer service interface to focus service delivery. I have found that staff quickly grasp the idea of the four logics and the explanation of customer needs in these terms.

Strategic Alignment

> *In the case of the SPL Group, we researched the needs of the new market — the major hardware retailing groups.*
>
> *After analysis and interpretation, we were able to summarise the customers' needs as essentially 'AI'. They displayed a preference for a consultative partnering approach that would deliver efficiency and lower prices to their chains.*
>
> *This was easily communicated to sales and customer service staff. We developed a "picture" of the 'AI' customer, and staff quickly learned to modify their own behaviour and sales processes to suit this need. We were also able to give this market segment a name – "Consultative partners". This made the communication process easier still.*
>
> *As the previous examples have illustrated, this was supplemented by a comprehensive culture change process to enable SPL Group to better align with this new market segment. But a key factor remained the way we were able to communicate a fairly complex concept in simple, easy-to-understand terms.*

PADI can provide a shorthand method for communicating information about customer needs. It does so by creating archetypes that enhance understanding and provide comparisons.

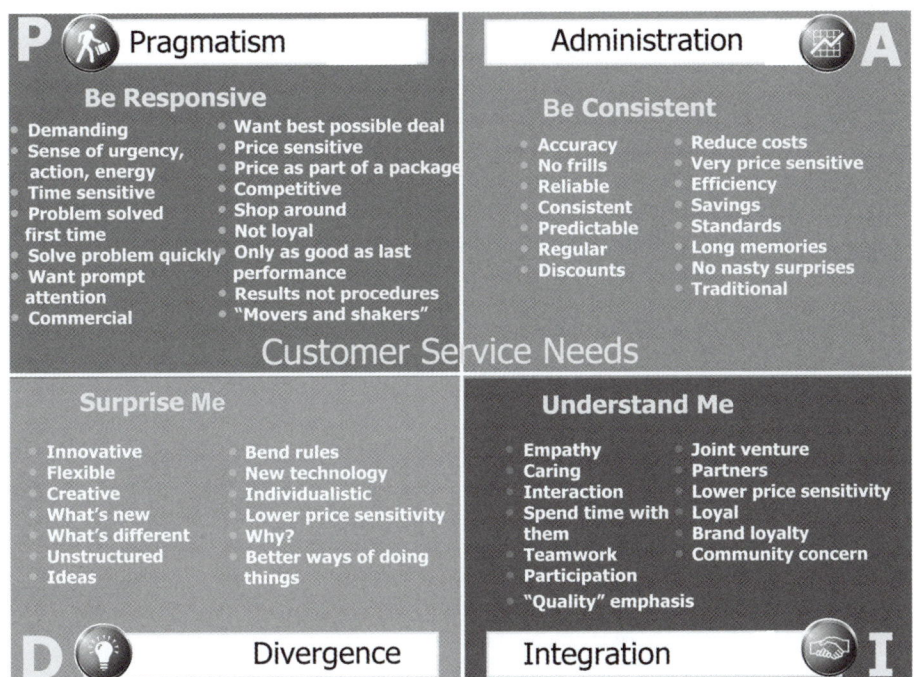

Segmenting your market

So far, our discussion and examples have referred mainly to the description and interpretation of whole markets. In practice, however, most markets are characterised by different segments that display different needs. We know that market segmentation allows us to identify these separate segments in order to provide a more "targeted" solution or strategy to each.

Often, these segments are characterised by different market logics, and PADI can be useful in understanding these differences.

Previously, we outlined the example of the hotel that serviced both business guests (during the week) and leisure guests (on the weekend).

Business guests have greater requirements for "P" service, while leisure guests have a clear preference for "I".

The challenge for the hotel was to recognise the different customers and to shape their service delivery to meet the needs of the different segments.

> *In a case I worked on some years ago, we were asked to assist the management of a major transport business. They had several divisions who all operated in the general and express freight markets.*
>
> *The business was not performing very well due to a variety of factors. One of the contributing reasons was the fact that the six operating divisions all operated in the same market space, and often ended up competing against each other. Aside from frustrating each other's efforts, there was considerable overlap and duplication in resources.*
>
> *We began with analysing the markets that these six divisions served. We found that there were some 37 different markets/market segments served by these operations. A partial list of these markets appears below:*

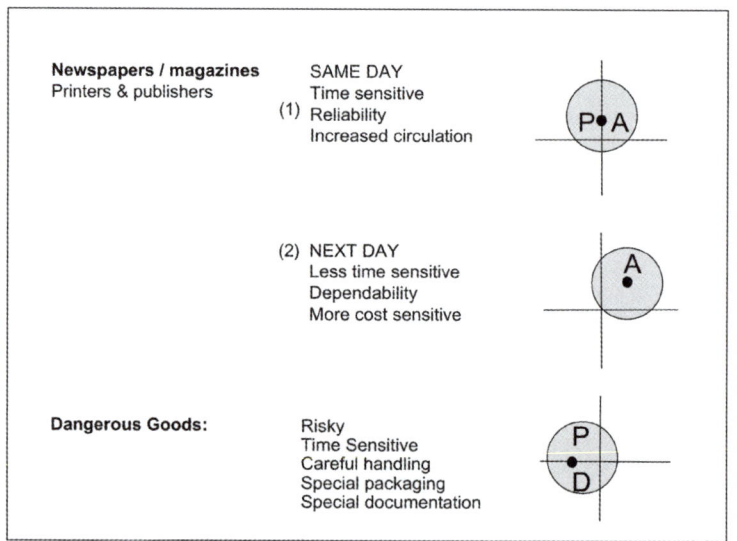

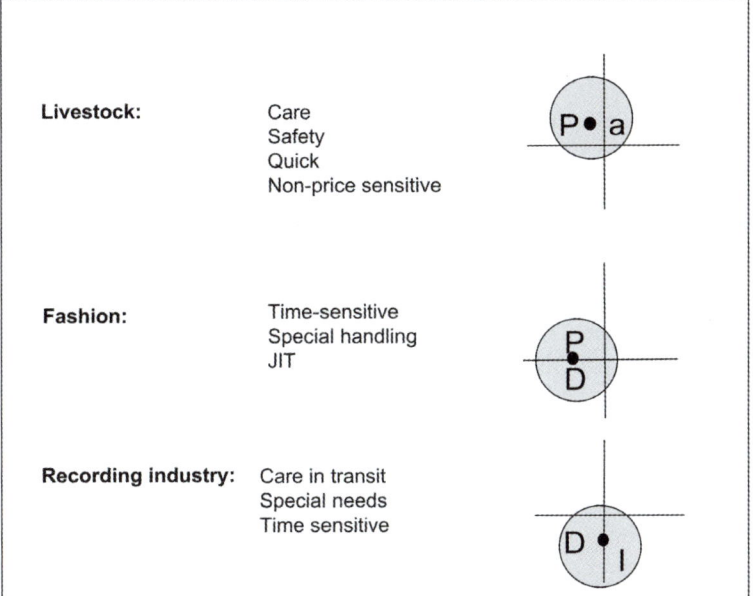

Management was keen to bring some order into the way that the divisions served the various markets. After analysing the needs of these markets by way of the PADI logics, we found that we were able to describe the market in a somewhat different way – by referring to the overall pattern of needs that linked all 37 markets.

We were able to identify three overarching market segments – each with a somewhat different pattern of needs and customer requirements:

Strategic Alignment

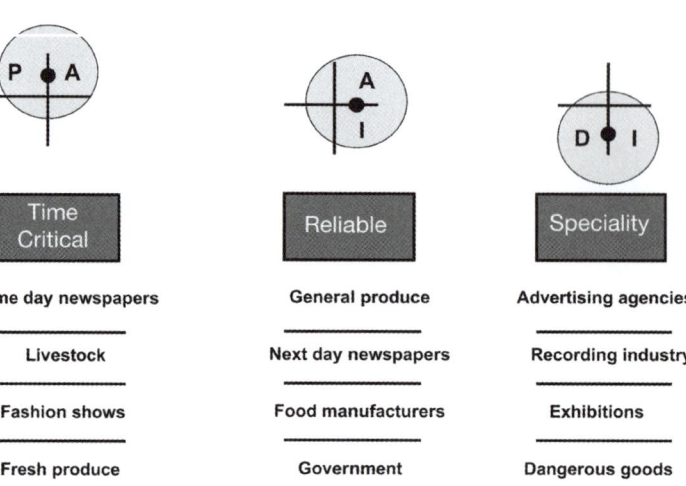

Each market segment was characterised by way of an internally consistent pattern of needs. This allowed each division to develop an overall strategy for dealing with their customers.

The divisions obviously had to cope with the differences between customers and meet each one's needs, but the "spread of difference" between the different customers was somewhat smaller, as they had been segmented according to similar needs. This has important implications for setting and implementing strategy as we will see in the next chapter.

Chapter 3

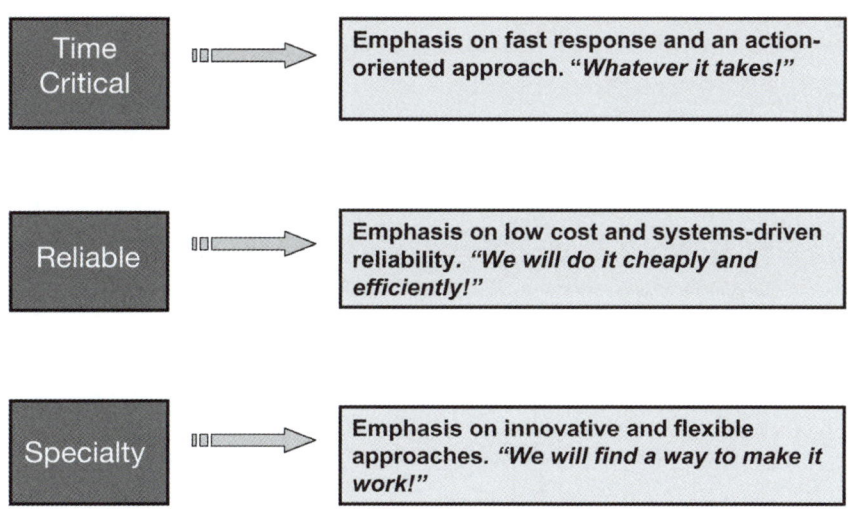

In time, this arrangement led to the restructure of the group into three business units, using the original rationale of the segmentation:

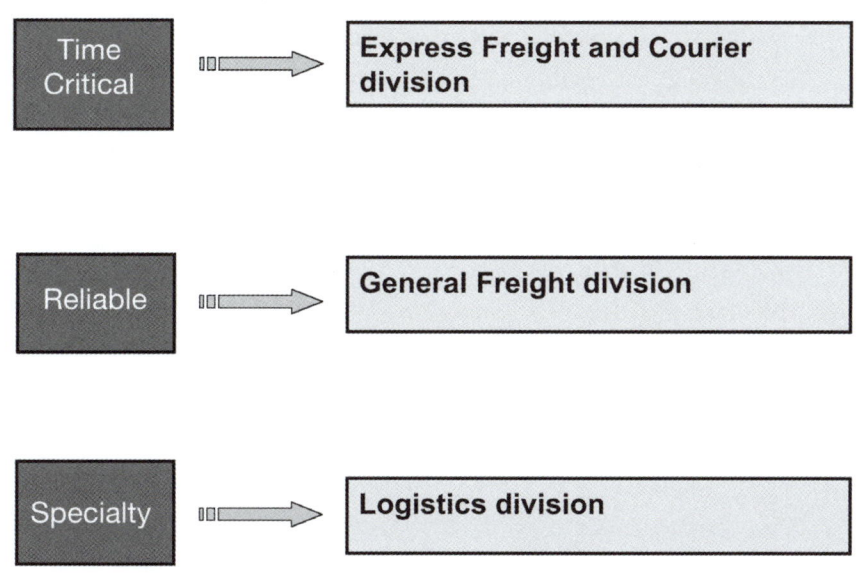

Key points in summary

Some of the key points to remember about describing your customers' needs are:

➤ Customers' needs may be described by way of their overall patterns of behaviour in the purchase situation. We can use archetypes to capture these patters in rich, holistic ways.

➤ The PADI model is a useful archetype to describe these behaviour patterns. Moreover, it allows us to understand the priorities and trade-offs made by customers as they express their needs in purchase or usage behaviour.

➤ The PADI model can be used to build shared understanding of the markets' needs throughout the organisation. It provides a shorthand method of communicating the needs of customers in different market segments.

➤ As we know from marketing theory, market segmentation allows us to group together customers with similar needs. These groupings, or segments, can then be "targeted" with more precise offerings that match the customers' needs. PADI offers a way of segmenting the market according to the patterns of behaviour of these customers.

Question 4: What effect do other environmental factors have on customer needs?

What are the other forces operating in my environment?

In the beginning of this chapter, I stated that I like to start my analysis of the environment with an understanding of customer needs. We recognised, however, that there were many other factors in the organisation's environment that had to be addressed.

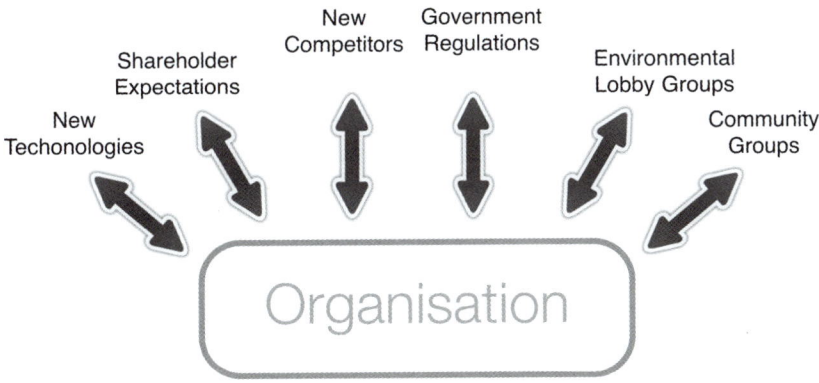

Many of these factors have an impact on your customers' needs and also on the way the organisation goes about its business. For example, the development of new technologies might mean that the organisation has to change the way it operates. Or new competitors might enter the market and provide a product or service that better meets the customers' needs.

How do we account for these forces? What impact do they have on our customers' needs and our ability to service them?

Scanning the environment

There are many techniques for scanning the environment, but Gary Hamel and CK Prahalad (1994) point to a useful approach for dealing with the major forces at play in the environment.

1. Identify the key forces in you environment that may have an impact on your organisation. Be as specific as possible, so that there is a common understanding of the implications of these forces. Identify the direction and pace of the force. You need to include both:

    i. Industry issues (eg, competitive forces, new technologies, legislation etc);

    ii. Trends (eg, social, political, economic).

2. Divide the forces into three categories:

    i. Forces that will decline;

    ii. Forces that will continue;

    iii. Forces that will emerge in the future.

3. Focus on three to five of the continuing or emerging forces that you believe will have the greatest impact on your organisation and customers. For each force ask:

    ➤ What causes this force?

    ➤ What threats are posed? Now and in the future?

    ➤ What opportunities are presented? Now and in the future?

    ➤ What do we need to do?

Chapter 3

Developing Market Foresight

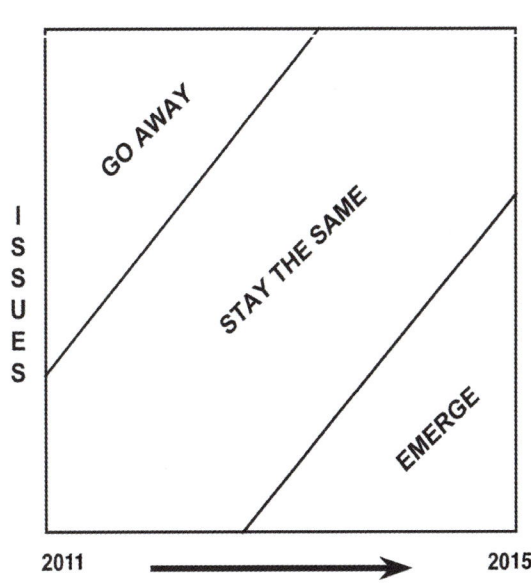

Issues
- Market rules
- Customers
- Channels
- Competitors
- Basis for competition
- Margins
- Distinctive competences
- Product markets

4. Finally, for each force ask:

   ➤ What is our preferred outcome?

   ➤ What key uncertainties still exist?

   ➤ What future shocks may be in store for us?

> Through a scan of the environment, new markets and segments are anticipated. The "Green" movement sparked the development of new "I" flavoured markets such as green electricity products, cleaning products and recycled paper products.
>
> In Australia, anticipation of electricity, telecommunication and airline deregulation signalled to organisations a need for a radical change in service delivery required to succeed in the new market.

The environmental scan allows you to move your field of vision beyond the present to issues that may emerge in the future. You should be more alert to emerging change and be able to seize opportunities and defend your organisation against threats through early detection of forces in the operating environment.

Assessing the impact on customer needs

I am often surprised by the resilience of the fundamental drivers of customer needs. Anecdotally, I am often told that "customer needs are changing so fast", or *"we don't know where the market is going".*

In reality, when we take the trouble to analyse and describe customers' needs, we often find that the basic needs have stayed the same, but that the customer is considering alternative products and services that do a better job of meeting these needs! Usually it is the organisation that has failed to keep up with customer needs that makes these complaints!

However, there are numerous cases where the forces described in the section above will have an impact on customer needs. And in most cases, we can understand these and work them out from first principles.

> ### Use of walk-in medical clinics
>
> *When I was a young boy, my uncle was a general practitioner in a middle-class suburb of Cape Town. He had a large practice and was clearly a very well liked and trusted doctor in the community.*
>
> *I recall many stories he told where he estimated that approximately half of his consultations were with patients who had no real medical complaint. They visited him to get his advice and counsel on matters that included marital problems, financial difficulties and business decisions! The defining*

factor in those interactions was the close, intimate relationship they shared with Dr Benjamin Chorn.

Nowadays, a number of factors have emerged that has changed these "customer needs". These include:
- *The time-pressures of a modern lifestyle;*
- *Greater patient knowledge of medical conditions from other sources such as the Internet;*
- *The ability to obtain specialist advice from other sources such as accountants, counsellors etc.*

As a consequence, customers have a different set of needs from general practitioners these days. These needs include:
- *Conveniently located clinics;*
- *Opening hours outside normal working times;*
- *Efficient, low-cost provision of quality services.*

This shift might be graphically represented as follows:

Medical services

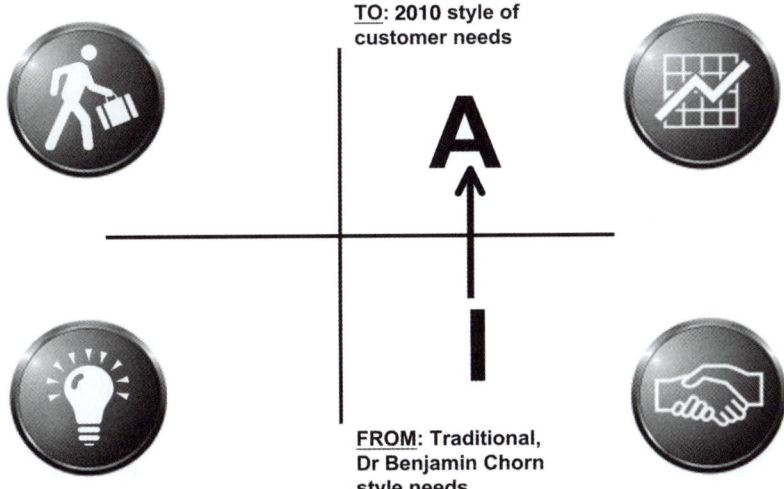

SPL Group's customers

The SPL Group experienced a significant shift in the forces within their operating environment. With the arrival of the major groups and chains into the hardware market, many of the "rules of the game" shifted.

Their traditional market was quite fragmented and regional. It was made up of many, small independent stores who did not hold much stock and ran their business along very simple lines.

The buyers in the major groups and chains, on the other hand, were far more sophisticated and demanded well thought through retail programs to suit their strategic positioning in the market.

Accordingly, management recognised that the whole "logic" of the market was changing and that they needed to develop a very different strategic response.

The shift in the market could be seen as follows:

The hardware buyer's market

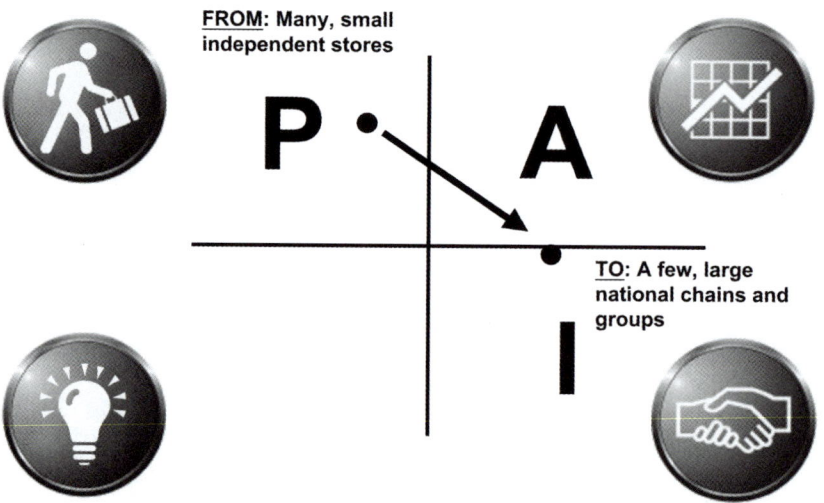

FROM: Many, small independent stores

TO: A few, large national chains and groups

> *In this example, the needs shifted from a fast-response "hit and run" style of representative, to a collaborative, partnership approach that built long-term strategies and joint programs.*

Both of these cases can be explained by the use of the PADI framework. In each case, the analysis reveals that:

➤ The change in environmental forces caused a shift in the needs and behaviours of customers.

➤ These changes resulted from a change in priorities and the trade-offs made by the customers.

Key points in summary

The key factors to remember in considering the impact of other forces in the environment are:

➤ There are a number of forces in the operating environment that can impact on the needs of customers and, therefore, strategic response.

➤ Scanning the operating environment and assessing which of these forces will change or increase in intensity is a useful way of analysing the impact on customer needs.

➤ The impact on customer needs may often be worked out from first principles by using PADI to understand the new priorities and tradeoffs made by customers.

Strategic Alignment

As we complete our assessment of the customers in our operating environment, it is time to turn to the issue of strategy: How do we respond in a manner that takes into account what we have found out from the analysis of customer needs?

Chapter 4
Developing a winning strategy

Strategy is about choice

Strategy is all about choice. It is choosing which games to play and how you wish to play them, which industries, segments and markets you will address, which products and services you will deliver to the market, how you will combine your resources and which technologies you will use.

It is about deciding how you will manage the interface between you and your operating environment. Because, after you have done all the analysis and understood the needs of your customers, you still have to make a choice about meeting those needs.

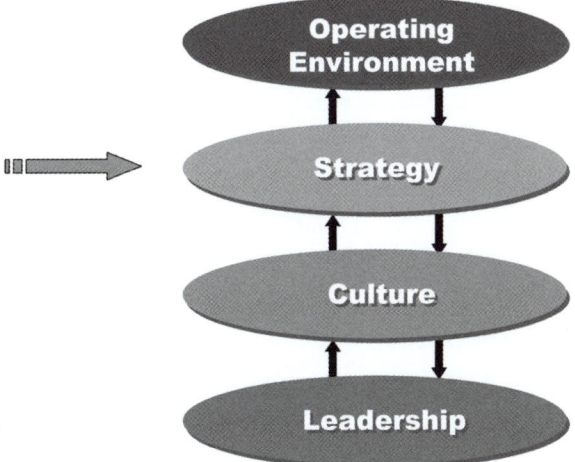

Effectiveness depends on fit

Strategic Alignment

Earlier, I raised the issue of your strategic stance – whether you elect to be a:

➤ Rule taker: You operate within the "rules" of the market and meet the customer's needs as they expect;

➤ Rule breaker: You break the rules of the market to do something different and attract the attention of the customers;

➤ Rule maker: You set out to change the rules of the game by delivering a radically new approach to meeting the needs of customers.

While we know from the research (Chandler, Rumelt, Burns & Stalker, Lawrence & Lorsch, Emery & Twist, Chorn) that the organisation's effectiveness is related to the extent to which it is aligned to the market (strategic alignment), management still needs to choose which of these positions it will adopt.

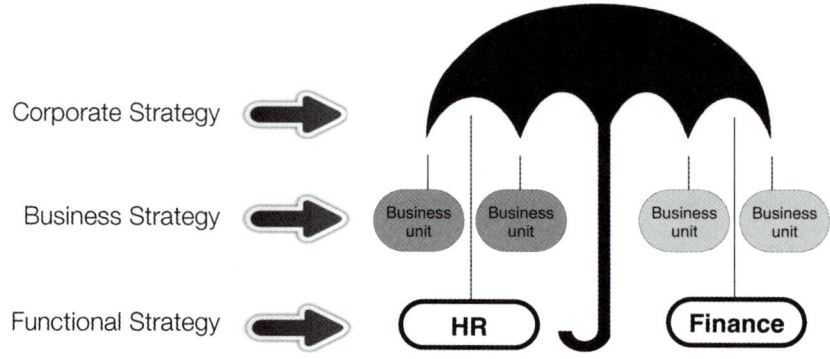

As shown above, strategy exists at three levels within the organisation, and it takes on different forms at each of these three levels.

Corporate strategy Focuses on overall shape of the portfolio and the allocation of resources among the different business units. Key question = **What business are we in?**

Business strategy Focuses on how to operate and compete within the business area that has been defined by corporate strategy.
Key question = ***How do we compete effectively in this business?***

Functional strategy Focuses on how the support areas will add value to the business unit they are part of or servicing.
Key question = ***How can we add value to the efforts of this business?***

Balance or focus in the strategy?

One of the most fascinating dilemmas that I have encountered in my career is the different positions adopted by the human resources and marketing strategy fraternities on the position of effectiveness. I spent parts of my career in both human resources and marketing positions and have experienced both of these perspectives in action.

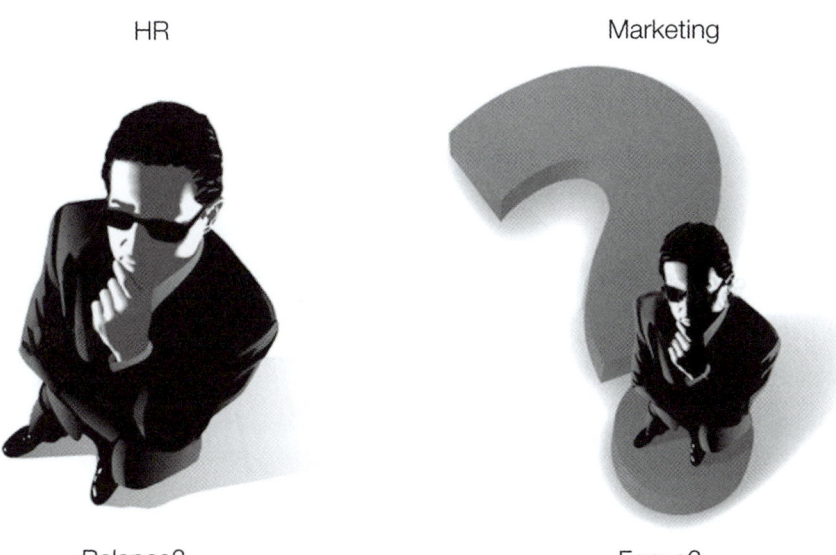

HR — Balance?

Marketing — Focus?

The human resources and organisation development area is interested in developing the capability and effectiveness of the organisation through the use of its people and skills (Mintzberg (1978)). One of the key issues they address is the notion of *balance* within the organisation's human resource capabilities.

More particularly, they advocate that people, teams, and organisations should strive for balance in their make-up and the way they operate. For example, if you are a details-oriented person, it is good to work in collaboration with a big-picture thinker. If your team is full of "starters" who can launch new projects, you need to add "finishers" who can see the projects through (Belbin (1981), Hunter (1998)).

The marketing and strategy research, on the other hand, is full of evidence that suggests that effective organisations are *focused* in their efforts (Miles & Snow (1984)). They advocate that organisations should be clear about their goal and commit resources to it.

However, it strikes me that *focus* is *imbalance*. Focus is the deliberate over-allocation of resource and effort into an area in the expectation of above-average return.

FOCUS ⇨ IMBALANCE

If I look around at people I know who have made an extraordinary contribution in a field – they have usually done so by way of an imbalance in the way they have allocated time and effort to the other parts of their lives. So, the focus comes about as a result of a deliberate trade-off of certain things in favour of others.

IMBALANCE ⇨ TRADE OFF

> *Bruce Fordyce – ultra-marathon athlete*
>
> *Bruce Fordyce was an extraordinary athlete in an extraordinary event – the ultra-marathon road race.*
>
> *The Comrades Marathon is run every year in South Africa between Durban and Pietermartizburg. It is a 96 kilometre race that includes a large number of challenging hills between the inland city and the coast. Only the very fit compete, let alone do well.*
>
> *Between the years of 1976 and 1988 Bruce Fordyce dominated the event. He was by far the most successful athlete ever to compete in this race – winning nine times in succession. And he followed an extraordinary fitness and training regime. In fact, he designed much of his life at the time around his ultra-marathon career and this race.*
>
> *Perhaps the most telling trade-off he made was his choice of work. He worked in the university library because this job allowed him to spend most of his working day sitting down! Although he held a Master's degree from the same university, he was prepared to trade-off his working career in favour of his career as an ultra-marathon athlete.*

Strategy and the PADI logics

We can use the PADI model to describe strategy and also to address the issue of focus versus balance.

As we know, the organisation's strategy is how it chooses to respond to the market in which it operates. We can use PADI to describe and understand the basic choices facing management in an organisation.

Strategy types

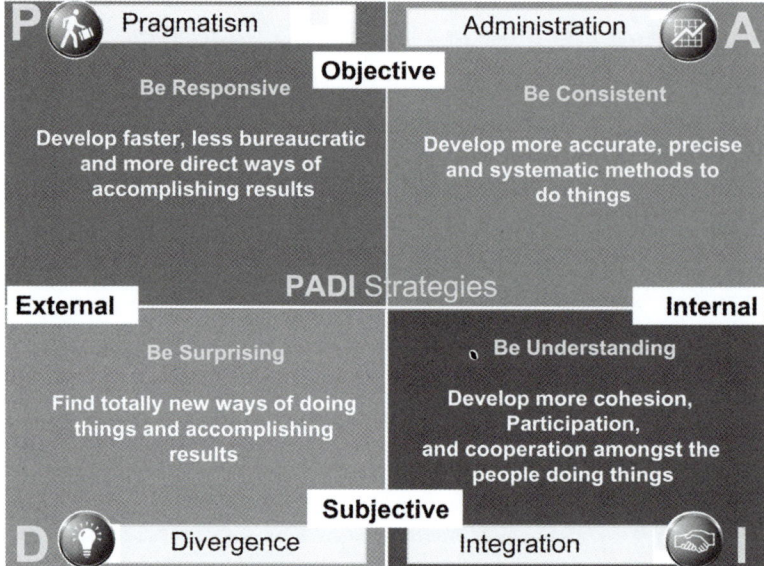

As we can see, each of the four strategies emphasise a particular direction and platform. As we will examine later, each of these strategy types involves a series of trade-offs in the way the organisation is designed, resourced and managed.

We have defined effectiveness as the ability to be relevant to your market and meeting customer requirements – that is, being strategically aligned with the market. Therefore, a "P" strategy is best suited to a "P" market, and so on.

The "P" strategy

In a "P" environment, the organisation's ability to respond rapidly to customer needs is key. Time is always of the essence.

The strategic platform of an organisation within a "P" market is likely to:

➤ Respond very rapidly to customer needs and changes in their requests;

➤ Attempt to solve problems quickly and first time;

➤ Develop and address market niches that value the need for fast response and a "can-do" attitude.

Express courier companies typically have a "P" strategic approach. All of their systems are geared for maximising their responsiveness to their customers.

Their phone booking systems have customer details recorded on a data base for speedier processing; couriers are equipped with phones and walkie-talkies for rapid pick-up and delivery. Tracking and tracing systems are in place for prompt feedback. Motor bikes and push bikes are used where possible for quicker movement through traffic.

Strategic Alignment

The "A" strategy

In an "A" environment, the key competitive response is the ability of the organisation to put systems and procedure in place for maximum efficiency and low cost.

The strategic platform of an organisation within an "A" environment is likely to:

➤ Develop systems and procedures to standardise operations;

➤ Provide a consistent solution for customers and achieve economies of scale through higher volumes of this solution;

➤ Focus on segments where low cost, value for money products and solutions are valued;

➤ Focus on continuous improvements to ensure that the organisation maintains its position as a low-cost supplier.

The low cost airlines in Australia, Virgin Blue and Jetstar, are good examples of organisations that have focused on systems and procedures to standardise operations.

Both airlines have standardised their fleets to simplify servicing and spare parts, and make use of Internet-booking systems to maximise their efficiencies.

Their market proposition is no-frills, low cost and value-for-money air travel. It appeals to travellers who have standard requirements and economy travel as a primary need.

The "D" strategy

In a "D" environment, the strategy of the organisation is concerned with always seeking newer and more innovative approaches to meeting customer needs. The organisation seeks to surprise their markets.

The strategic platform of an organisation within a "D" environment is likely to:

➤ Focus on R&D and new product development in markets that value innovation and leading-edge technologies;

➤ Encourage and develop creative and flexible solutions to organisational and customer issues using high levels of technical expertise and personnel;

➤ Often seek first-mover or first-to-market advantages in markets.

Many advertising agencies have obvious "D" strategies. They work flexibly to generate high levels of creativity in their work.

Their objective is to generate innovative approaches to communicate a client's proposition in order to "win" a particular position or space in the market.

The key staff – who are highly valued and have primary decision-making roles in the organisation – are often technical experts in their various fields (media, copywriting, art etc).

Advertising agencies are often seeking the "big idea" that will re-define the rules of the game for their clients.

Strategic Alignment

The "I" strategy

In an "I" environment, the organisation seeks to build long-term, loyal relationships with its customers. It has a strong partnering stance that promotes collaboration and "joint venture" type initiatives.

The strategic platform of an organisation within a "I" environment is likely to:

➤ Have a high level of internal team work, collaboration and participatory style of management;

➤ Have a consultative and partnering style of customer relationship – requiring ongoing and long-term commitment to partnering principles;

➤ Focus on loyalty and adopting a long-term view – decisions and actions are based on consultations with both customers and staff.

The Qantas frequent-flyer membership is an example of an "I" strategy. Qantas attempts to retain its customers by offering free flights for loyalty and support.

The program is graded to offer increasing benefits to more frequent fliers – from "silver" members who have access to the lounges to "Chairman's Lounge" members who have their own exclusive facilities and are offered upgrades on a frequent basis.

The strategy of the frequent flyer program is to make Qantas customers feel like important partners in the business. Hence they provide newsletters, regular offers for discounted merchandise and other personalised give-aways.

The four PADI strategies

Following the discussion above, we can assemble the four PADI strategies to complete the matrix:

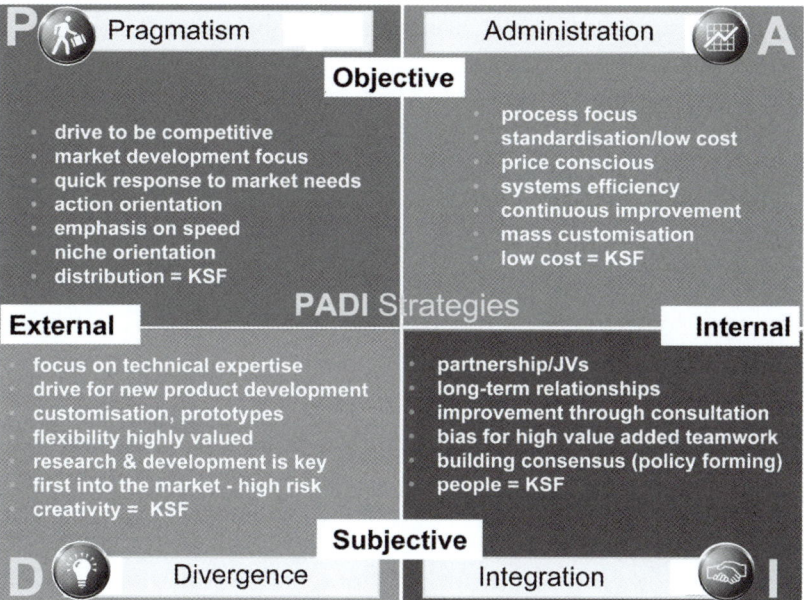

The matrix highlights the key features of the four strategy types. It also identifies the "Key Success Factors" (KSF) in each strategy.

Strategy is about trade-off

In discussing the concept of balance versus focus earlier, I alluded to the fact that successful endeavours usually involve some sacrifice or trade-off.

My experience suggests that effective strategy is imbalanced. It is this imbalance that allows the organisation to put above-average effort into one area (usually at the expense of another).

Is this completely necessary? Can't we find a way to get the organisation focused and successful in all areas?

Pathways to competitive advantage

Let's begin by exploring how an organisation achieves competitive advantage in its market or operating environment.[1]

An organisation achieves competitive advantage by being better than its competitors. In other words, the organisation has to outperform any rivals in its choice and execution of strategy.

---

1 Public sector organisations, or those with a captive market, may find it difficult to consider "competitive advantage". However, my experience suggests that this is still a powerful consideration, since all organisations would want to be in a position of the "preferred supplier". Where organisations are not overly concerned about achieving this status, most economies will find ways of removing those organisations or their captive market status.

Chapter 4

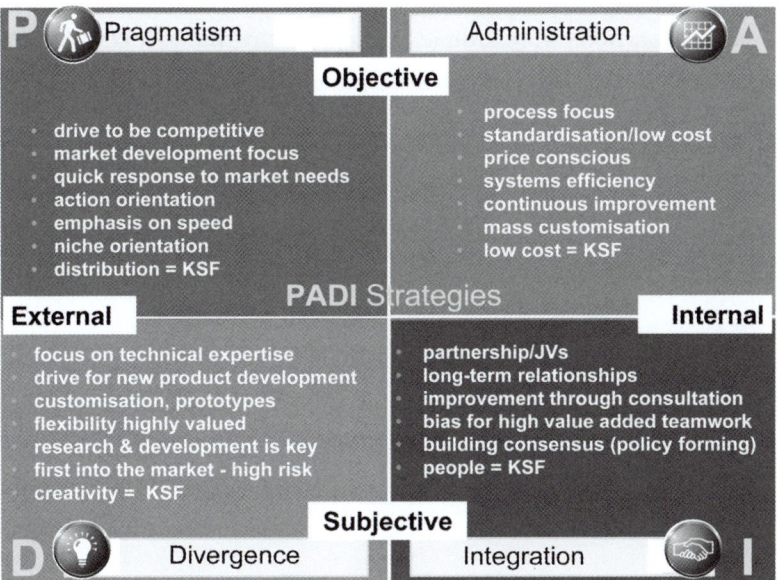

So, an organisation could achieve competitive advantage by:

➤ *Being faster and more responsive than competitors and having a very sharp focus on the market niches it has chosen to serve.* An example might be the emergency plumbing service that gets to your premises within an hour of being called.

➤ *Being more efficient and more reliable than competitors and achieving a very low cost of supply that appeals to economy-minded customers.* An example is a direct-sales (over the phone) insurance company that provides very cheap car insurance.

➤ *Being more innovative and flexible in meeting customer's needs and having high levels of technical expertise and problem-solving.* An example is an IT firm that is known for its ability to develop and deliver complex systems to meet client needs.

➤ *Having better long-term relationships with customers and developing a strong partnering approach that builds interdependency and profitable collaboration.* An example is a legal firm that has become a trusted business partner and really understands the business of its client.

➤ So far, so good. But why can't an organisation successfully pursue a strategy that combines speed and fast response with customer intimacy and partnering with clients? Why can't we combine lowest cost of supply with innovation and flexibility?

Trade-offs in strategic capability

The difficulty in attempting all these strategies simultaneously lies in the fact each strategy requires different resources and capability.

As we can see, each strategy requires a fundamentally different configuration of resources, skills and capabilities within the organisation:

➤ The "P" strategy has to be supported by high levels of activity and energy within the organisation. This is usually facilitated by flat organisation structures with high levels of autonomy. Staff near the customer interface are highly empowered, have broad job descriptions and are expected to take fast decisions and be accountable for them (eg, the emergency plumbing service).

➤ The "I" strategy emphasises relationships, partnering and teams in a highly collaborative mode. In order to support this approach, the organisation will have a very consultative and participative approach that ensures all opinions have been considered before actions are taken (eg, the legal firm).

➤ The "D" strategy is driven by innovation, creativity and flexibility. These capabilities are facilitated by high levels of personal autonomy, flexible working arrangements and a style that emphasises finding new ways and approaches for doing things.

The organisational form is extremely fluid and uses few systems and controls (eg, the IT consulting firm).

➤ The "A" strategy emphasises systems, controls and procedures in order to achieve high levels of standardisation and reliability. The organisational form is more hierarchical and staff have precise job descriptions with clear lines of reporting. There is a strong focus on expense management and cutting costs (eg, the phone sales insurance company).

Focus in resource & capability

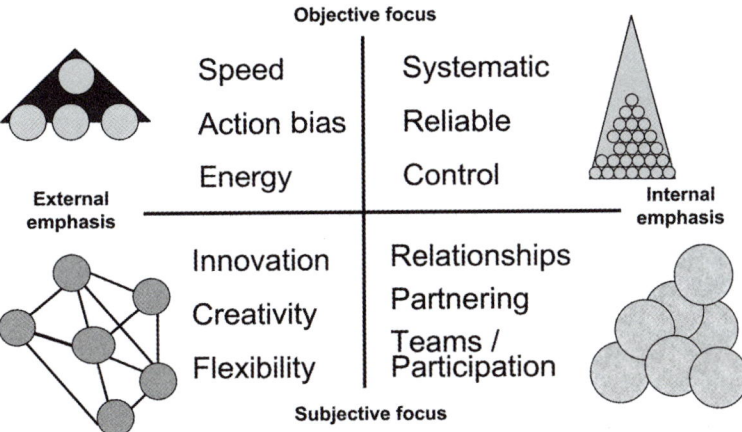

The configuration of resources and capabilities that are required to support an effective "P" strategy (speed and fast response in order to deliver quickly) are fundamentally opposed to the arrangements that are required for an "I" strategy (customer intimacy and long-term relationships, that is, time spent with the customer).

And the same goes for the "D" / "A" combination. "D" strategies (innovation and creativity to deliver new solutions) are supported by flexibility and fluid organisational form, while "A" strategies (low cost and reliability to deliver standardised solutions) are supported by strong systems and controls.

Strategic Alignment

So, we can't get effective diagonal combinations if we wish to produce the high levels of effectiveness required for competitive advantage. Remember the issue of diagonals in the earlier chapter?

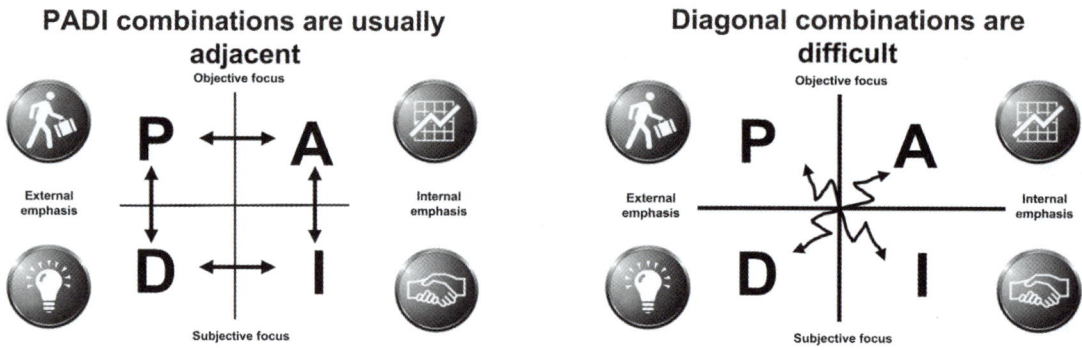

> **The airline industry and trade-offs**
>
> Consider the case of Southwest Airlines in the US domestic air-travel market.[2]
>
> Southwest offered low-priced flights through minimising their costs. They maximised flying time by choosing routes between mid-sized cities and secondary airports in large cities in the US. By doing this they avoided the more congested, delay-prone, 'hub' destinations and maximised their turn-around times. They maximised efficiency of maintenance by using a standardised fleet of Boeing 737 aircraft.
>
> Southwest did not offer meals, assigned seats, interline baggage checking or premium classes of service to their customers. Their ticketing system encouraged customers to buy direct rather than through a travel agent to avoid commissions. Southwest was able to offer low-cost travel by limiting the range of services offered to its customers and so maximising flying hours.

Continental launched a new service called "Continental Lite" in response to the success of Southwest Airlines. Continental Lite, however, was unable to make the type of trade-offs that allowed Southwest to keep its costs down. Its planes were delayed leaving the congested city airports that Southwest avoided. Gate turn-around was slowed down by baggage transfers that Southwest didn't offer.

Continental could not compete on price and still pay commissions to travel agents, but it needed travel agents for its full-service business, so it cut commissions for all its services. It also reduced its frequent flyer bonuses to all its customers because it could not afford to offer the same bonuses to the lower priced, "Lite" tickets. The result was dissatisfied travel agents and dissatisfied full-service customers.

Continental was unable to compete in the low-price market and its full-service position was also compromised. Continental Lite lost hundreds of millions of dollars and the CEO lost his job.

Southwest had tailored its activities to provide an excellent low-cost, no-frills, reliable travel between secondary destinations. Continental failed because its activities were geared to servicing a different market with a different strategy.

Continental's full service offered flexibility of full destination choice, ease of purchase through travel agents, price as part of a package of other services, convenience of meals, baggage transfers and assigned seats and service class options. The activities required to produce the low-cost service were incompatible with those required for excellent service in Continental's traditional markets. Continental had not made the necessary trade-offs in their service delivery.

What does this mean for effective strategy?

Effective strategy embraces the trade-offs inherent in retaining focus. Rather than avoiding the trade-offs and trying to cover all bases, certain trade-offs have to be made and managed.

The Southwest/Continental example illustrates the danger of attempting to be all things to all people. It illustrates that there are often penalties associated with trying to cover all the bases. At best, the organisation will not be truly competitive in any area of its strategy. At worst, the organisation can cease to be relevant to any market and fail.

Vertical and horizontal combinations can be achieved, since the capabilities that are sought are not incompatible. So, the organisation can be:

- Fast and low cost ; or
- Low cost and intimate with customers; or
- Intimate with customers and innovative; or
- Innovative and fast.

I have spent many years attempting to understand these issues of trade-off. It seems pretty harmless to set a strategy that combines speed and intimacy, or innovation and low cost. And in many cases it makes sense to do so! But I have found that the real problems occur when you try to successfully implement the strategy.

Without embracing trade-offs, the different elements of the strategy somehow fail to achieve synergy. Or they cause real friction within the organisation. Or even worse, the strategy never gains traction inside the organisation and life continues as if nothing has happened!

Chapter 4

So, if management recognises the need to develop and implement an effective strategy, the issues of focus and trade-offs have to be considered and managed.

"But, can't I develop different strategies for different parts of the organisation?" is a question I am often asked by senior managers. Yes, you can. But this produces some challenges in the area of organisation design. We need to ensure that we design the organisation appropriately so that we can accommodate the different areas of focus within the structure.

We will deal with this topic in a later chapter. But I do want to mention, however, that the solution is *not* simply to create a functional structure with each function having its own PADI strategy. This produces difficulties in other ways.

Key points in summary

- ➤ Strategy is about choosing the way in which you wish to operate in your market. A "P" strategy in a "P" market is more likely to produce an effective organisation.

- ➤ Competitive advantage is usually achieved by focusing on a particular approach to strategy and implementing it well.

- ➤ Focus in strategy usually requires an imbalance in your resource allocation – you have to trade-off certain attributes for others.

Strategic Alignment

Chapter 4

Chapter 5
Developing an appropriate culture

Culture in organisations

I vividly remember 2 January 1987. It is the day I sat down and began writing up the findings from the biggest research program I had yet undertaken – my doctoral thesis.

The title of the thesis was *"The Relationship between Business Level Strategy and Organisational Culture"*.

Certainly, there had been much written and researched about strategy – but the concept of "organisational culture" was relatively new and there was a great deal of excitement about this new way to understand our organisations.

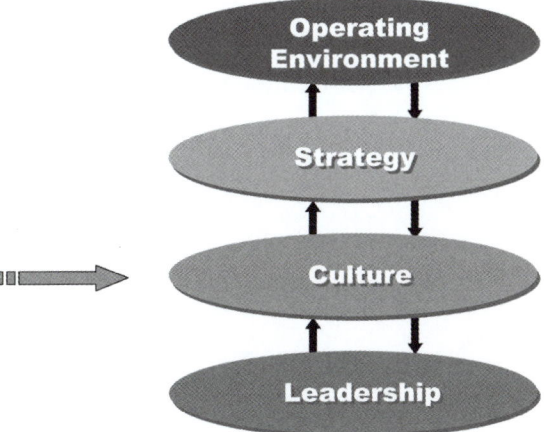

Effectiveness depends on fit

Consultants did culture surveys, managers spoke of culture change and the human resources practitioners had a new rationale for arguing that organisations needed to manage their people more effectively.

But the term "culture" was, and still is, often misconstrued. Managers still launch major change initiatives that are focused on achieving "a change in culture", but no-one actually knows what this means and life goes on as usual!

Put simply, culture means "the way things are done around here". It refers to the patterns of behaviour that occur within the organisation when people go about their work. As we know, these patterns are quite robust and they affect much of what goes on inside the organisation.

> References to "culture" are focused on "organisational culture" – the culture that occurs within the organisations in which we work and interact with. This is also sometimes called "corporate culture", but this term confuses the concept of the corporate entity and the business entity. I will deal with this in more detail in the later chapter on organisation design.

Organisational culture includes a number of elements or factors within the organisation which are useful for researchers and consultants in describing and diagnosing the culture. Some of these include:

➤ The way communication occurs;

➤ The way decisions are made;

➤ The way change is managed;

➤ The way the organisation responds to external influences;

➤ The way work is organised.

Culture is neither "good" nor "bad"

My clients are often tempted to describe an organisation as having a "good" or a "bad" culture. But this is not a useful way of thinking, since we know that a culture is only appropriate or inappropriate for a given situation: what works in one situation need not necessarily work in another. Remember the advertising agency and gold mine in Chapter 1?

Culture should be aligned to the business strategy

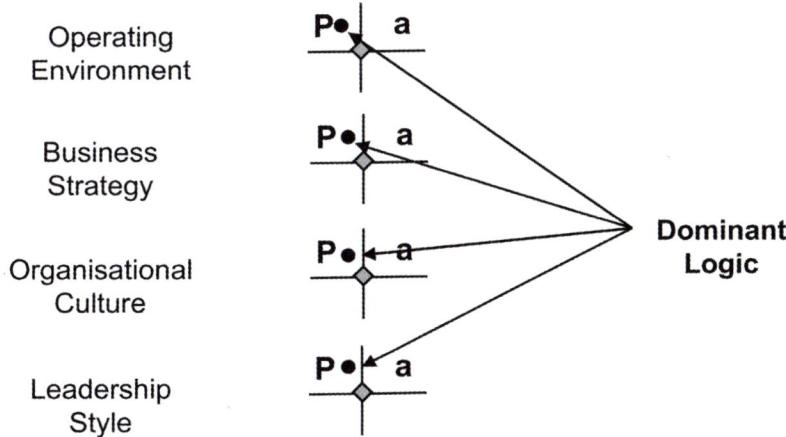

Strategic alignment allows us to say that an appropriate culture is one that is suited to the operating environment and the organisation's strategy. And similarly, an inappropriate culture is one that prevents or inhibits the organisation from implementing its strategy.

Closely related to this is the confusion that often exists when senior managers try to create a "common culture" across their organisation. *"I want our organisation to have a single, strong culture that binds us together"* is something I am often told by my clients.

Why is this not appropriate?

Culture is a multiple concept in organisations

Many organisations have more than one market in which they operate. And accordingly, they employ more that one business strategy to address these different markets. For example, the case of the Transport Company (see Chapter 3) identified that the organisation faced three major market segments:

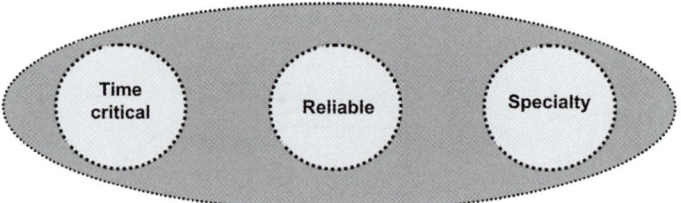

They developed a specific business strategy for each of these markets and individual business units to deliver these strategies:

Chapter 5

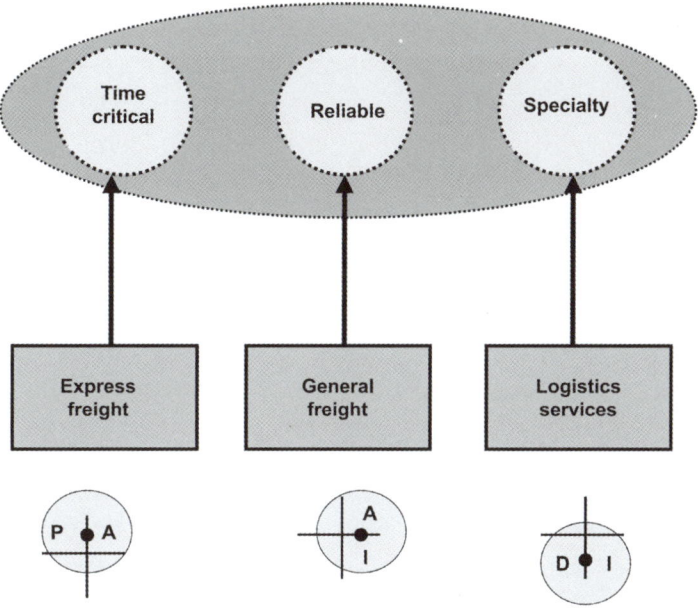

Each business unit had its own appropriate strategy and culture in order to allow it to properly implement the strategy and operate in the chosen market.

It would have been inappropriate for the CEO of the organisation to decree that all the business units needed to have the same culture. Indeed, the business units were designed with different cultures in mind. They used different organisation structures, different performance measures and employed different types of staff.

So, rather than having a single culture, organisations are a portfolio of different cultures – each culture (hopefully) suited to the needs of the business unit and/or strategy in that part of the organisation.

I have many conversations with senior managers about this issue. Many seem intent upon building a common culture across their diverse organisations in order to get the required integration and "corporate perspective".

But this is not only hard to achieve, it may be detrimental to the effectiveness of the organisation! If we liken culture to the "capabilities to play the game", then a common culture is a straight-jacket that forces the whole organisation to operate in the same way. Like Ford's Any colour you want, as long as it's black!

Having dealt with this issue, however, there are two more to address:

1. What binds a diverse organisation together, particularly one with different business units operating in different markets?

2. How can we design and build an organisation that embraces diverse cultures without fragmenting the organisation and losing effectiveness?

These issues are covered in detail in Chapter 7. However, I will submit two short answers for your consideration at this point:

1. The organisation's strategic vision binds the organisation together. This usually operates at the Corporate Strategy level and should define the role and place of each business unit.

2. The organisation design should, ideally, group together parts of the organisation that serve the same market: a business unit. That way each business unit has a culture appropriate to the market it serves.

Note, however, that this is not the same as grouping similar functions together (eg, the accounting unit or the human resources unit) and then allowing them to develop a unique culture for their function.

Culture is both seen and unseen

Culture exists at different levels inside organisations – some seen and others unseen. Perhaps the best way to visualise culture is by using Edgar Schein's (1986) model of the iceberg:

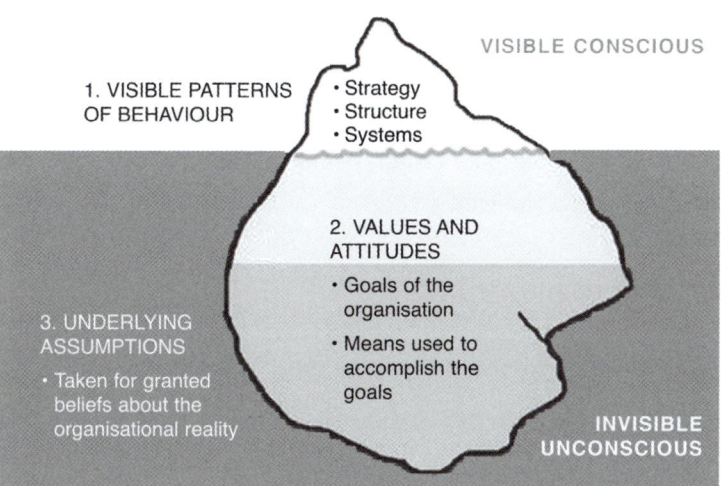

1. Visible patterns of behaviour
The visible parts of the culture are observable and most amenable to change. They include elements such as structure, how work is organised, reporting and control systems and the strategy that is being pursued in the market.

2. Values and beliefs
The invisible components are more difficult to describe and have a powerful effect on the behaviour of staff within the organisation.

These values and beliefs relate to the "real" goals of the organisation and how the organisation is committed to achieving these goals. For example, I work with a number of organisations where the executive calls for the different divisions to collaborate and take a "corporate" (whole of business) perspective.

However, when the staff observes the behaviours of their managers, they see them making "selfish" decisions that may be detrimental to the whole organisation, but beneficial to the division in question and the bonuses of the specific individuals.

These behaviours and actions determine the "real" values of the organisation – that the way to get ahead in the organisation is to look after your division and your job, rather that the interests of the organisation as a whole. These are the values and beliefs that drive the behaviour of staff and managers. (Sometimes these "selfish" behaviours are exacerbated due to the reward systems in the organisation – for example, emphasising individual performance at the expense of team performance).

3. Underlying assumptions

These are the taken-for-granted assumptions that people make about the organisation and the way it works. More deep-rooted than values and beliefs, they are very difficult to change.

An example of underlying assumptions is well illustrated by a consulting project I had in the late 1980s.

> *The state government utility*
>
> *A major state government utility in NSW was keen to implement a quality management initiative in order to improve the overall effectiveness and responsiveness of the organisation. I began working with a small team in order to identify the key cultural barriers to change.*
>
> *One of the key findings was the organisation's underlying assumptions about "rate payers". When we began to question the use of this term in their business plans and reports, senior management suggested that we simply change the*

word to "customers" in all future versions of the business plan and annual report!

But, of course, the problem was more deep-seated than simply the use of outdated language. The issue was around the assumptions made by the organisation about the citizens they "served".

We showed management an analysis of the different underlying assumptions that supported the use of the two terms:

"Ratepayer"	"Customer"
They pay us a rate for the service we provide	We charge a fee that represents the value of the service to the customer
They are fortunate to have professionals like us provide these services	We are pleased and grateful to have their business
If they don't pay their rates, we will cut off their service	If we don't look after them, they will take their business elsewhere

Although we had much debate about the nature of public sector versus private sector organisations, we were able to demonstrate to management that a significant cultural shift was needed to re-orientate the organisation.

Incidentally, our efforts were assisted by the public outcry several months later when the organisation responded very arrogantly to concerns about environmental pollution. We were able to point out that the underlying assumptions of the culture were a powerful driver of this behaviour.

Real cultural change is only possible when these underlying assumptions are surfaced and challenged. I will discuss this further in Chapter 8.

Culture is not climate

I find it useful to distinguish between the concepts of culture and climate. Climate can be thought of as the 'mood' of the organisation. Climate is often the focus of employee opinion surveys and relates to employees satisfaction with their working conditions and general morale. Climate can change rapidly and does not have a long-term effect on the ability of an organisation to successfully implement its strategies.

Culture, on the other hand, is a more enduring phenomenon that is more difficult to change as it consists of a range of institutionalised behaviours and underlying attitudes and values that are widely shared in the organisation.

If climate is the mood of the organisation, culture can be thought of as the personality. Culture directly relates to the long-term capability of the organisation to implement its strategy.

Why make the distinction? I have found it important to do so, particularly when considering the results of a staff survey.

Culture vs. Climate

CULTURE	CLIMATE
• Internal reality of the organization – the personality	• "Mood" of the organization
• Drives the strategic capability	
• Long term	• Short term
• Difficult to change	• Easier to change

Culture influences Climate

Often, these surveys show that staff is unhappy about aspects of management or issues inside the organisation. These have to be interpreted carefully, as I have encountered a number of situations where the climate (staff satisfaction) is poor, but the culture is appropriate. Managers have to be careful not to change the culture of the organisation just to make the staff happy!

I experienced a case some years ago with a major public sector organisation. The organisation had recently implemented some much needed reform and a major cultural change program.

As a consequence, work and jobs were organised very differently, and staff were far more accountable for their decisions. In addition, they had instituted a service level agreement that outlined the maximum response times their clients could expect in certain categories of work.

While the new culture was appropriate for the new strategy and requirements of clients, large numbers of staff were very unhappy with the new arrangements.

When the results of the staff survey were completed, certain members of the executive were keen to reverse the restructure because of the adverse effects on climate. We worked through a number of issues and managed to agree that this was not the appropriate solution.

It seemed more appropriate to look at the way that the culture had been changed, rather than whether the new culture was appropriate. In this case, there were approaches that could assist the staff to come to terms with the new culture (ie, improve the climate), rather than changing the culture.

Defining culture using the PADI logics

As we have said, the effectiveness of the organisation is enhanced when the culture is aligned with the strategy and operating environment. Indeed we know when the culture is not aligned with the business strategy, this strategy is unlikely to be fully implemented.

I am often amused by the public announcements of "a new strategy" we see in the newspapers, television advertising and public statements. How many times do we then encounter that organisation's service for ourselves and become very disappointed?

Sometimes, this new strategy has not been effectively reflected in any culture change within the organisation. Although the firm may have introduced new products and services, the behaviour within the organisation has not been altered. Accordingly, nothing changes with respect to the way staff interacts with their external environment – there is no change in the way they "play the game".

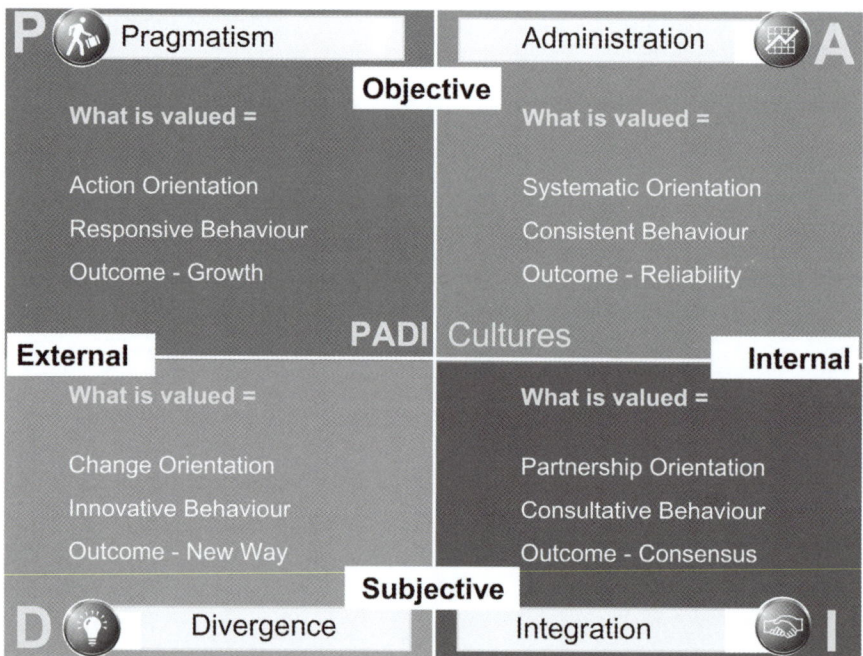

Chapter 5

Organisation culture can be described by using the PADI logics – in much the same way as for customers and strategy.

In the next section, I have detailed the features of the different culture types. In order to do this, I have used the various culture factors that were mentioned earlier. Ten factors have been used to describe each PADI culture type, but, of course, there are several others.

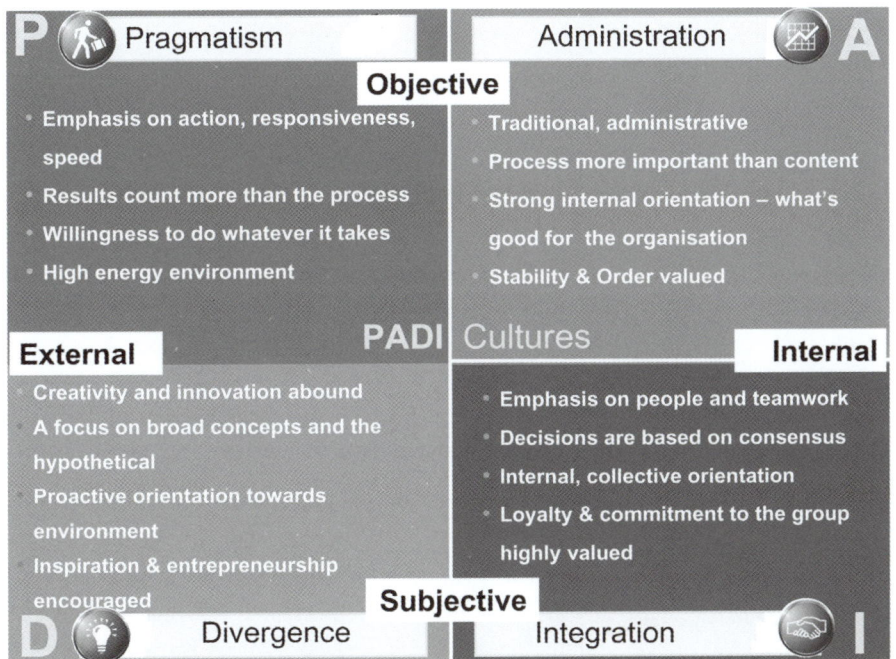

"P" cultures

"P" cultures are dominated by action, high energy and fast response. They focus on achieving the outcomes by doing whatever it takes, and will place the ends above the means. A sales team is a good illustration.

They can be characterised as follows:

Culture factor	"P" Culture
Autonomy	Limited by the need to perform to set objectives and to prove the validity of decisions
Control	Achieved by individually negotiated and agreed performance standards
Performance rewards	High value is placed on the individual's ability to meet short-term operational goals
Identity	Based on pride in what the organisation can and will achieve in the market
Communication	Planned, impersonal, regular – information widely shared and easily accessible
Conflict tolerance	Conflict arises when individuals perceive barriers to the achievement of objectives; usually resolved by negotiation
Change tolerance	Change is tolerated if the logic for it is fully understood and action is planned
External coping	Obstacles and opportunities are dealt with by attempting to beat the opposition
Internal organising	Goals are provided and staff are motivated in order to achieve best results
Management support	Focus is on results and setting performance targets to be achieved

Chapter 5

"A" cultures

"A" cultures are dominated by a need for control in which systems are used to achieve order. They have an internal perspective, focused on incrementally perfecting procedures to produce reliable, efficient and low-cost products and services. A good example is a continuous production manufacturing facility.

Culture factor	"A" Culture
Autonomy	Minimal, task-specific and limited by the need to make decisions according to tried and trusted formula
Control	Achieved through conforming to explicit rules and procedures
Performance rewards	High value is placed on the ability to maintain productivity and efficiency
Identity	Based on protecting an established history
Communication	Systematic, directive, regular – information shared on a need-to-know basis only
Conflict tolerance	Conflict arises when there is deviation from processes, it is suppressed and only resolved by enforcement
Change tolerance	Change is not well tolerated but can be implemented indirectly by aligning systems and infrastructure
External coping	Opportunities are dealt with as threats and minimised where possible
Internal organising	A clear structure of rules and procedures are provided to achieve maximum efficiency
Management support	Focus is on controlling information flows and budgets

"D" cultures

"D" cultures are dominated by a drive for innovation, flexibility and the desire to find new answers. They are externally oriented and attempt to stay ahead of the competition by being the leader in innovation. They aim to be ever ready to grasp opportunities in a turbulent and unpredictable environment. A good example is an R&D laboratory.

Culture factor	"D" Culture
Autonomy	Limited only by an individual's creative response to organisational ideals
Control	Achieved by individual's commitment to a shared vision of the future
Performance rewards	High value is placed on the individual's ability to be flexible and creative
Identity	Based on affiliation with the organisation's leadership role
Communication	Spontaneous, interactive, irregular – information must be discovered by the individual
Conflict tolerance	Conflict arises often as a result of individual expressiveness but it usually resolved quickly and easily
Change tolerance	Change is implicit in the cultural make-up but implementation of specific programs can be hazardous
External coping	Opportunities are dealt with in a flexible and creative way
Internal organising	Staff are allowed to work on their own to fulfil their potential
Management support	Focus is on mainly on organisation's future direction and opportunities for development

"I" cultures

I' cultures are dominated by a drive for cohesion. They have an internal orientation and see cooperation and morale-building efforts as central to optimising the development of the organisation's human resources. They reflect a relationship-oriented approach. In their dealings with the external environment, they attempt to forge close bonds and enduring relationships. A good example is a team of social workers.

Culture factor	"I" Culture
Autonomy	Limited by the need to obtain consensus about the way things should be done
Control	Achieved by collective adherence to a set of common values and beliefs
Performance rewards	High value is placed on group harmony and human interaction skills
Identity	Based on belonging to a group which shares a common set of values
Communication	Participative, team-based continuous information is accessible to group members but inter-group sharing is poor
Conflict tolerance	Conflict arises when there is no consensus on values and is usually resolved through the formation of a new coalition
Change tolerance	Change is valued for its own sake, but can only be implemented if there is consensus on how it should be done
External coping	Opportunities are dealt with by considering if they are compatible with existing values
Internal organising	Staff are organised into supportive teams to ensure participation and commitment
Management support	Focus is on building teams which work together

Developing cultural alignment

Despite frequent referrals to culture in organisations, I have found that senior management often fail to give it due consideration. It is quite simply forgotten in the excitement over new technologies, organisational structures, or products.

As a consequence, I have found that culture, if not in alignment with strategy, can operate as a "silent but deadly" force that inhibits the successful implementation of appropriate strategy.

That may sound somewhat melodramatic, but we need to remember that culture is "the other side of the coin" to strategy. The strategy in the market is a reflection of the patterns of behaviour that occur within the organisation:

So, whatever culture and patterns of behaviour prevail inside the organisation, the strategy delivered to the market will reflect this. Indeed, my earlier research (Chorn (1986)) showed that the internal culture was a far better predictor of actual strategy than the plans held up by management!

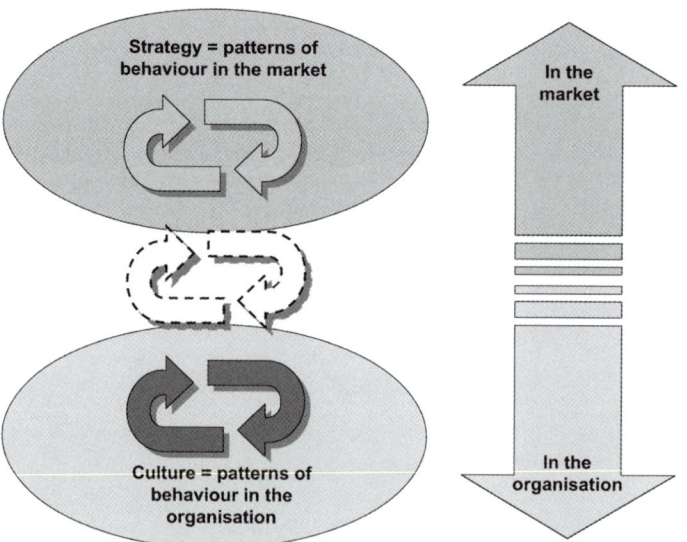

Chapter 5

At the outset of this book, I mentioned that strategic alignment is an elusive state – it is not easy to achieve or maintain. Because organisations do drift "off course" over time, it is important to stay vigilant to ensure that your organisation is always on track.

Andrew Grove, the founder and CEO of Intel (the computer chip manufacturer) has an interesting way of viewing this. In his book, *Only the Paranoid Survive* (Grove, (1996)), he outlines his philosophy that the successful organisation is one that is always looking over its shoulder and testing its basic assumptions about business and customer needs.

I'm not so sure about the use of the term "paranoid", but I do agree that management should always watch for the signs that the something may have slipped out of alignment.

Most of the assignments I have worked on involve a shift in culture to match the strategy of the organisation. Either something has "drifted" and the organisation is no longer in alignment, or there has been a conscious and substantial shift in strategy which has to be supported by a similar shift in culture.

Given these scenarios, I find it useful to address four broad questions:

1. What are the forces that shape culture in organisations?

2. What can we do to reinforce our existing culture to avoid "cultural drift"?

3. How do we recognise cultural misalignment?

4. How do we go about shifting the culture in the organisation?

1. What shapes culture in organisations?

There are many excellent texts that have dealt with this topic. See, for example, Schein (1997), Johnson (1992), Miles and Snow (1978), and Handy (1997). In developing my own view, I have been heavily influenced by these "masters", although I recognise that everyone approaches the subject in their own way.

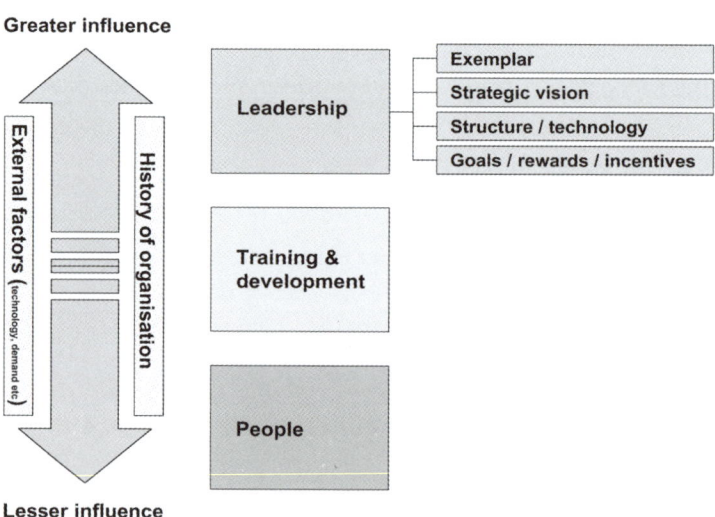

I regard leadership as the greatest influence on the culture in an organisation, followed by training and development, and then the staff themselves.

I outline these influences below, along with examples. NB. I have included external factors such as technology, customer needs and the history of the organisation for sake of completeness. However, since we are dealing with controllable elements for the present, I do not develop these any further.

Leadership

My experience and research suggests that leadership has the greatest bearing on the culture in the organisation. This is covered in more detail in the next chapter, but for the moment it is sufficient to say that leadership is powerful because:

> Leadership behaviour, particularly in the Australian context,[1] has a powerful role modelling effect in setting the example for staff;

> Leadership sets and communicates a compelling strategic vision for the future —-creating meaning and clarity for staff and explaining why things are being done the way they are;

> Working relationships are defined by the organisation structure and design;

> Goals and how they are rewarded provides a powerful incentive for the organisation and individuals to behave in certain ways.

A good example of the impact of leadership on culture was the tenure of James Strong at Australian Airlines. When he joined the airline in 1988 (then known as Trans Australian Airlines) he caused a near revolution in the manner in which he set about changing the culture.

> *At the time, the organisation was a somewhat bureaucratic, slow-moving government business enterprise that was desperately trying to ready itself for the impending de-regulation in the domestic airline industry.*
>
> *Strong made a number of strategic changes in the business. But, in the opinion of many, the most significant impact he had was related to his personal behaviour within the organisation. He certainly altered the organisation structure to produce tightly-focused business units and instituted changes to the incentive structures to match, but the most telling element was his visibility to the staff.*
>
> *He provided a good role model for what he wanted the organisation to be – customer-focused, action-oriented and responsive to the market. He travelled frequently on flights – usually without the entourage that had accompanied previous senior managers. And he spoke openly to staff, communicating his vision and talking honestly about the prospects of the business. Many commentators would regard these aspects of his personal style as being the most significant influence on the culture of the organisation as it simultaneously shifted its strategic focus.*

Training and development

The training and development of staff is always a popular method of shaping the culture and inducing change in organisations. However, I believe it to be far less effective in bringing about change than most managers believe!

I have to be very careful in presenting this argument. I don't want people to think that I am not in favour of training and development. Of course I am! *I just don't believe it is a very effective tool to use when seeking to shift the culture.*

Training and development will equip people with a different set of skills and outlooks to perform their jobs. It will certainly give them a broader repertoire of behaviours from which to choose. But on its own, it is very unlikely to cause them to change or shift their patterns of behaviour. Research shows that behaviour is very robust and resistant to change even when individuals are assigned roles that are different to their types they generally default to their personality i.e. robust patterns of behaviour (Hunter (1998)). Therefore, it is not such an effective driver of culture as we sometimes believe it to be.

In general, we know that people need three things in place before they change:

- The opportunity to change;

- The desire to change;

- The skills and competencies to change.

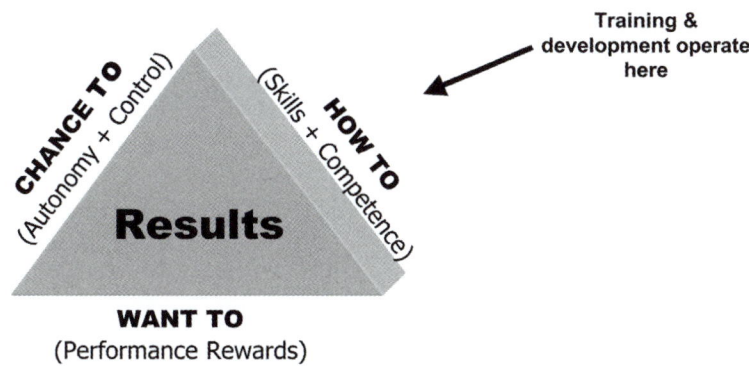

So, the use of training and development as a major culture or change driver is rarely enough. Perhaps I am a little cynical, but I believe that the reason it is used frequently as a major change driver is that it does not threaten or confront the status quo – and often the senior managers don't have to go through it themselves or do very much to put it in place!

People

There is no doubt that the people in the organisation themselves have an impact on the organisational culture. Obviously, if all the individuals in an organisation were very risk averse, that would have some bearing on the risk profile of the organisation.

But, culture is not simply an aggregation of the individual personalities of the people. Culture is the pattern of behaviour that prevails in the way the people interact and work with each other. While the individual personalities of the people are a factor in this, the culture of the organisation embraces far more.

The cultural patterns are shaped by the job roles assigned to people, the structure they find themselves in, and the technology they work with. Goals, rewards and incentives all play a part.

So, even if we could change all the staff of the organisation (and this is neither practical nor legal), this would not be as significant a driver of culture as the contextual issues of leadership and training.

History of the organisation

The history of the organisation is a driver of organisational culture, but while the organisation's history has a significant influence on its culture, it cannot be readily changed or managed.[2]

I have known organisations where the history has had a profound impact on the culture. In the case of Encyclopaedia Britannica, history taught the organisation that it was a successful printing and publishing company that

---

[2] In some cases, leaders have sought to "re-interpret" the history in a manner that suits their purposes. If it can be successfully achieved, it can have a modifying effect on the culture. For example, people may begin to think differently about a past mistake or phase of their history. But, in general, re-writing the history is not a tool of the modern leader in organisations.

achieved much success through its unique form of direct sales and marketing. This was so powerful a lesson, that the organisation could not readily re-invent itself to cope with the onslaught of digital technology.

The history of the organisation helps to form the underlying assumptions in the culture – those deep-seated, taken-for-granted beliefs about the way the organisation works (remember the culture iceberg!) As we have seen, they require a lot of conscious effort to change.

So, we see that the key shapers of culture are leadership, training and development, and the people within the organisation. Clearly, if we want to bring about a shift in the organisation's culture – these are the levers to work with.

Once again, I want to re-iterate that all three groups of factors are important. However, in the management of cultural change, we should recognise that some of these are more effective than others.

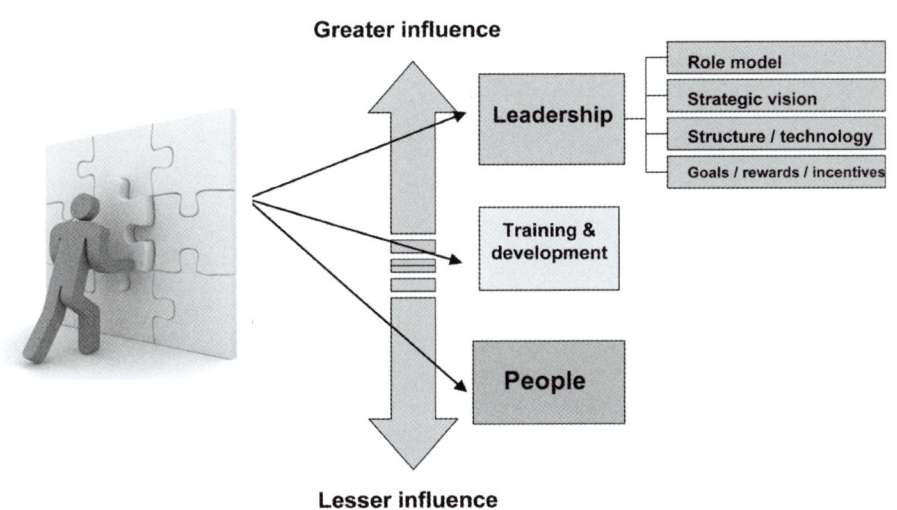

2. How can we reinforce our existing culture?

Organisations can "drift" off course over time. This often happens to those organisations experiencing a period of success. Dan Miller (1990), in his book The Icarus Paradox, outlines the process whereby organisations can become the victims of their own success.

In essence, management stop questioning the reason for their success, preferring instead to focus on operational efficiencies and meeting the shareholders' requirements for a steady stream of dividends.[3] They lose sight of the specific "recipe" that embraces their organisation's alignment between the market, strategy and culture. And, because culture is dynamic and is always influenced by the context, it slowly shifts.

There will be signs that this shift and misalignment is occurring, but management is often blinded by other concerns such as profit and bonuses.

The key is to recognise that culture is dynamic – it is constantly evolving and changing in response to context and to management actions. Accordingly, it has to be managed and reinforced to prevent drift.

Following is a series of steps that management can take to ensure that they are reinforcing the culture in their organisation:

---

3   See Greiner's account of the changes that occur in organisations as they develop. He demonstrates that the initial concerns for effectiveness (alignment and relevance to market) give way to a focus on efficiencies and financial returns. This is similar to Miller's view of the Icarus effect.

Chapter 5

P

Reinforcing the 'P' Culture

- Ensure that job descriptions allow latitude to individuals in the way they work
- Control performance through achievement of outcomes – don't become overly prescriptive
- Reward individuals on achievement of operational goals
- With any change – let people know what you want to achieve
- Keep communication brief and to the point
- Define the goals clearly – let people know "what they are fighting for"

A

D

I

For example, management in an express freight/courier business should avoid becoming too prescriptive and burdening the staff with unnecessary administrative controls. It is important to keep the energy high inside the organisation, and this is achieved by developing a level of *healthy* competition between individuals in the way they work.

By keeping the organisation tightly focused on the key goals, but allowing individuals some latitude to find their own approaches within this, the culture will remain responsive and energetic.

These cultures do not respond well to lengthy debates and consultative processes about change. Management should do its homework and work out what needs to be achieved. The goals and objectives can then be clearly outlined and people will generally find their own way.

Developing an appropriate culture

Strategic Alignment

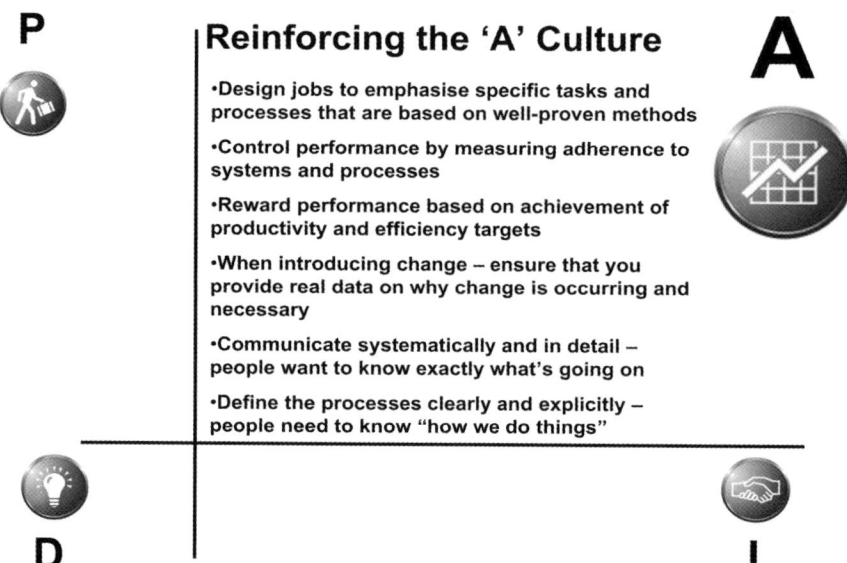

If we consider a continuous production manufacturing facility, for example, the aim of management is to maintain a focus on doing things systematically, in line with proven processes. Accordingly, they should ensure that job specifications and operating procedures reflect current best practice and that they are explicit and highly detailed.

Efficiency and adherence to specific standards are the key performance measures, and results against these should be publicised and widely communicated. Staff who perform well against these criteria should be rewarded – and the reasons made public.

When introducing any process changes, these should be carefully explained and the rationale for the change made very clear. The communication should include detailed information and evidence to support any decisions.

Chapter 5

Reinforcing the 'D' Culture

 P

 A

- Design jobs and roles around the individual's specific skills and interests
- Performance is managed by ensuring the person is committed to the vision of the organisation – and then given freedom of expression
- Reward individuals on the long term contribution they make to the organisation
- Allow people an opportunity to develop their preferred view of the future for the organisation
- Communicate when you have something significant to say – and then do it in significant ways
- Spend time reviewing and discussing the vision for the future – get people involved

D

 I

I consulted to a R&D laboratory a few years ago. It illustrates clearly the principles of reinforcing a "D" culture. The laboratory management had a process for monitoring the progress of scientists within the organisation. Key features of the individual's skills and preferences were used to design job roles.

Individual performance contracts were negotiated with staff, and these catered for preferences in work style and research interests. All interested staff were involved in the planning process, and much attention was given to regular reviewing of the vision in light of emerging technologies and environmental factors.

Instead of holding regular staff meetings, management held impromptu meetings when a member of the team had some significant results to share, or when an important milestone was reached. They also focused on keeping the communication fresh and interesting.

Strategic Alignment

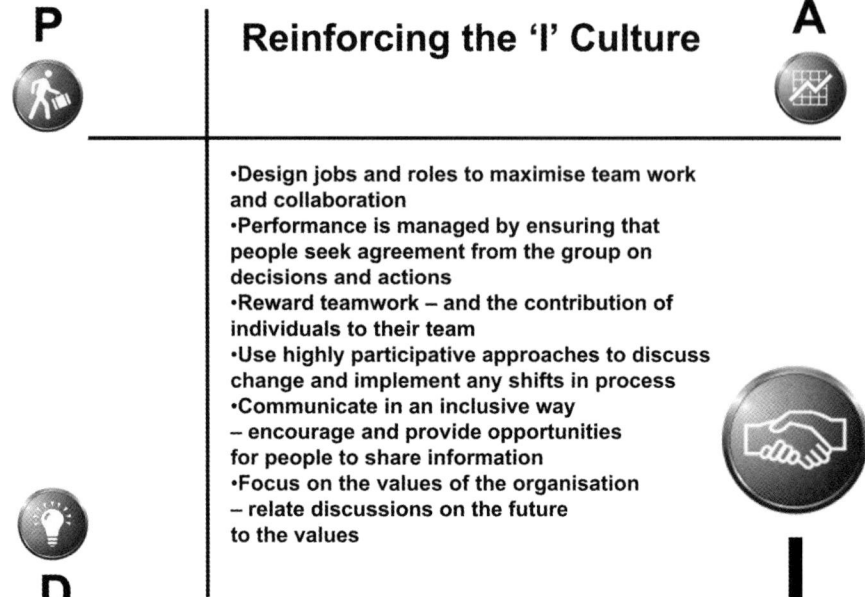

In the case of an "I" culture, we might consider the example of a social welfare agency. A key emphasis is on collaboration and teamwork so that they are able to provide a holistic approach to client care.[4] This collaboration is achieved by creating a strong "teamwork" culture.

Accordingly, team performance should be rewarded. Staff should be encouraged to share information openly by having their reward systems based not on achievement of individual goals, but on the contribution they make to the team.

Staff should be actively involved in decision-making and any plans for the future – care should be taken to get full support before any changes are made. The values of the organisation should be continually referenced in making tough decisions.

---

4   This is sometimes termed a "case-work" approach, whereby a member of staff assumes overall responsibility for a client. Because no single member of staff possesses the complete range of skills to deal with different aspects of the client's welfare, staff have to collaborate closely to ensure that different perspectives are brought to bear on the client.

3. How do we recognise cultural misalignment?

First, we have to recognise that the culture is out of alignment. Often there are symptoms that suggest that something is not right in the organisation. But, as we saw in some of the examples above, management does not always hear the message clearly.

I have included, as Appendix 3, a short questionnaire that will give you an indicative cultural profile for your organisation. The questionnaire is generic, rather than tailored to your organisation, but will provide useful indications. Try to focus on a specific business unit when answering the questions, rather than the whole organisation. It may be useful for the management team to work through to help them understand their current culture.

> Please note that this generic questionnaire will only give you an indicative profile. It is based on management perceptions only. In order to obtain a more accurate reading, we would design a specific instrument for your organisation.

In the tables below, I have outlined the major signs and implications of different types of cultural misalignment. They should help to get a fix on what is happening in your organisation.

In each case, I have started with the prevailing culture (eg "P", "A", "D" or "I"). I have then posed the question – *what would happen if the strategy or customer needs were different?*

You may recognise some of the symptoms in your organisation. With the help of the diagnostic questionnaire in Appendix 3, you can begin to identify the specific problem and work out ways to address it.

The "P" culture

If Culture is		Implications, if strategy or customers are
A	☞ ☞ ☞	not enough attention to detail not consistent enough too fast
D	☞ ☞ ☞	not enough new ideas not innovative enough too commercial
I	☞ ☞ ☞	not consultative enough not enough focus on people's needs too commercial

These organisations can become misaligned because they are so intent on action and doing things at speed. If we imagine our hypothetical sales team, they can get into trouble by:

- Doing things too quickly;

- Not spending enough time planning and thinking things through;

- Not considering the needs of their customers (or staff) carefully enough.

> *I remember the start-up phase of mobile telephone companies in Australia. The key issue was to sign up as many new subscribers as possible, without too much concern about understanding their needs or whether the package sold to them was capable of meeting those needs.*
>
> *No wonder the average "churn" rate in those halcyon days was about 25% – they lost a quarter of their customer base each year! This only changed when the growth slowed and the companies began focusing on understanding customer needs and customer service.*

The "A' culture

If Culture is	Implications, if strategy or customers are
A 📊	**P** ☞ too slow ☞ too focused on process, not responsive enough ☞ not commercial enough
	D ☞ too bureaucratic and slow ☞ not enough innovation ☞ too rigid
	I ☞ not enough concern for people ☞ not focused on systems ☞ not consultative enough

These organisations can become misaligned because they become overly focused on process when the market is changing. Some of the issues arise because:

▶ They are too concerned with maintaining the efficiencies generated by standardisation – they don't like changing their products or the way they operate;

▶ They are not concerned enough about the people' needs – staff or customers;

▶ They take their time in responding to requests – too slow.

> *A good example is the "wage-packet" business run by security and armoured car operators. For many years they focused intently on improving the operational efficiency of their operations in order to secure new business, but failed to respond to the shift towards "plastic" and electronic banking. Most Australians now have their wages paid directly into a bank account.*

The "D' culture

If Culture is	Implications, if strategy or customers are
D P	☞ not responsive to customers needs ☞ too rhetorical, theoretical or impractical ☞ not quite fast enough
A	☞ too radical ☞ not consistent enough ☞ not enough attention to detail
I	☞ not enough consultation ☞ not enough concern for people ☞ disregard for the customers way of doing things

These organisations become misaligned because they are too concerned with finding new ways of doing things and fail to bed down any processes – they keep re-inventing the wheel! Referring to our example of the R&D laboratory, issues can arise because:

➤ They are more interested in developing a better solution than listening to client's needs;

➤ They change things before they are shown to be either effective or ineffective;

➤ They can be very inefficient.

I know a number of IT whiz kids who really have something to offer the business community in terms of their approach to networking and websites. These folk specialise in coming up with really innovative solutions that are at the leading edge of developments in their field.

However, they rarely manage to get business organisations interested in their work, because they can't be bothered perfecting their new solution or system, and prefer to start working on the next "breakthrough".

Chapter 5

The "I' culture

If Culture is	Implications, if strategy or customers are
P	☞ too slow/unresponsive ☞ not commercial enough ☞ lack of goal clarity
A	☞ not systematic ☞ not enough hard measurement ☞ insufficient controls
D	☞ not enough innovation ☞ too slow to new ideas ☞ not customised enough to suit market needs

"I" organisations can lose alignment because they are very focused on the "family" – their staff and inner circle of clients that they partner with. Problems can arise because:

➤ They are too concerned with meeting everyone's needs and so often fail to make the tough decisions;

➤ They may suffer from "groupthink";

➤ They can be very opinionated and judge others from their own values perspective.

> *Encyclopaedia Britannica failed as a business because they were captive to their own ideas and did not want to upset their direct sales force.*
> *Despite the evidence that CD ROM versions of encyclopaedias were gaining popularity, they convinced themselves that the content was "not as good" as theirs. Their sales force also resisted any moves into a digital format because it would reduce their commissions and change their style of selling.*

4. How do we change culture in an organisation?

If I had a dollar for the number of times I have had this conversation with an executive, I would be very wealthy indeed. All of them want to transform their organisation's culture so that it becomes:

- Responsive to customer needs (P)
- Cost and efficiency conscious (A)
- Innovative and creative (D)
- Team-oriented and collaborative (I)

Seen in terms of the PADI model and its compatibilities/discrepancies we can see the above is impossible to achieve. I sincerely believe that one of the reasons managers are often so disappointed about the results of culture change programs is that the nature of change is not specified clearly enough. We tend to use generalisations such as a "high-performance" culture, a "commercial" culture, or an "entrepreneurial" culture. No one seems really sure what these terms mean specifically, so, it's very hard to put a program into place that actually achieves any change. The PADI model allows us to specify the systems and behaviours required in each different culture.

Though dealing with the topic in detail is somewhat beyond the scope of this book, here are a few guidelines that can help you address these issues:

(a) Be specific about the nature of the change
Identify where you are starting and where you want to end up so you can navigate the journey you are embarking upon.

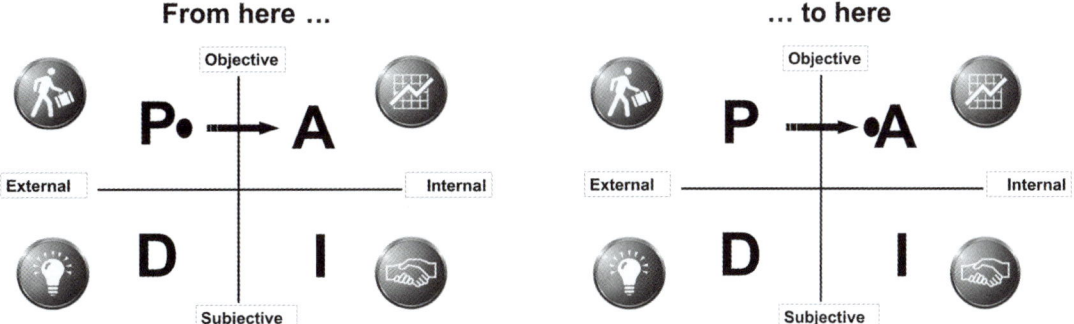

(b) Identify the extent of the change needed

Generally, we distinguish between change that is evolutionary versus revolutionary (Balogun & Hope Hailey (1999)). The key distinction is whether we simply modify key aspects of the culture (evolutionary change) or whether we have to fundamentally alter and reorientate its basic structure (revolutionary change).

This is significant since the amount of time, effort and direct management involvement increases greatly with revolutionary change.

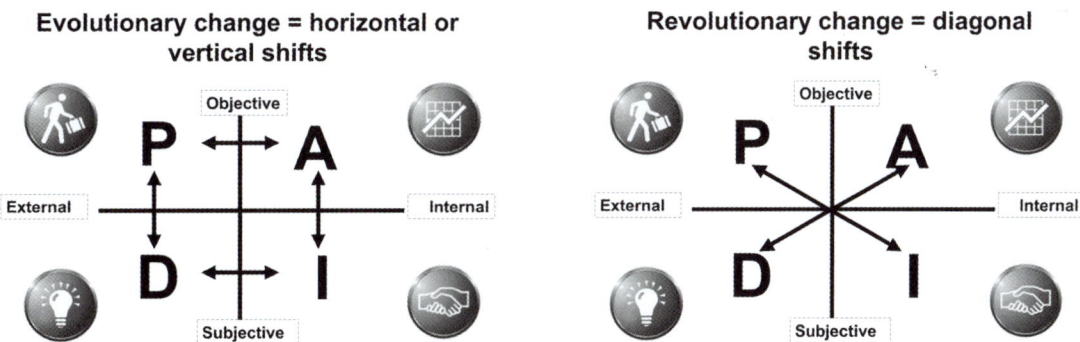

(c) Use the "levers for change" in the culture

Within the different factors that comprise culture in an organisation, there are three "levers for change". These factors exert a significant influence on the shape of the overall culture (see the list of ten factors used to describe the PADI cultures on page 92 of this chapter).

Strategic Alignment

AUTONOMY — What people are allowed to do

Objective

P — Autonomy is determined by the need to perform to set objectives

A — Autonomy is task specific and limited by the need to make decisions according to tried and tested formulae

External ——————————————— Internal

D — Autonomy is limited only by the individual's creative response to organisational ideas

I — Autonomy is limited by the need to obtain consensus about the way things should be done

Subjective

By ensuring that these three factors are closely aligned to the culture you want to achieve, you are likely to achieve the desired outcome. For example, if you want to move towards a "P" culture, then ensure that:

➤ Jobs are re-designed so that staff are given the freedom to do what needs to be done in order to achieve the agreed outcomes. Do not be over-prescriptive in the way they ought to *perform* their duties. Simply make the *outcome* very clear.

➤ Set up the performance management system so that staff are controlled and measured in terms of the *outcomes* they achieve and not how well they followed due procedure.

➤ Reward staff primarily on their ability to meet these short/medium-term operational goals

Finally, ensure that you have alignment between these three culture factors. Misalignment here can cause friction and stress within the organisation – and ultimately lead to a significant deterioration in performance overall.

Chapter 5

For example, if you *expect* a specific set of results from your staff, make sure you *inspect* the appropriate performance measures.

CONTROL — What is *inspected*

Objective

P — External
Control is achieved by individually agreed performance standards

A — Internal
Control is achieved through conforming to explicit rules and procedures

D — External
Control is achieved by the individual's commitment to a shared vision of the future

I — Internal
Control is achieved by collective adherence to a set of common values and beliefs

Subjective

PERFORMANCE REWARDS — What is *expected* of people

Objective

P — External
Value is placed on the individual's ability to meet shorter term operational goals

A — Internal
Value is placed on the ability to maintain productivity and efficiency

D — External
Value is placed on the individual's ability to be flexible and creative

I — Internal
Value is placed on group harmony and human interaction skills

Subjective

Developing an appropriate culture

129

Strategic Alignment

> *I came across a case in the poultry industry where the general manager was keen for his sales staff to prospect for new business. He was continually disappointed that they did not do much calling on prospective customers, preferring instead to call on their regulars.*
>
> *After some analysis, we found that the finance manager was measuring the sales force on their "sales effectiveness" ratios. He measured the number of sales they made in a month against the travel and entertainment expenses they incurred. Sales representatives falling outside the required ratios were hauled over the coals and given a hard time on their expense claims.*
>
> *Clearly, while they were being expected to prospect for new business, they were being inspected on how efficiently they used their time and vehicles. This was a no-brainer! It was far more sensible for the sales representative to call on customers they knew (and get a sure order) that to drive across town to a prospective customer that might not buy anything.*
>
> *People will do what is inspected rather than what is expected.*

Key points in summary

- Culture is neither "good" nor "bad". It is simply appropriate or inappropriate to the organisation and context.

- Organisations can have more than one culture – culture is not the unifying factor in organisations. Different business units are likely to have different cultures that are suited to their strategies and markets.

- Culture has both seen and unseen elements. It is usually the invisible parts of culture that trip us up and prevent strategy from being implemented.

Chapter 5

➤ When the culture of the organisation is misaligned with the strategy, the strategy is unlikely to be effectively implemented.

➤ The major shapers of culture are leadership, training/development, staff, the history of the organisation, and other external factors such as technology, customer demand etc.

➤ Unless the culture is actively reinforced by management action, it is likely to drift over time – and misalignment can occur.

➤ Shifting the culture requires managers to be *specific* about the change, recognise the extent of the change required, and use the required "levers for change".

Chapter 5

Strategic Alignment

Chapter 6
Leading the organisation to strategic alignment

Defining leadership in organisations

I have to open this chapter by making two confessions. First, leadership is the area with which I am most fascinated and in which I have the most to learn.

Secondly, this chapter does not attempt to cover this vast and complex area.

My objective is to focus on the role played by leadership in creating strategic alignment within organisations. Within the scope of this book, therefore, I will only address those aspects of leadership that are pertinent to bringing about alignment between the market, strategy and organisational culture.

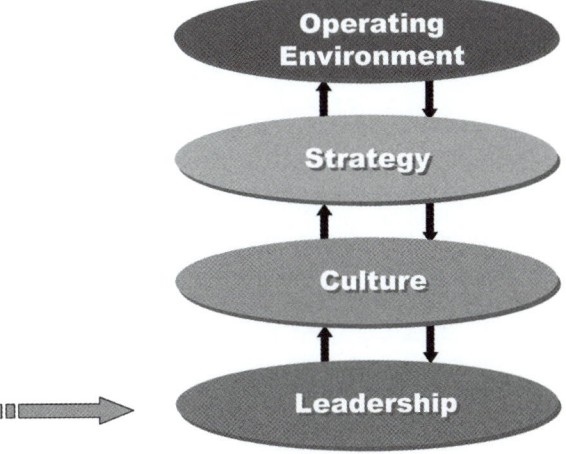

Effectiveness depends on fit

I define leadership as the process that gets people to move, in a competent and committed way, in a particular direction, or towards a particular goal.

In this definition, I am very influenced by the work of Elliot Jaques and his colleagues (Jacques & Clement (1994)). Following on from this, I have made eight observations and assumptions about leadership in organisations.

1. Leadership is a function and process

Rather than view leadership as a role per se, it seems more appropriate to view leadership as a function that takes place in many roles. It is the function that gets other people to move in a particular direction or towards a specific goal. When these functions are well coordinated, the overall process produces effective leadership.

This means that many roles incorporate leadership accountabilities. Teachers, parents, managers and military commanders would all have responsibility for leadership in their roles – they all seek to influence others to move in particular directions.

But there is another key implication of seeing leadership as a function and process. This view allows us to move away from the common focus of "personality" as an important element of leadership effectiveness. Instead of viewing characteristics such as "bold", "strong" and "courageous" as essential to effective leadership, we begin to recognise that competence in the role, reasonable intelligence and a good value system are probably more important.

I am reminded of the exercise I often run in senior management strategy workshops. I ask the participants to identify a few of their "ideal leaders". We get the usual list of leaders such as Branson, Churchill, Mandela, Gandhi and the like.

> *Then I ask them to name a few people who have had a profound impact on their lives and have been influential in helping them to achieve the success that they have. This produces a very different list.*
>
> *The people who have influenced, taught and equipped them for their future roles in life often include people that we would not necessarily view as "leaders": teachers, the local parish priest, an uncle, or the coach of the local netball team usually figure in these lists.*
>
> *We begin to understand that many people can play a leadership role and influence others around them. This helps executives realise that their notions of the "great leader" are often founded on unrealistic (but supposedly ideal) personality characteristics.*

2. Leadership is an elitist activity

This statement, although controversial, is true in two senses. First, leadership is the process whereby a few people influence the actions and behaviours of many. In this sense, it is an elitist activity.

Secondly, the leadership process can sometimes create an "apartness" between those setting the directions from those having to follow them. Where the decisions are unpopular, there will be a time lag between the decision and its acceptance by the organisation. This is a very lonely period for those involved in the leadership process, as it requires them to stand "apart" from other staff.

I have seen many competent people in an organisation who steadfastly refuse to be part of the leadership process. All the evidence suggests that they have the necessary qualities to excel in this, but they are unwilling to be "separated" from their work-mates by having to stand apart.

Strategic Alignment

I came across a case in a major financial institution some years ago. We were conducting a training course for "individual contributors" (non-managers or supervisors) in the organisation and we noticed a very articulate and well-read individual in her mid-40s who had assumed a clear leadership role in a number of role plays and exercises.

After some enquiries, we found out that she was a leading figure in the Girl Guides movement in Australia, but had steadfastly refused to accept a leadership role in her financial institution employer as this would separate her from her friends and colleagues.

For those who enjoy the leadership challenge, it can be hard to understand why another does not want the promotion that would take them up the ladder. Terri and I often discuss this topic as her experience of formal leadership positions showed her that the "apartness" of being a leader did not suit her style or her needs from the workplace. This is an issue of which leaders should be aware as good people can be lost to an organisation simply because they are pushed into leadership positions they do not desire.

3. Leadership is a multiple concept

Leadership occurs throughout the organisation. While the leadership process may be established and maintained by a few in the organisation (the so-called dominant coalition), many people display leadership in their roles.

An effective leadership process will elicit leadership contributions from many people through the organisation. Depending upon the specific context or demands at the time, certain people will have more to contribute than others – and this will require them to display a leadership function.

We have learned to call this phenomenon "empowerment", but I'm not sure how many managers really understand what this means.

In essence, empowerment is the process where we create the conditions, capabilities, and incentive for individuals to assume leadership in the performance of their job role. In reality, creating a successful empowerment process requires a number of key actions from others, particularly those in senior roles within the organisation.

4. The leadership process embraces "followership"

It may seem to you that the second and third observations are somewhat contradictory. How can leadership be simultaneously elitist and multiple?

I believe that empowerment holds the key to this apparent contradiction. As we said, empowerment is the process whereby people throughout the organisation are encouraged and enabled to display leadership in their job roles. And empowerment is, in turn, enabled by "followership".

Followership is the practice whereby an individual, assigned a senior role within the organisation, is prepared to stand aside and let a subordinate take the lead on a particular task.

The key issue is that the subordinate may be approaching the task in a different manner to that normally undertaken by the senior. For followership to occur (and therefore, for empowerment to occur), the senior has to accept this leadership, even though he or she may have performed the task differently.

> *I have observed senior managers, with traditional styles of leadership, experience difficulty in this area. Typically, these senior managers will regard democratic approaches as signs of weakness, and are loathe to admit that they don't know the answer to a particular conundrum.*
>
> *Often, these managers will not be able to hold back when they observe a subordinate performing a task in a different manner to that which they would approach it. This inability to "step aside" and follow the lead of another can undermine the leadership processes in an organisation.*

5. Leading is a function of management

There is a lot of discussion in the popular management literature about the so-called differences between management and leadership.

We are told that managers control complexity, while leaders produce change, and so on. While this is useful in highlighting some of the functions that make up a modern managerial role, I have not found it useful to make a distinction between a management *role* and a leadership *role*, per se.

What seems to happen is that we begin to classify someone as a good manager, but not a good leader, and vice versa. I am not sure that this is very helpful, because both the control of complexity and the introduction of change are important elements in a successful senior manager.

In organisations, the leadership function is nearly always undertaken within the context of management. In other words, the individual is usually performing a management role and they display leadership in it – they are able to influence others to move in a particular direction. The movement of others in a direction that promotes organisational effectiveness (leadership) *is* a function of good management.

6. Leadership is about self-awareness

Being able to demonstrate leadership in an organisational role requires a level of self-awareness. This is because the leadership function is not merely a role that is played during working hours, but rather an important part of the way you go about your job.

In other words, the leadership function will reflect who you are, your values and attitudes to people and the organisation around you.

A wise man once said that *"who you are shouts so loudly in my ear that I cannot hear a word you say!"*

I believe that who you are shines through in what you do. Others around you observe *the person* as much as they do their words and deeds. Indeed, if they perceive authenticity in what you do and say as well as in *who* you are, you are likely to be more effective in your leadership activities.

Being self-aware is an important part of understanding what (or whom) you

> *A client of mine has a saying that "leaders bring themselves to the table". He argues that a manager cannot play the role of a leader during working hours – it isn't a mantle that can be donned when required.*
>
> *Instead, he points to the fact that whenever you interact with your colleagues, they will register "who" you are in the way you perform your duties and go about your job. So, the "whole you" gets brought to meetings and into interactions with colleagues.*
>
> *And it is the "whole you" that determines how effective your leadership is within the job role you play.*

Chapter 6

bring to the table as a leader. And it is also an important step in ensuring that you are happy with *whom* you are bringing to the table.

There are a number of steps you can take to improve your self-knowledge and to make the changes that you feel may be necessary. Some of these include:

> ➤ Keeping a learning journal to record and reflect what you have learned about your organisation, your role and yourself;

> ➤ Using a trusted mentor, external to your situation, to give you feedback on your style and approach;

> ➤ Using feedback instruments such as employee surveys and 360º questionnaires to understand your impact and influence on others around you;

> ➤ Using various psychometric instruments such as the MBTI (Myers & Briggs (1962)) and OPQ (Saville & Holdsworth 1978, 1993) to help you understand your own approach and style in the roles you perform.

7. Leadership is understanding the strategic context of the organisation

In addition to the required intellect and the desire to perform a leadership function, a necessary requirement is the understanding of the strategic context of the organisation.

If we return to the notion that forming strategy is like a "conversation" within the organisation, then leadership must participate in that conversation.

Indeed, effective leadership is about actively participating in and influencing the strategic conversation. Obviously, this is not really possible unless the leader has an understanding of the market, the organisation and its goals.

> *I am not convinced by the argument of the "super-leader", that is, someone who has great management and leadership skills who can be successful in leading any organisation.*
>
> *The essence of this argument seems to be that this super-leader surrounds him or herself with people who are competent and who have a good knowledge of the technicalities of the organisation and its market. They then focus on coordinating the efforts of these people.*
>
> *My experience is that this fails as often as it succeeds. Where it does succeed, it is because the individual has managed to learn the nature of the industry and organisation very quickly and therefore is soon able to play a major role in shaping the strategic conversation.*
>
> *Politeness prevents me from identifying the list of super-leaders who failed in their new organisations because they could not succeed in making a meaningful contribution to the strategic conversation.*

8. Leadership is about producing strategic alignment

I consider this the ultimate legacy of leadership – to create a relevant organisation and to leave it in a state of alignment with its environment.

In many respects, that is what this book is about: creating an effective organisation that is relevant to the market is serves and has the processes necessary to maintain that state of alignment.

In terms of strategic alignment, that means that management has to:

- ➤ Understand the nature of the environment;

- ➤ Form a strategy that is appropriate to the needs of customers;

- ➤ Shape the culture so that it facilitates the effective implementation of strategy;

- ➤ Ensure that the approach to managing and leading the organisation is appropriate for the needs of the aligned organisation.

With this in mind, we can now turn our attention to analysing the different approaches to leading organisations towards strategic alignment.

Strategic Alignment

Leadership and PADI logics

In much the same way as we have been able to describe customers, strategy and culture using the PADI logics, we can describe different approaches to the leadership process.

In essence, what this means is that the leadership function can be performed in many different ways. However, if we wish to lead people in a specific direction or towards a specific goal, we need to perform the leadership function in a particular way.

The PADI model identifies where the focus (dominant logic) lies in a particular approach, and how this approach might lead to a specific organisational outcome.

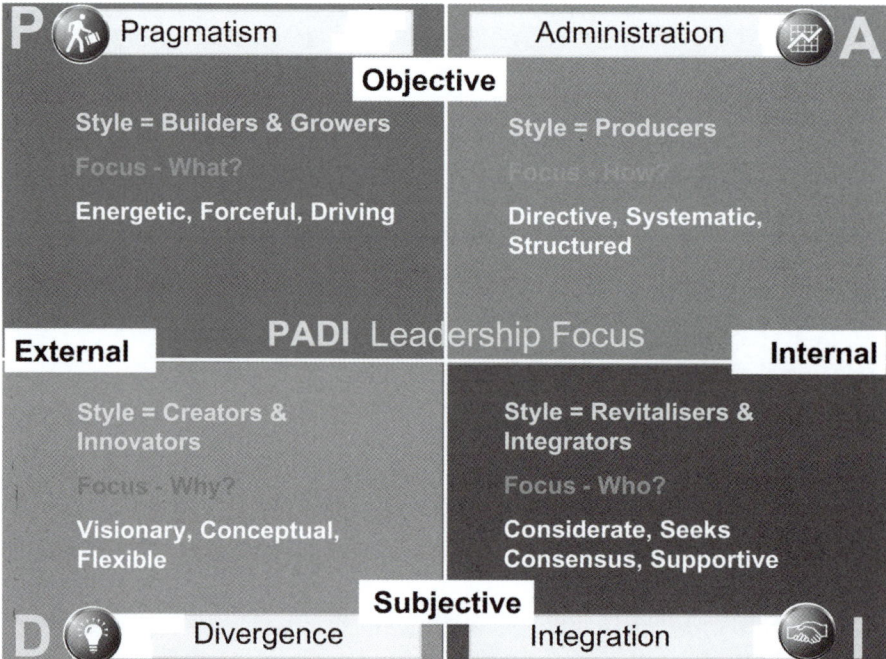

In each case, these focuses rest on a range of different values regarding leadership within the organisation:

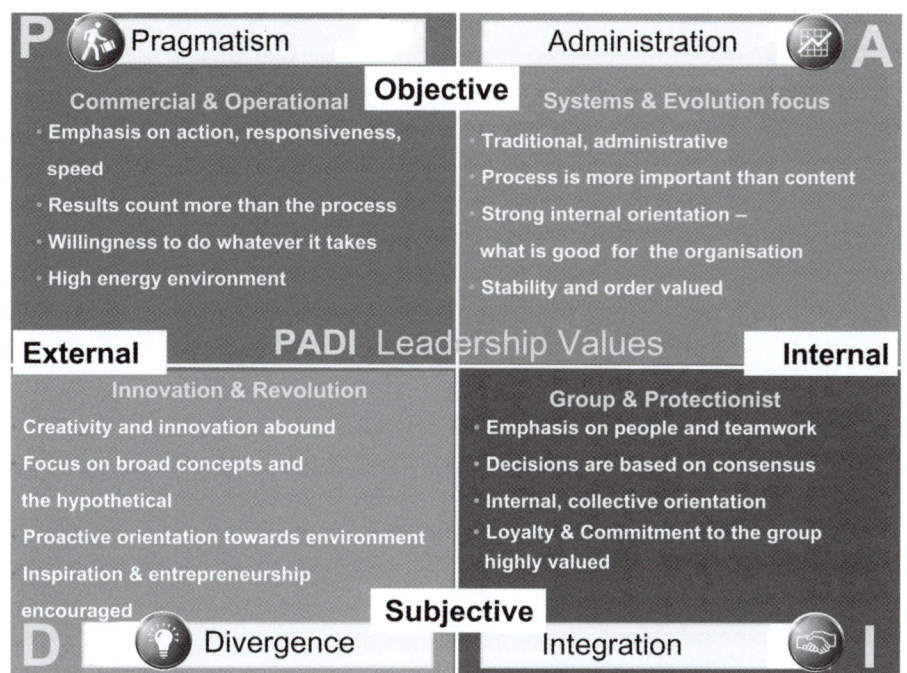

"P" Leadership

"P" leadership has an unwavering focus on achieving the end-point (as opposed to the *process* of achieving it). It sets unambiguous, challenging targets and provides an environment where people are unencumbered by rules and procedures to deliver results.

This approach demands action and has a low tolerance for ambiguity or personal feelings. Cultural change programs are focused on building capabilities to rapidly respond to customer needs and problems within specified market niches.

Strategic Alignment

"A" Leadership

"A" leadership continually improves the organisation's knowledge and experience base. It focuses on designing processes to create explicit control systems to ensure uniform outcomes in the organisation.

Seniority and experience is highly valued, as this helps to eliminate surprises. Cultural change programs focus on creating workable systems and bringing people into line with these systems. This style is effective in highly regulated, relatively stable industries or where safety is a key issue and there is no margin for error.

"D" Leadership

"D" leadership creates and implements strategies for the expansion of the organisation. Much of the time is spent on external matters such as customers, competitors, technologies and trends.

This form of leadership embraces ambiguity, expects upheaval and publicly acknowledges breakthroughs. Day-to-day matters are delegated and people are inspired with speeches and face-to-face meetings. This approach is effective in environments characterised by complex technologies and industry turbulence.

"I" Leadership

"I" leadership emphasises shaping and imparting values, modelling the appropriate interpersonal behaviours and managing personal growth. Human resources activities – recruitment, performance management, career mapping, climate surveys, succession planning, mentoring and coaching – are integral.

This approach is effective in environments where relationships and adherence to values are prized above all.

Horses for courses

Just as there is no universally desirable strategy or culture, the validity of a particular leadership approach depends on its alignment with the rest of the organisation and operating environment. Each approach is valid in the appropriate context.

An "A" approach (sequential, analytical, conservative) will be ineffective if the operating environment is turbulent and uncertain. However, in a mature market when an organisation needs systematised processes and cost efficiencies, it can be very effective.

Similarly, a "P" approach (emphasising speed and results at almost any cost) will be ineffective in a situation when an organisation needs to invest time and effort in building strategic partnerships.

> *My earlier example of the SPL Group in the hardware industry illustrates this point. Management would not have been able to build strategic partnerships with new buyers if they had continued emphasising the hard, driving style ('Pa') that previously characterised the organisation.*
>
> *In order to shift the organisation towards a more consultative, partnering strategy, management had to adopt a leadership approach that emphasised more participation and relationship building ('AI').*

Further specifics of each leadership approach are identified below

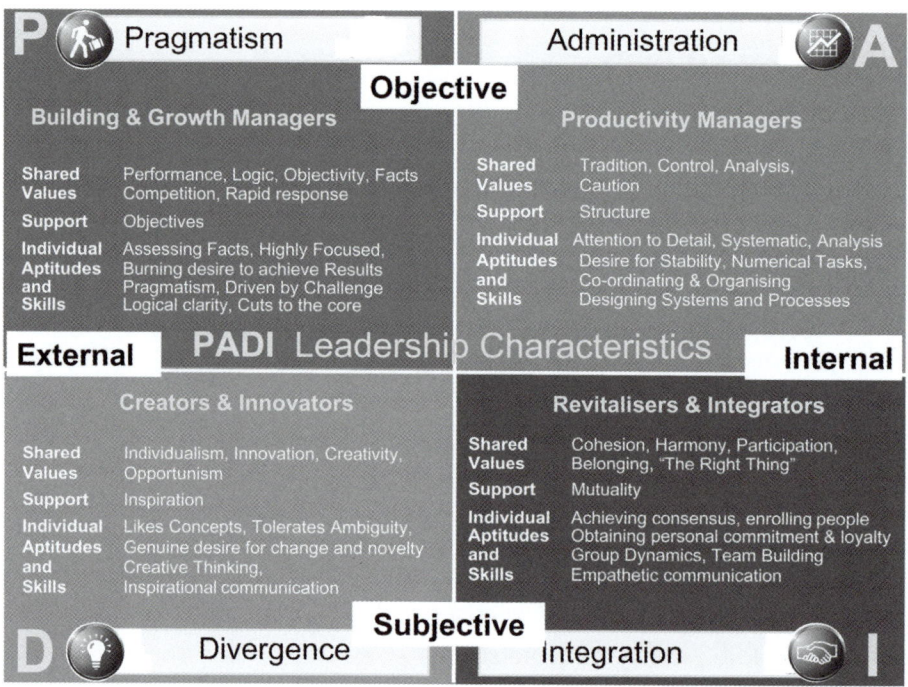

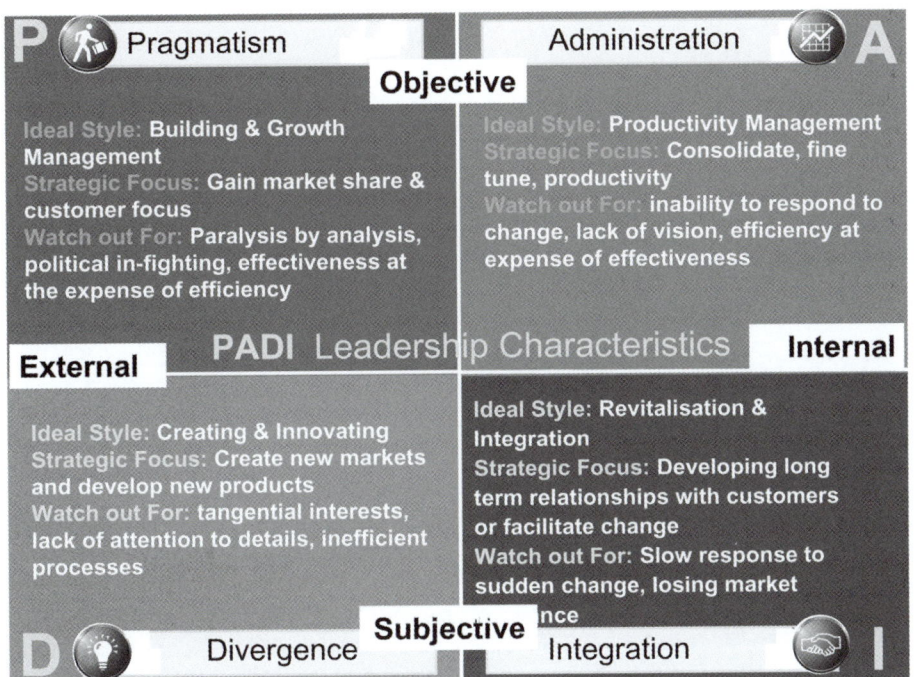

Too much of a good thing

Throughout this book I have spoken about the need to achieve some form of focus in the strategy and efforts of the organisation. We have now said much the same thing about leadership. Leadership is the process that influences people to move in a particular direction. In other words, leadership focuses the efforts of the organisation.

But Leadership must also be focused. There should be a distinct and recognisable flavour in the leadership approach used in the organisation so that the staff understands where they are going and what is to be achieved.

However, we have to guard against over-zealous attempts in leadership – where the leadership function is performed with such enthusiasm and energy that it approaches dogma.

There are some danger signs when any of the four leadership approaches is pursued too vigorously:

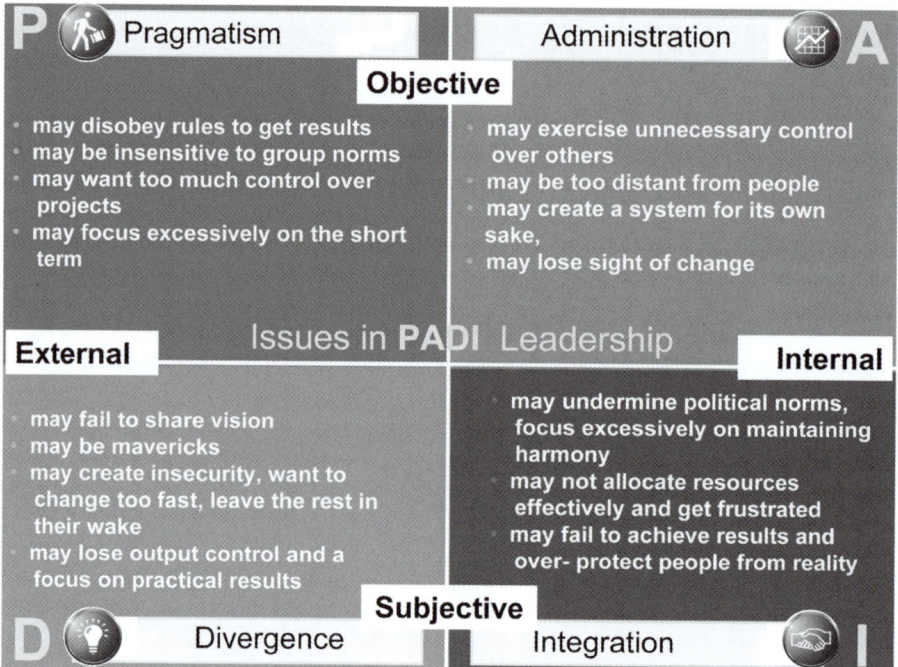

Key points in summary

> ➤ Leadership is the process that gets people moving in particular directions and towards particular goals.

> ➤ The process view de-emphasises the concern about personality traits and suggests that there are many effective ways to lead.

> ➤ Participating in the leadership process can be lonely as it sometimes requires the leader to stand apart from colleagues.

Chapter 6

➤ Leadership is a multiple concept that recognises many people show leadership in the way they perform their roles. The concept of empowerment embraces the contributions that all people can make in the leadership process, but it has to be supported by a willingness for followership in senior management.

➤ Leadership is a function of management. It is therefore not very useful to think in terms of leaders versus managers.

➤ Effective leadership requires self-awareness, an understanding of the strategic context of the organisation, and the creation of strategic alignment for the organisation.

➤ There is no approach to leadership that is more effective than another. PADI helps us to identify which approach is appropriate under different conditions.

➤ A degree of moderation must be exercised in implementing a particular leadership approach – too much of one particular approach can be detrimental to the organisation.

Chapter 6

Strategic Alignment

Chapter 7
Designing your organisation for strategic alignment

What is organisation design

The design and structure of the organisation is an important part of the organisation's effectiveness – and yet it does not always get the attention it deserves.

I find that management doesn't always think about the linkages between the strategy and the structure. Often it seems as if they have simply designed the organisation for administrative convenience or the ambitions of a single executive!

In a way, it reminds me of my time in the advertising industry. Most people have an opinion about a particular advertisement, but few can spell out the principles that they use to form their opinion. The same seems to apply in the case of organisation structure!

I have alluded to the concept of organisation design and structure several times through this book. My experience suggests that it is an important part of achieving effectiveness and strategic alignment in the organisation. I have found that an appropriate organisation design and structure can:

> ➤ Focus the organisation towards its customers and make it relevant to the market it serves

> ➤ Ensure that the organisation is not hindered by the "straightjacket" of having a "one-size-fits-all" approach to the way it does its business

> ➤ Introduce necessary change into an organisation and allow it to address shifts in the market or strategic direction

My purpose in this chapter, therefore, is to outline some of the key principles in designing and structuring organisations to enhance their overall effectiveness. I will be using the concepts of strategic alignment to assist in that analysis.

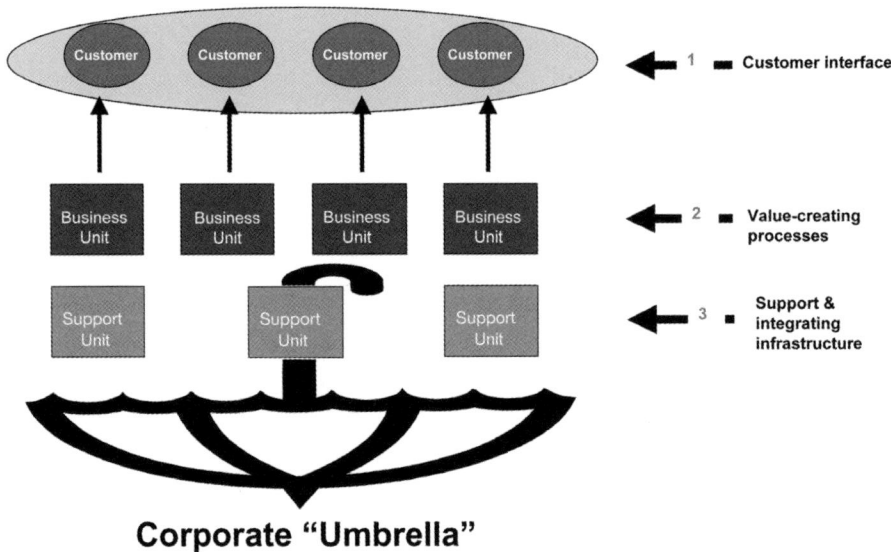

Corporate "Umbrella"

In the above diagram, I have tried to capture the key elements and challenges of the organisation design and structure process:

1. How do you set up and manage the interface between the organisation and its major customer groups (how do the business units, that are part of the organisation, serve the customer segments?)

2. What is the configuration of resources that produces the value-creating processes in the organisation (how do you actually create something of value for the customer?)

3. What is the infrastructure that supports and integrates the efforts of the different parts of the organisation (how do you create a coherent organisation and develop synergy between the different parts?)

Why bother with organisation design?

This is a good question that I am asked quite often. In order to answer it, here are some important issues that we should examine regarding the very nature of "*organisation*" itself.

"Organising" and "organisation" drives behaviour

When we "organise" something, we do so in order to reduce the complexity and risk in that situation. Organising is, therefore, an approach to managing complexity and risk.

> *Think of the time you may have assembled some "flat-pack" furniture. Let's assume that you had five sets of shelves to assemble.*
>
> *You might begin the first assembly without really focusing on the specific process you used and the order in which you put the various parts together. After you realise how much time the whole operation will take and how difficult it can be, you re-think the situation.*
>
> *You now work out the best way to do things. You get the various tools and components ready and you lay out the parts in the order they will be needed. This, you know, will simplify the whole operation and ensure that you assemble the rest of the shelves properly.*
>
> *You have now organised yourself in order to make the whole exercise run smoothly and reduce the chance of things going wrong.*

In a similar fashion, "organisations" are vehicles for reducing risk and complexity in situations where the efforts of people have to be coordinated.

Strategic Alignment

> *Now assume that you decide to go into business as a shelf assembly and installation company. Having learned from your own experience as a shelf assembler and installer, you will know the critical steps and processes.*
>
> *You will organise your team so that someone is responsible for each of these critical steps. Perhaps you will even appoint a supervisor who will coordinate and integrate the efforts of the individuals in the team.*
>
> *The "organisation" you have created is now a means of achieving tasks of shelf assembly that is larger and more complex that an individual could perform alone. And you probably build in checks and controls to ensure that mistakes are eliminated or spotted quickly and corrected.*
>
> *You have created an organisation that has reduced the risk and complexity of large shelf assembly projects.*

Organisations involve social interactions between the members – but these interactions are not simply random contact. The organisation imposes a certain structure to the way the interactions occur (ie, by grouping people together in certain ways and giving them specific objectives to meet).

> *As the shelf assembly business grows and becomes more successful, you start planning the development of the organisation in a conscious way. You identify the critical processes as:*
>
> - *Business Development – selling new contracts to assemble and install shelving for clients;*
>
> - *Project Planning – designing the projects, ordering the components and delivering them to the site for assembly and installation;*

> - Administration and Accounting – keeping track of the costs and ensuring that clients are billed accurately for the work performed;
>
> - Assembly and Installation – doing the actual assembly and installation of the selected shelving on site according to customer-approved plans.
>
> Each of the four functions listed above now have a manager and a set of relationships that have been defined.
>
> For example, the Business Development Manager has a team of sales representatives that report through to him/her. Their objective is to follow up on leads and to sell new shelving installations.
>
> The Assembly and Installation group has a number of teams – each managed by a supervisor that takes charge of the jobs on site. Each installation team is organised so that the critical processes of shelf assembly and installation are performed efficiently and accurately.
>
> And so, each group develops their own style of interaction. The sales team is structured very loosely, thereby giving each sales representative the maximum flexibility to achieve sales targets.
>
> The assembly teams are structured very tightly. There are specific processes that have to be performed very precisely, and each team member has a defined role that has to be performed in a precise way at a precise time. This creates very tight-knit teams in which the individuals develop very close working relationships.

The way these interactions are structured reflects the way we have chosen to control and coordinate the resources of the organisation.

The way you have chosen to structure the business reflects the choices you have made with regard to the various resources in the organisation. It suggests that:

- *You believe that the assembly and installation crews have to be controlled very tightly due to the high risk of something going wrong in this part of the business.*

- *You have decided that the decisions about design and installation procedure should not be made by the installation crews. Instead, you have chosen to have these decisions made centrally by the people in Project Planning as you choose to have a standard approach, perhaps because you believe you can control costs and quality better in this way.*

- *You also believe that the sales representatives are best suited to make decisions about the way in which they secure new business. The loose control exercised by the Business Development Manager suggests that there is not much value they can add in this part of the sales process.*

Finally, the nature and structure of these interactions will shape the outcomes that flow from the organisation.

How will the design and structure influence the outcomes that flow from the organisation? A number of things can be identified:

- *The sales and business development process is likely to be fairly opportunistic and quite "shotgun" in focus. You are likely to pick up business from a variety of sources. You may also be generating a wide spread of expectations from customers.*

- *The design of your product is likely to be standard and will follow a particular formula and "look". Costs will be tightly controlled but the design may not always fit the requirements on site.*

> - *The assembly and installation process will be tightly regimented and the on site crews are not likely to have much flexibility in the way they operate. Standard orders will be handled competently, but anything out of the ordinary will present problems for the crews (and probably customers).*
>
> *So, the strategy actually implemented by this hypothetical shelving company will be shaped by the structure that is designed into the organisation. The structure shapes the relationship and behaviours inside, and this is manifested in the strategy implemented by the business outside.*

Organisation design IS important

While the example above has been hypothetical, it does demonstrate the close relationship between the structure of the organisation and how the organisation actually goes about its business.

It suggests, therefore, that managers should carefully examine what they want to achieve (their strategy), and then design an organisation that is likely to reflect that strategy and result in specific behaviours.

 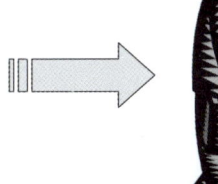 

But, I have found that many management teams do not necessarily see these linkages. Moreover, I have found that there are a number of misconceptions about structure that contribute to it being pushed to "the bottom of the pile".

Some of the more *common* misconceptions are:

Misconception 1: "A good attitude and willingness to work is more important than structure."

This misconception holds that people can work "through", or despite, the structure and that their positive attitude and willingness to collaborate will drive their behaviours.

The assumption is that the structure may not reflect the behaviours and relationships that management want within the business. While people can certainly overcome the limitations of the structure, *they do so at a cost to themselves and the organisation.* Some of the consequences of this are:

- There is stress and tension within the organisation as people work outside some of the required lines of reporting and communication;

- Some of the structural elements, such as autonomy and performance measurement, will be out of "synch" with the required behaviours, ie, staff will not be measured or rewarded for the work they are required to do;

- The organisation will be difficult to understand, particularly for newcomers and outsiders. This means that the level of complexity and uncertainly rises, with a resultant fall in efficiency and a simultaneous increase in risk;

> *I have encountered this phenomenon in a number of public sector organisations where the structure is inappropriate to the tasks that are required.*

Chapter 7

> *Because the majority of public servants are hard-working and conscientious, they strive to achieve the goals and outcomes of the organisation within the constraints of inappropriate structure. However, the costs are high and are subsequently reflected in a lack of efficiency and high levels of work stress.*

Misconception 2: "Good process can overcome the inadequacies of an inappropriate structure."

Sometimes when a structure does not deliver all that the strategy requires, management sets up a process to correct the deficiencies. Examples here are the Total Quality Management processes (TQM) or processes designed to "integrate" the strategies of different divisions within the organisation.

This misconception has much in common with the first, but there are a few specific issues that occur in this situation.

- ➤ Structure is more "powerful" than process. Because structure determines who you work with, the reporting relationships you have and way you are measured /remunerated, it tends to have a greater effect on shaping behaviour than any processes that have been implemented (Chorn (1991)).

- ➤ Processes that are designed to "cut across" the organisation, such as matrix management, can cause confusion and tension as a result of the additional lines of reporting. These can often be in conflict with each other (Chorn (1991)) and result in sub-optimum outcomes.

- ➤ The primary shaper of outcomes will be the structure of the organisation. At best, processes such as TQM and "coordinating committees" can only moderate the behaviour of the organisation. "Quality" and "integration of effort" are outcomes that should be designed into what the organisation does, rather than being added as a secondary process.

I worked with a financial services client some years ago that mounted an all-out assault on Quality Management as a means of reducing the error rate in their processing of client queries and claims. The management team believed the problem was that staff in the different departments were too focused on their own narrow part of the total process, and did not adopt a "whole-of-client" perspective.

For political reasons, they were unwilling to re-structure the organisation in a way that would group the parts of the process together more logically. Instead, they implemented a TQM initiative and appointed a senior manager to oversee the process. They gave him the authority to introduce processes that would ensure the different departments collaborated more effectively.

In a number of cases, the processes he recommended clashed with the established ways of running the various departments. This threatened the departmental managers who subtly resisted the initiatives by managing their staff's behaviour a little more closely in vital areas.

When the TQM manager realised this, he got the senior management team to force the compliance of the departmental managers. Ultimately, the departmental managers fell into line, but at the expense of their own managerial authority and accountability for their results. The departmental managers now had an "excuse" to blame for the shortcomings in their own departments – they were no longer fully accountable for their performance.

The situation has not yet resolved itself, but a number of the departmental managers have since left the organisation because they believe that they have been stripped of their managerial autonomy. And the level of errors and inefficiency continues as the departments still do not collaborate as effectively as the strategy requires!

My lesson from this, and other unhappy experiences, is that the structure of the organisation is more powerful in shaping behaviours than a (TQM) process. Although the structure was inducing (in some cases) inappropriate behaviours and strategy from the staff, the TQM process overlaid on top was not able to modify these sufficiently.

Indeed, when you "push" the process so that it is powerful enough to overcome inefficiencies in the structure, this only succeeds in undermining the structure so that the organisation becomes even more inefficient!

Misconception 3: "Flexibility implies a lack of structure."

This misconception is not always voiced explicitly, but it is implied in the actions of some managers.

In rapidly changing and uncertain environments, managers usually want to retain maximum flexibility in their repertoire of strategies and responses. And so they resist defining or setting a clear structure in the belief that this will allow them to retain maximum flexibility.

But flexibility is not produced by a lack of structure. Flexibility is produced when the structure appropriately reflects the complexity and uncertainty in the environment. Indeed, a lack of structure generally results in uncoordinated effort and a lack of focus in the way resources are deployed.

This lack of coordination and focus does not assist in coping with the demands of a complex and uncertain environment. In fact, the opposite usually occurs.

This counter-intuitive insight is well presented by Raymond Miles and Charles Snow in their work on different structures and strategies (Miles and Snow (1978)). Miles and Snow identify four different forms that capture the different configurations of structure and resultant strategy.

These are:

The ***Prospector*** (characteristics of "D")		Entrepreneurial organisation that is structured around broader job descriptions and a clear understanding of the strategic pathways they want to explore
The ***Defender*** (characteristics of "A")		A tightly controlled and efficiency-focused structure that seeks to standardise and perfect processes for product and service delivery
The ***Analyser*** (characteristics of 'Pd')		A combination of the above two forms. One part of the organisation is structured to pursue entrepreneurial opportunities, while the rest is structured to look after the core business
The ***Reactor*** (no clear form)		A fluid form that does not adopt a particular structure, preferring instead to react quickly to whatever opportunities are presented in the market

Their research shows that while the first three forms enjoy varying levels of success, the *Reactor* is consistently the worst performer.

Since the *Reactor* does not adopt any particular form, preferring to "be prepared" for any eventuality, there are no regular patterns of behaviour that develop. As a consequence, the organisation has no real capabilities that can be brought to bear on the opportunities in the environment.

While individuals within the *Reactor* organisation may have high levels of skill, the lack of "organisation" and structure renders the organisation somewhat ineffective.

Chapter 7

What are the key influences on organisation design?

"What are the things we need to consider when looking at the structure and design of the organisation?" This is a question I am often asked when we examine organisations that have structure or design problems.

I have developed a summary of the most important factors for consideration. This is by no means an exhaustive list, but it does provide a way to begin exploring the issue of structure.

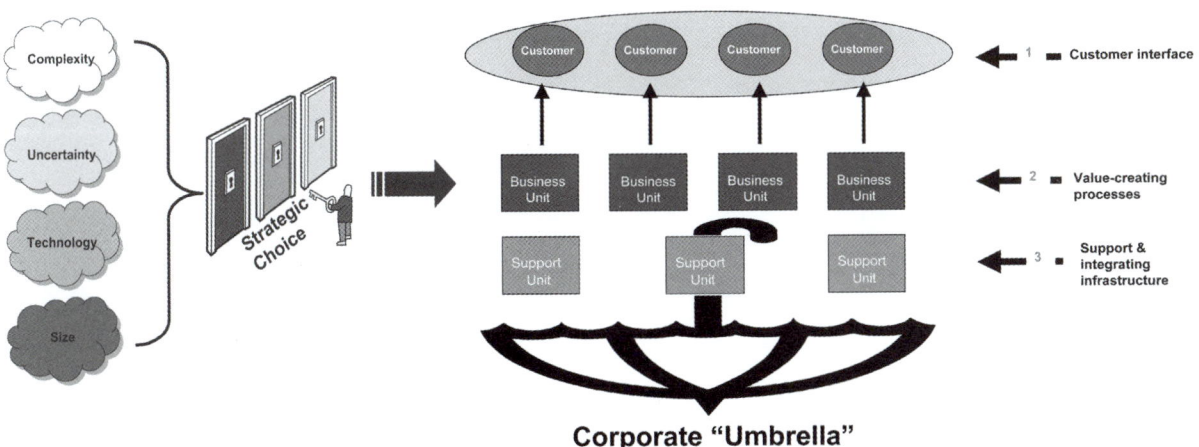

Essentially, the matter boils down to *strategic choice* (it often does), but there are four key factors that have to be taken into account before making your strategic choice:

- ➤ The level of uncertainty in the environment and within the organisation;

- ➤ The degree of complexity and/or fragmentation in the situation – both inside the organisation and in the operating environment;

> The technology that is used in the value creating process – what demands does it make on the people and organisation;

> The size of the organisation – how many resources you need to coordinate and control.

Uncertainty in organisation design

The concept of uncertainty is usually experienced within the operating environment of the organisation. It refers to issues such as changing patterns of demand, new technology and shifts in the regulatory environment.

But it can also refer to aspects inside the organisation – such as uncertainty in the outcomes of certain activities and processes. An example might be the findings of research and clinical trials within the pharmaceutical industry.

The level of uncertainty has a major influence on the way the organisation is able to control and coordinate its resources. In general, the greater the level of uncertainty, the more the organisation structure should rely on an *indirect/ subjective* form of control (Burns & Stalker (1961), Lawrence & Lorsch (1967) Wilkins & Ouchi (1983)).

Chapter 7

Low uncertainty

Direct/objective control

Explicit and formal standards

Control by rules, regulations and standard operating procedures

Roles and decision authority specified precisely

High uncertainty

Indirect/subjective control

Implicit and informal standards

Control by staff's participation in a common set of values and vision for the future

Roles and decision authority specified broadly and generally

We can relate the concepts on "direct" and "indirect" control with our earlier references to PADI.

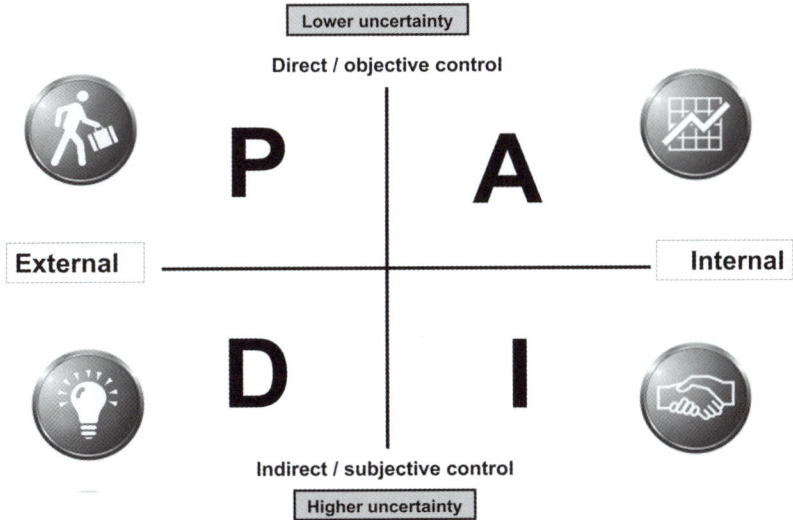

167

Let's examine some of the implications of this analysis:

➤ The diagram suggests that "P" and "A" organisations use direct/objective forms of control, while "D" and "I" organisations rely on more indirect/subjective forms of control

So, "P" and "A" organisation structures will have formal standards and will rely on precise roles and decision authority, while "D" and "I" structures will have more implicit standards and rely on fairly broad role descriptions.

➤ Another implication is that "P" and "A" organisations have a lower tolerance for uncertainty than "D" and "I" organisations. While this is true, you should recognise that we are talking of *relative differences*.

For example, a sales representative in a "P" structure will not have the minutiae of her role outlined in great detail and she will have to be relatively creative in securing new business. But, the range of possible outcomes is well defined, that is, whether she gets the sale or not, what the product range is, what discretion she has in pricing etc. Contrast this to a researcher in an R&D laboratory who has fewer guidelines and a much broader range of outcomes that are possible.

➤ **Direct/objective control** organisation structures seem better suited to conditions of relative certainty. The explicit and formal standards used can cope with situations where the range of variations and options is relatively contained. Staff can refer to the standard processes and procedures to deal with most of the contingencies that arise.

Examples include:

- Production processes where variations are allowed within pre-determined guidelines;

- Sales activities where the customers' needs fall within a range of requirements – you have a product range and will use the "standard" components in various combinations to meet these needs.

➤ **Indirect/subjective control** organisation structures can cope better with situations of relative uncertainty. In these situations, there are no standard rules and regulations that can cope with the wide array of contingencies that may be encountered by the organisation. Staff cannot refer to a manual of procedures that outline their course of action.

People and teams rely on their understanding of the strategic intent and values of the organisation to guide them in developing approaches to meet customer needs and solving problems.

Examples include:

- Advertising or marketing professionals who seek ways to attract new customers and meet their needs. The only guidelines they have are the strategy of the organisation and a set of general principles on aspects of consumer behaviour and psychology;

- Aid workers who deliver relief and emergency aid to victims of war and natural disasters. They are guided by the general aims and goals of their organisation, but have to decide on the best approach based on the local conditions. Each situation is truly unique and they have to respond to the specifics of each situation as they find it.

So, in conclusion, we are saying that indirect/subjective control structures are better suited to coping with conditions of relative uncertainty. "D" and "I" organisations are best structured using these *implicit* means of control and coordination.

Strategic Alignment

"P" and "A" organisations, with their more direct/objective control structures, on the other hand, are better suited to conditions of lower uncertainty where control, co-ordination and outcomes are more *explicit*.

Complexity and fragmentation in organisation design

Complexity generally refers to the number of occupational or process specialties within the organisation. For example, a chemical manufacturing plant would include a great number of different processes in order to produce the end product. In addition, there would probably be a large number of different chemists and specialist chemical engineers working on the overall process.

Fragmentation usually refers to the number of different segments or groupings in the environment or market. An example of a fragmented operating environment is where the organisation faces a number of different customer segments (with different needs) and a range of stakeholders (unions, lobbyists) with different agendas.

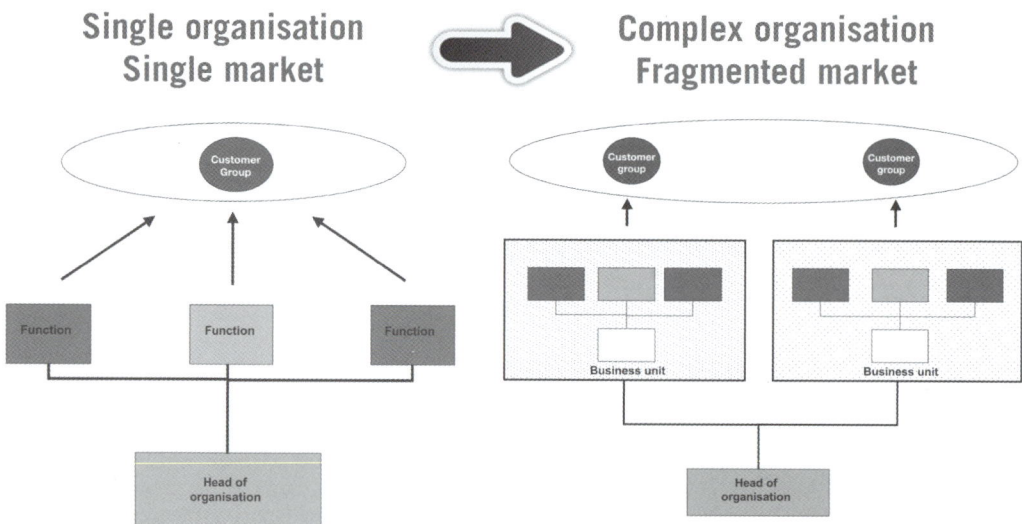

Organisations deal with complexity and fragmentation by introducing *differentiation* into the structure. Differentiation is where additional functions and units are created to deal with the different aspects of the organisation or market (Hall (1982)).

Importantly, the more differentiation that is created in the organisation structure, the more *integration* has to be achieved by other means (Lawrence & Lorsch (1967)).

In conclusion, we can argue that the more complex the environment or organisational task, the more differentiation we are likely to create in the organisation. This differentiation will manifest in greater numbers of different functions, business units or processes. And, the more of these we have in the organisation structure, the more we are likely to use integrating structures to achieve overall coordination.

Technology in organisation design

When we consider technology use within an organisation, we usually are referring to more than just the equipment or machinery that is used. We are interested in the way the whole value-creating process works inside the organisation (Hall (1967)).

I find that the classification systems used by many researchers quite useful here, in that it helps to understand the processes that take place within the organisation (Burns & Stalker (1961), Lawrence & Lorsch (1967) Perrow (1967), Wilkins & Ouchi (1983), Woodward (1965)).

Generally, technology has the following characteristics:

Level of routine

Routine technology
Highly repetitive procedures and processes that can be closely specified and controlled. Example = an assembly line in an automotive plant

Non-routine technology
Procedures and processes that depend on the situation and can only be specified in relatively general terms. Example = an interior decorating business

Level of uncertainty

Low uncertainty technology
Technologies that produce the same outcome on an ongoing basis. Example = a continuous production facility in a chemical manufacturing plant

High uncertainty technology
Technologies where the outcome is highly dependent on conditions. Example = complex medical surgery

Level of complexity

Low complexity technology
Technologies that have only a few elements or constituent parts. Example = house painting

High complexity technology
Technologies that have many elements or parts that may be combined in many different ways. Example = laboratory research

These dimensions of routine, uncertainty and complexity usually manifest in five different 'types" of technologies as follows"

Type	Routine	Uncertainty	Complexity
Continuous production	High	Low	Low-moderate
Mass production	High	Low-moderate	Moderate
Engineering	Moderate	Moderate	Moderate-high
Crafts	Low	Moderate-high	Low-moderate
Unit production	Low	High	High

Continuous production is where there is an ongoing process for converting materials or information to a higher state. An example is the chemical production plant that works on an ongoing basis converting raw oil into refined petroleum and lubricants.

Mass production is the technology used to produce large volumes of a standard unit – for example, a vehicle assembly plant.

Engineering is the technology that uses the properties of physics and mathematics to convert/fabricate materials from one state to another. An example would be the construction of bridges or the manufacture of sophisticated equipment.

Crafts are skill sets that are used in highly individualistic ways to produce outcomes that are non-standard. There is usually an artistic component to the task. Examples are cabinet-making, jewellery-making and acting.

Unit production is a catch-all description that includes those technologies that produce "one-off" or "one-at-a-time" products and services. Examples include prototypes or specialised consulting assignments where the approach is non-routine, highly complex and uncertain.

I have outlined these different technologies because it is possible to relate them to our previous discussion on organisation design – particularly with regard to the focus on *Direct Control* versus *Indirect Control*.

In general, we can show the following relationship:

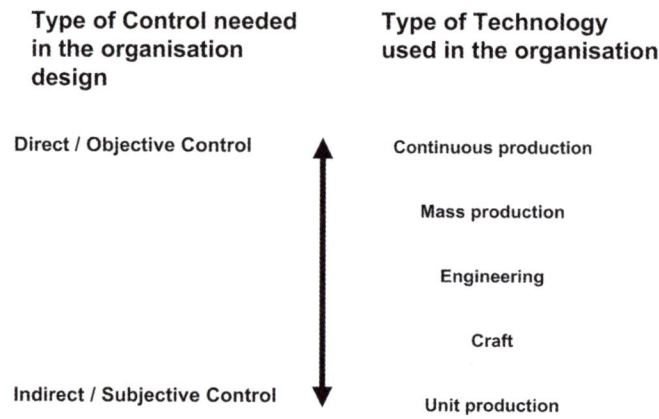

This means that we need to use different organisation structures and designs as the technology differs within the organisation. For example, the production facilities in the organisation are likely to be very differently structured from the engineering unit, and so on.

We can also link this to the discussion on PADI types and identify what type of culture and organisational form these different parts of the organisation are likely to have.

Size and organisation design

I am often involved in discussions with colleagues and friends about the size of their business or organisation. More precisely, they are usually telling me why they wish to keep their operation small.

Their argument is usually connected to the view that with size comes additional complexity and bureaucracy — that is to say that the organisation becomes more cumbersome and rigid.

It's an interesting argument, but it is only partially correct.

Additional size is often associated with greater complexity, but the research shows no necessary link with being cumbersome and rigid. Let's explore the arguments briefly.

First, there is some evidence to show that size is associated with increased complexity in three ways:

1. **Size — more hierarchical differentiation.** With more people and resources, the organisation often has to have more levels in the organisation structure.

1. **Size — more spatial differentiation.** The increased size may mean a greater number of business units dispersed over a larger distance. Again, this introduces more complexity in the way the organisation is controlled and coordinated.

1. **Size — more role specialisation.** The increased size may require a greater division of labour and role specialisation. This introduces greater complexity into the organisation.

However, we need to be careful of making generalisations about these relationships. Larger organisations are not necessarily more complex than smaller organisations. Accordingly, the larger organisation need not be more difficult to manage, nor more cumbersome in its response to change.

Complexity is not always linked to size. For example, it may be more complex to manage a small, multi-technology organisation than a larger, single-technology one. Therefore, we may add more complexity by introducing another small product line into a business than by simply doubling the size of the original, single product business. Because of this, the smaller organisation can be more cumbersome and rigid (because of the complex internal relationships) than the larger organisation.

So, the general implication of greater size on organisation design and structure is this:

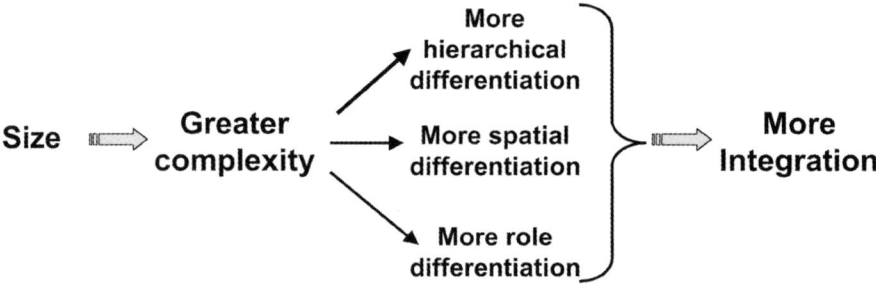

The greater the size of the organisation, the more likely we are to introduce complexity into it. Since the complexity manifests by way of hierarchy, more business units and greater role specialisation, we need to introduce more integrating mechanisms to "pull the organisation together".

In organisation design terms, this means that we need structures and processes that integrate the various parts of the organisation.

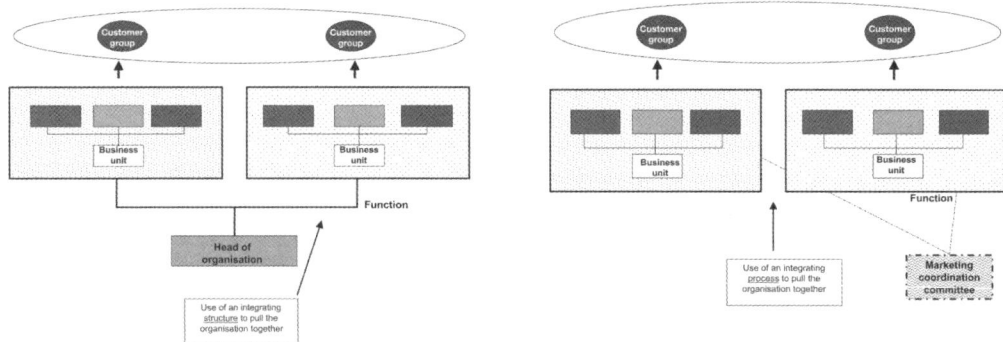

Chapter 7

In the example above, I have shown the use of an integrating *structure* – this is the appointment of an overall "head of the organisation". This role has the responsibility of integrating the efforts of the two business units. Although the two units serve different markets and, therefore, operate in different ways, the role of the "head of the organisation" is to ensure that they operate within the parameters set for the organisation.

Secondly, I show the use of a "marketing coordination committee". This is obviously an integrating *process* where the marketing managers in the business units attempt to coordinate their marketing efforts.

Earlier, I mentioned that structure is more "powerful" than process. This means that the integrating efforts via the structure (the "head of organisation" will be more effective that that via the process (the "marketing coordination committee"). So, if we need to integrate the different parts of the organisation, structure produces better results.

However, if you wish to give the business unit managers more autonomy and are not so concerned with an integrated organisational effort, an integrating process will produce a looser form of coordination.

However an organisation must ask itself which is more appropriate-structure or process? Both can produce results but in different ways.

So, in overall terms, I am suggesting that size is not as important a factor as people often believe. In the grand scheme of things, it is not a prime determinant of the organisations' design and structure.

Strategic choice in organisation design

The argument I have presented suggests that while uncertainty, complexity, technology and size do place certain constraints on the organisation's design and structure, management still exercise some choice about the final outcome of the design.

However, the design and structure that emerges often does not seem like the optimum solution under the circumstances – at least to the outside observer. Why is this so?

The major reason seems to be that management operates within what is known as "bounded rationality" (Handy (1994)). Herbert Simon (1957) identified this interesting phenomenon when he observed that organisations operate within a boundary that defines their knowledge and understanding of themselves and their environment. (This is no different for me or you).

Bounded rationality

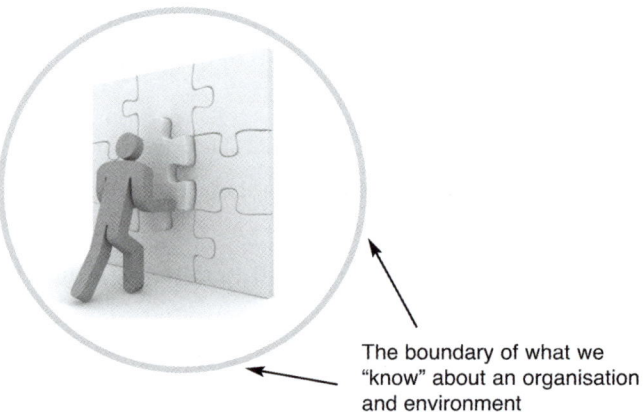

The boundary of what we "know" about an organisation and environment

At any point in time, executives are attempting to make rational decisions in the best interests of the organisation and its stakeholders – at least we hope so! But they are doing so *within the limits* of what they know, or what their culture will accept at the time.

I have found that there are a number of factors that can determine the boundaries of their rationality:

- ➤ Political and power factors within the organisation – where certain privileges and advantages have to be maintained. For example, where the financial officer has always controlled marketing expenses.

- ➤ Cultural factors – where the organisation "believes" in a particular approach and has trusted in it over the years. For example, where the organisation has always employed an engineer to head the organisation.

- ➤ Knowledge limitations – where the systems and processes in the organisation can handle only certain types of data. For example, where the organisation does not measure customer satisfaction and therefore cannot detect unhappy customers.

The management behaves "rationally", but within the current boundaries of the knowledge and understanding that have been created. That is why, when we study decisions taken some years before, we cannot always understand why certain courses of action were taken as with our new knowledge (or boundaries) they seem illogical. Our tendency is to call these past actions "irrational", but it is often the case that they were operating within different boundaries and so were completely rational at that point.

After considering all the environmental factors such as uncertainty, complexity, technology and size, we have to make a strategic choice about the design and structure of our organisation. We may be fortunate enough to have broad limits to our rationality, and so be able to optimise the decision. In other cases, we may have to accept that there are limits to what can be done with respect to this sensitive issue of organisation design.

Alternative forms of organisation design

At this stage, I would like to outline a few of the more typical forms of organisation design and structure to illustrate how these various principles may be applied.

Type	How achieved	Where best used	Example
Functional	Grouping similar functions together into organisation units	In single market or single product organisations	A manufacturing organisation that sells glass bottles to beverage plants
Product	Creating business/organisation units that focus on a single product	Where the products are very different and are sold to different customer groups	An importing business that sells hardware, small goods and electronics to hardware stores, gift shops and department stores respectively
Process	Creating organisation units that control a particular process(es)	In complex organisations where different processes re combined in various ways to produce different products and services	A management consulting firm that has skills in operations management, HR assessment, market research and strategic planning
Geographic	Creating business/organisation units to serve a particular geographical segment	Where the regions served are very geographically dispersed and have distinct requirements	A multinational pharmaceutical company that markets into different countries with different disease regimes
Market	Creating business units to serve a specific product-market	Where the markets served have discernable differences in terms of customer needs	A transport company that has different divisions for courier business general freight

Key principles in designing organisations

Over the years I have read a number of texts on organisation design and structure. They have all offered me valuable insights and understanding of the topic. Coupled with the experience I have had in working on many such assignments, I have attempted to draw together those principles that have helped me most in approaching the issue of designing an organisation.

Again, this is not an exhaustive list, but rather an outline of the key lessons I have learned when working in this challenging area.

1. Beware of generalised principles

This may seem a strange principle to start with, given that this is exactly what I am doing! But one of my major gripes is the crude checklists that often appear in articles and presentations on organisation design.

They usually include simplistic slogans such as:

> *Never have more than five layers of management between the CEO and the customer.*

> *Never have more than seven people report to you.*

> *Keep the organisation below 100 people.*

> *Managers should not be allowed secretaries and have to answer their own phones.*

While these principles may work in certain specific organisations in specific settings, they are dangerous to apply across the board. Our whole discussion about organisational effectiveness and the contingency approach has suggested that the appropriate form always depends on the situation at hand.

2. The organisation design should be understandable to most people in the organisation

I am often confronted by organisations with such complicated designs and structures that many within the organisation cannot understand how it works! As a rule, I find that this is often a good indication that the organisation is not operating as effectively as it could.

When staff do not understand the various parts of the organisation and how they work, they will operate within a severely "bounded rationality". In other words, they will be making decisions based on a very incomplete view of the organisation and its strategy. From an outsider's perspective, there will be many "irrational" decisions being made.

If I were a manager inside an organisation whose staff did not understand the organisation design or structure, I would ask myself two questions:

> ➤ *Is the organisation design too complicated or illogical for it to work effectively?*

> ➤ *Am I doing all I can to ensure that staff understand the bigger picture?*

3. The organisation design should reflect the "strategic intent" of the organisation

There is much debate about whether strategy leads structure or the other way around. The theoretical merit of either argument is not of interest to me at this juncture. What I am concerned about is whether the organisation design and structure gives effect to the strategy of the business.

For example, if your strategy is to offer the customer a totally seamless and one-stop experience, then your structure should reflect this. Your structure should, for example, integrate all the elements of your offer and manage the various linkages inside the organisation, rather than expecting the customer to speak to several different departments in order to have their problem solved.

4. The organisation design should reflect the appropriate levels of uncertainty and complexity that are found in the operating environment

The internal structure of the organisation should in some way reflect the conditions of the operating environment within which it operates. One cannot expect a highly routine set of processes to work effectively in a highly uncertain and complex environment.

As the levels of uncertainty and complexity rise, so the nature of the controls and systems within the organisation should shift towards a more *indirect/ subjective* approach. As we saw in the earlier discussions, this will mean that we have to forgo some of the *efficiency* concerns in favour of a focus on *effectiveness*. The 'PA' focus will give way to a 'DI' approach.

5. Don't confuse responsibility for Corporate Level strategy and Business Level strategy

In Chapter 4, I spoke of the differences between corporate level and business level strategy:

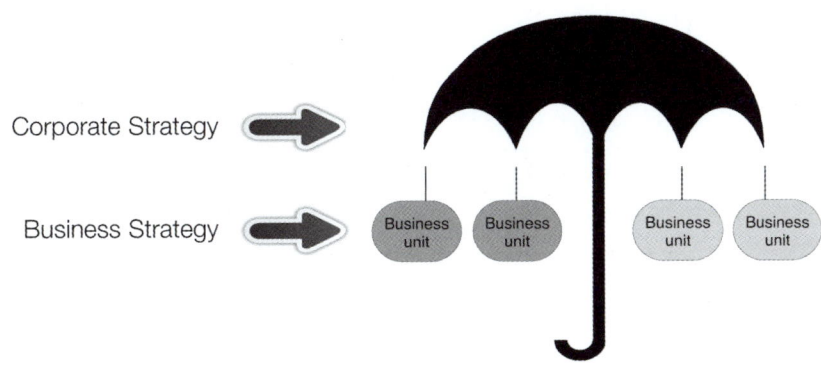

Corporate strategy involves the integration of the whole organisation and addresses three key areas of responsibility:

- Defining the shape of the overall portfolio of businesses and activities within the organisation (*what business are we in?*);

- Allocating and deploying resources across the business areas so as to optimise the performance of the organisation;

- Nurturing and developing the distinctive competencies of the organisation as a whole.

Business strategy, on the other hand, addresses the key issue of:

- How do we compete/operate within this business?

The two roles, therefore, have very different focuses and areas of responsibility within an organisation. Accordingly, it is not a good idea to create a structure that gives someone responsibility for both areas at the same time. In my experience, the breadth of the dual role is too great for most people – no matter how talented they are. The conflicts and trade-offs required are usually too great for one individual to overcome easily.

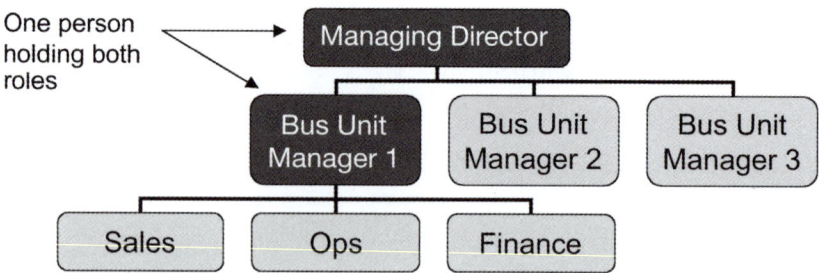

In the cases I know, this situation almost inevitably results in one of the roles being performed inadequately. The timing, pace and skills required at the corporate role are quite different to that of the business role. These differences make it very difficult to cover both appropriately.

6. In order for federal structures to work effectively, important conditions apply

Federal structures have become a popular design and structure model for complex organisations. In these structures, the organisation is designed into several business units with a head office that performs a corporate integrating function.

Charles Handy (1994) reflects on the federal structure and observes how effective this structure is when the organisation serves several customer groups and has a moderate to high level of complexity and uncertainty in its environment.

He notes, however, that the success of this structure depends on two important principles:

(a) **Subsidiarity:** This is the principle whereby all the supporting functions necessary to make the business unit effective should be included *within* the business unit. That is, the manager responsible for the business unit should have direct influence over the resources he or she needs to operate effectively in his or her market.

The exceptions to this rule are those functions that have a vital corporate role or those functions where the available skills are extremely limited or expensive. Even so, the head office roles should be confined to policy, leaving the application and implementation up to the business unit wherever possible.

In my opinion, this is the most misunderstood and abused principle in federal structures. Under the guise of "sharing costs", many organisations set up support centres/units whose role it is to "serve" the needs of the business units in those areas. Examples include human resources functions, finance functions and IT functions. There is obviously a case for setting up "shared service centres" in some cases, and I will deal with that below (see "The Case for Shared Services").

However, in many cases, the setting up of support units creates the dilemma of an "internal customer" and ends up sub-optimising the organisation's overall effectiveness – remember the argument against Internal Customers in Chapter 3!

(b) **"Twin citizenship"**: Another important condition to ensure the effectiveness of a federal structure is that managers adopt a corporate perspective in the decisions they make. Although they are a "citizen" of their business unit, and have to operate with the business unit's interests in mind, they are also a "citizen" of the overall corporate entity – and it is at this level that their primary loyalty should lie.

This means that decisions should be made in the long-term interests of the overall organisation – even though the short-term interests of the business unit may be compromised. Often, the incentives within organisations prevent this from happening, and to this extent, the federal structure fails to deliver optimum effectiveness.[1]

---

[1] The other good argument in favour of a corporate perspective is the fact that one cannot optimise the performance of an organisation by simply optimising the performance of the individual units. Organisational optimisation is, by definition, a top-down function and the corporate view has to be held as primary.

7. Approach the practice of outsourcing with care

The last decade has seen a rise in outsourcing, whereby organisations contract out processes that can be delivered more efficiently elsewhere.

This has certainly delivered short-term cost savings in most cases, but the rising number of policy reversals in this practice has led some to rethink the initial approach.

From the cases I have observed and worked on, I have assembled five key pointers managers should keep in mind when they consider outsourcing.

(a) **Make sure you understand the true cost of this service:** This is actually a good argument in favour of outsourcing, since organisations rarely understand the cost of a service until they explore the outsourcing option.

Consider the example of the office photocopier. Only when the total number of copies made are calculated and added to the cost of consumables, does the organisation know what the true cost is. In these cases, outsourcing can add real value to the organisation.

(b) **Protect the core elements of the value-adding process:** Those parts of the organisation that generate the real value proposition offered to the market should be protected, if possible, from the outsourcing process.

The value-adding process is that which generates "the organisation's business" or that which gives the organisation a competitive edge in the market.

For example, if the organisation's business is the supply of a "total kitchen solution" to your home, then they should not be outsourcing the delivery and installation. Similarly, if your competitive edge is that you offer "24-hour professional advice", then you should not outsource your after-hours telephone answering.

(c) **Ensure that variations in quality of the outsourced service will not impair the customer's experience:** If you have chosen to outsource part of your value chain, make sure that any variations in the standard of outsourced service will not seriously damage your value proposition.

Good examples here are those furniture retailers who do not keep stock of their products in store – preferring to keep them centrally warehoused for delivery direct to the customer. Often, the storage and delivery functions are outsourced to third-party providers who serve a range of similar organisations.

I can certainly recall a number of situations where I have purchased an item of furniture in the pleasant surroundings of the retail store – and then had my illusion of quality and care shattered by the experience of the "rough and tough" delivery people.

(d) **Ensure that you retain enough of the value chain to justify your position as the "supplier":** In most cases, the outsourcing takes place "behind the scenes" – you still offer and take responsibility for the whole value proposition to the customer. However, if you have outsourced the majority of the value chain and this becomes apparent to outsiders, you may lose the ability to legitimately represent the offer to customers.

If this occurs, you may have difficulty being the "main" contractor and retaining the customer relationship. Also, because you have outsourced so much of the value chain, you may have limited ability to add value and charge an acceptable price/fee for your services.

(e) Remain as close to the customer interface as possible: The research on customer value management (Gale (1994)) suggests that, in general, value migrates to the point of interface with customers. That is to say, the most valuable position for an organisation is to control and manage the relationship with the customer.

As a general rule, therefore, it is preferable not to outsource those functions that permit you to manage and control the customer relationship. This can seriously erode your ability to add value (and charge for your products and services accordingly) in the long run.

The case for shared services

On a number of occasions I have outlined my concerns with creating "internal customer" arrangements by having centralised support functions "serve" the business units. The discussion on federal structures also highlights Charles Handy's (1994) view that, wherever possible, support services should be devolved into the business units that require them (subsidiarity).

However, there are certain cases where setting up centralised, shared services is appropriate. In recent years, the practice has become quite popular as organisations attempt to cut costs and save on "duplication". And there are certainly a number of benefits that flow from this exercise, including:

➤ Cost savings as duplication is eliminated;

➤ Economies of scale as multiple smaller units are combined into a larger, more efficient unit;

> Increased focus on the core operations as some of the support activities are removed from management responsibility.[2]

I have tried to outline below some of the conditions under which the setting up of shared services is desirable and can produce significant overall benefit for the organisation.

Where critical mass of the service is not possible within the business unit

If the business units are not able to sustain or afford a critical mass in particular function, then it makes sense to centralise it as a shared service.

An example of this is a legal function within an organisation. None of the business units use the service sufficiently to warrant it as part of their organisation, so the best solution appears to be to create a "legal services" function and operate it as a shared service.

Where the service is not a critical part of the value chain of the business unit

We discussed this issue briefly as part of the outsourcing question. If the service in question is a true support activity – such as printing or office maintenance – then setting up a shared service is not likely to disrupt the operations of the business unit.

However, if the function is a core part of the business unit's value chain – such as the transport service in a courier business – then it could disrupt the ability of the business unit to meet the needs of its customers. In this case, we may be damaging the integrity of the value proposition to the market.

---

1 The banks have done this successfully by removing the transaction processing from branches and setting up centralised shared facilities. This has allowed the branches to focus on managing their customer relations and also allowed cost savings in the high-volume transaction processing facilities.

Where the business units have similar strategic logics

Where the business units in an organisation have similar strategic logics, their needs can be more readily served by a centralised shared service.

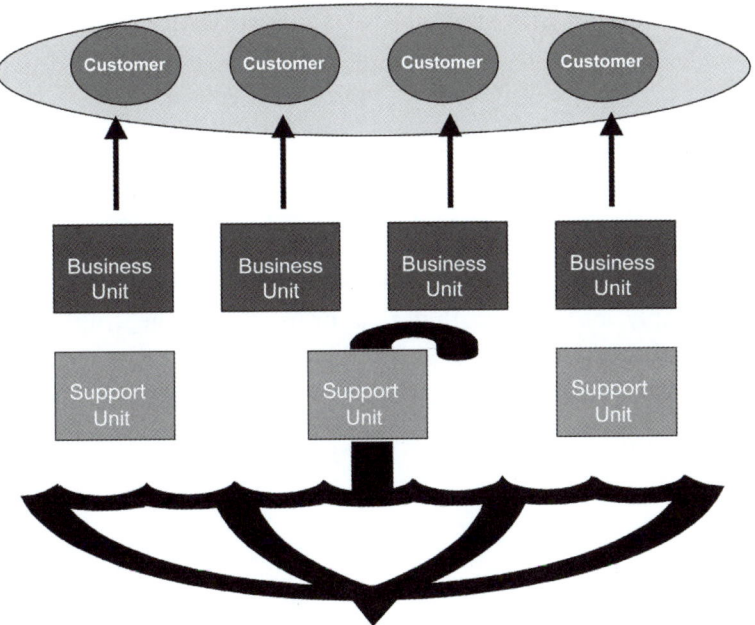

However, as above, where the logics of the business units *differ* markedly from each other, the shared service will have difficulty meeting these disparate needs with one basic type of service. In other words, the shared service will not be aligned to the needs of its different "internal customers"!

This usually results in dissatisfaction about the "captive" market state and business units complain that they are able to purchase more cost-effective services on the open market. So we end up with a less than optimal set up all around.

So, in conclusion, there are cases where the use of shared services will produce enhanced effectiveness for the overall organisation. However, my experience suggests that management is often too blinded by the short-term cost savings by eliminating what they see as duplication. Often, however, the real cost is a deterioration of the longer-term effectiveness of the whole organisation.

Key points in summary

- The design and structure of an organisation is important as it drives the strategic behaviour and outcomes from the organisation.

- Structure is more powerful than process in influencing behaviour within organisations.

- Flexibility in organisations does not imply a lack of structure – simply a structure that is appropriate to the conditions in the environment.

- Organisation design is influenced by:
  - Uncertainty
  - Complexity
  - Technology

- The more uncertainty and complexity in the situation, the greater the use of Indirect/Subjective Controls and 'DI' type organisations.

- Size does not necessarily increase the complexity in organisations, but it does increase the need for integration. Integration through structure is more effective that integration through process.

- Organisation design is ultimately determined by Strategic Choice, but this is, in turn, is limited by "bounded rationality".

➤ A number of key principles are useful when designing organisations:

- Beware of generalised principles

- Make sure the organisation is understandable to most people

- Ensure that the design reflects the strategic intent

- The design should reflect the conditions in the external environment

- Don't confuse corporate and business level responsibilities

- Federal structures are effective in complex, uncertain environment, but we have to remember the conditions of subsidiarity and twin citizenship

- Outsourcing should be approached with care, and remember to protect the core value-creating processes of the organisation

➤ Shared services can produce some shorter term cost savings in the organisation, but these can be at the expense of overall organisational effectiveness.

Chapter 7

Strategic Alignment

Chapter 8
Inducing change to create strategic alignment

The story so far

In the earlier chapters of the book we explored the various aspects of organisational effectiveness and how it is related to strategic alignment. We understand that increasing the levels strategic alignment is likely to lead to improved effectiveness and relevance for the organisation.

The earlier chapters also gave us insight into how the PADI model can be used to describe customer groups, strategy, culture and leadership. And we know that getting them all aligned will produce better results for the organisation:

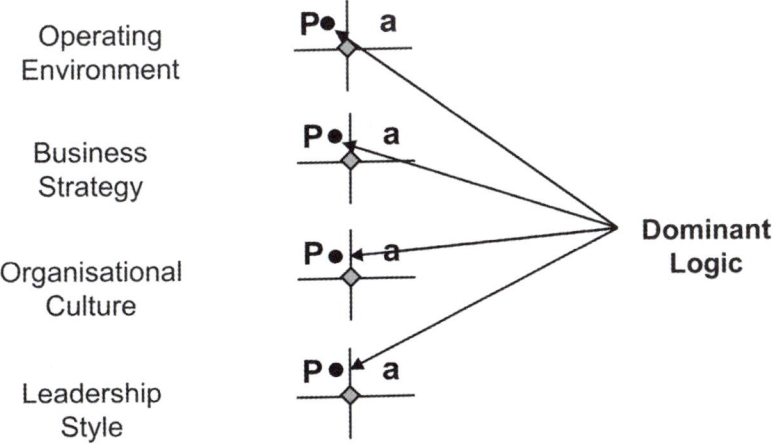

We have also discussed the issues of how culture can be shaped and how organisations can be designed. All of these are related to producing strategic alignment.

But how do we put it all together? How do we juggle all the pieces so that we end up with an organisation that is better aligned with its environment?

How do we create strategic alignment in our organisation?

In a way, this is the key question that I have been trying to answer. And now, I believe I can put all the pieces of the puzzle together.

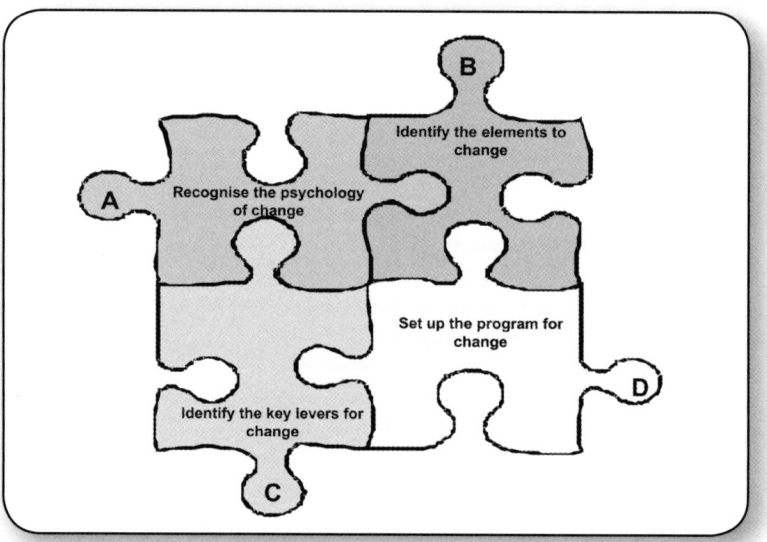

I have tried to keep it simple; because that's the way I can understand it! There are four key phases to creating strategic alignment – some are just brief pauses to reflect on what you are doing, while others involve a series of more intricate steps. These phases and detailed steps are outlined over:

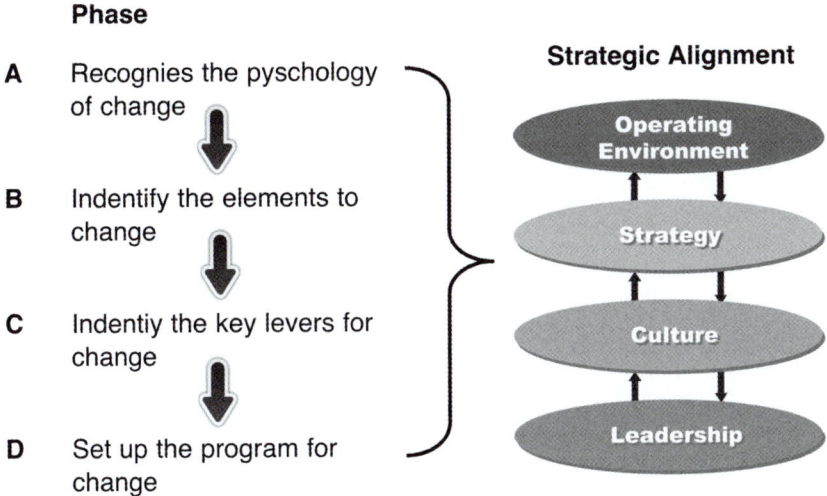

Before discussing each of these phases in more detail, it is worth noting a few points:

➤ The process of organisational change is complex (a full treatment of this subject is beyond the scope of this book);

➤ Although the four phases are presented in a neat sequential manner, change rarely occurs in an orderly fashion. In most cases, things occur in a haphazard way and progress is not orderly or predictable;

➤ Strategic alignment is a rather elusive state. Organisations move fleetingly from alignment to misalignment and back again. So change is an ongoing process with phases of "tinkering" (evolutionary change) interspersed by phases of more radical transformation (revolutionary change).

> **Phase A: Recognise the psychology of change**

In Chapter 5 we introduced the topic of change psychology. The key message is quite simple – if you want to re-align the organisation effectively, the initiatives have to eventually lead to a change of behaviour in the organisation. Research showed clearly that individuals act in patterns of behaviour that are directly consistent with their personality types. It also showed that individuals default to this type even when they are assigned roles that have behaviours different to their preferences (Hunter (1998)). This means that we have to address three focal points for individuals in the organisation:

Individuals need to have:

- ➤ The chance/opportunity to change;
- ➤ The incentives/motivation to change;
- ➤ The skills and competencies necessary to make the change.

The chance to change

The culture and organisation structure have to provide the opportunity for the individuals to try new behaviours. In particular, the way we design roles (autonomy) and the way we measure performance (control) have to support the new behaviours.

So, for example, if we want staff to use their initiative and take responsibility for solving customer queries on their own, then we must define their roles accordingly. Instead of listing the sequence of processes they should follow, the role should provide broad guidelines and specify the outcomes that are sought.

In addition, the performance measures used to control the organisations should measure these behaviours. Instead of measuring the adherence to specific procedures, we should be measuring the extent to which customer queries are being solved.

The motivation to change

Appropriate rewards and incentives should also be in place to encourage the required behaviours. If we are seeking team behaviours rather than individual behaviours, for example, then we should be rewarding people on a team basis and for their contribution to the team.

As we saw in Chapter 5 on shaping the culture, the key factors that have the leverage are autonomy (job design), control (what we measure) and rewards (what behaviours we encourage).

But there is another, broader issue at stake when we discuss motivation. Aside from the personal rewards and incentives, there is also the motivation to be part of an organisation whose goals you believe in. In this sense, the *vision* of the organisation is also important. Does it inspire people? Is it credible? Do the people care? These are all issues to consider when we plan the overall program for change.

The skills and competencies necessary for change

Staff need the necessary skills and competencies to support the new behaviours. This is where training and development (T&D) comes in. These initiatives give staff the "how to" element – and the all-important confidence – in order to embark upon the journey of change.

But, as I said in Chapter 5, T&D alone will rarely be sufficient to induce change in an organisation. And T&D should not be seen as a reward for good performance or long service.

T&D is best viewed as a tool that enhances the effectiveness and versatility of staff in performing their roles in the organisation. The more clearly the new context (the new culture or strategy) is defined, the more clearly the goals can be set for T&D. And, the more clearly the goals are set, the more effective the actual training and development can be.

Phase B: Identify the elements of change

As we know from the earlier chapters, a change in strategy may require a change in both culture and leadership. Therefore, it is useful to identify *precisely* what has to change:

Areas of potential misalignment

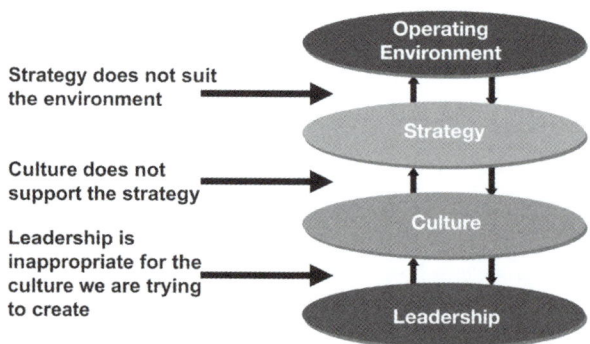

As you can see, there are three possible scenarios:

1. **The strategy does not meet the needs of customers:** If this is the case, we may need to re-think the entire strategy and the way we attempt to add value to our customers. Of course, if the strategy needs to change, then the other elements of culture and leadership may need to change as well.

2. **The culture does not support the strategy:** If we have a case of cultural misalignment (as discussed in Chapter 5), then we run the risk of having the implementation of our strategy impaired or even derailed completely. The goal is to achieve a cultural alignment with the strategy, so that the patterns of behaviour inside the organisation match those that are expected in the market.

3. **The leadership is not creating the culture we want:** This is relatively serious, as it implies that the way we are leading the organisation is inconsistent with the kind of organisation we are trying to create!

   Since leadership provides the role model for the rest of the organisation, this has a high leverage factor in shaping the culture and inducing change. You will have to think seriously about whether or not the leadership can change in the appropriate way – or you will have to reconsider the desired culture and strategy.

I believe that it is important to identify which of these elements require change and realignment. Being as specific as possible about the change process will help you achieve better results.

Strategic Alignment

> **Phase C: Identify the key levers for change**

Each of the elements of strategy, culture and leadership has leverage points that can induce the required realignment. For the purposes of this analysis, I will deal with organisation design as a major leverage point within culture.

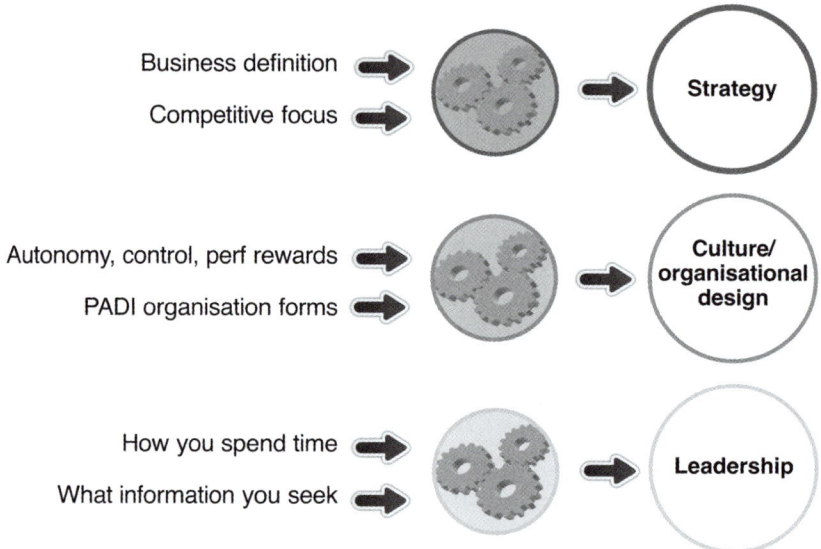

Strategy

I have found that the major leverage points in bringing about an alignment of strategy are to revisit the business definition of the organisation and the competitive focus in the market.

> **Business definition:** The definition of your business is the starting point of any strategic planning exercise. Derek Abell (1980) has defined a very neat and powerful way of capturing this important information. It makes a really useful planning tool as well.

Business Definition

Customer Groups (Who do we serve)

Products, Services or Technology (What do we provide)

The value added (How do we make a difference)

If your strategy is misaligned with the needs of customers, it is useful to review your business definition and make any necessary changes. There are three elements to the definition:

1. The customer groups you serve:

    ➤ Have you defined the market segments and customer groups correctly? Is there a better way to segment the market? (See the discussion on market segmentation in Chapter 3.)

    ➤ Are there customer groups/segments you have not addressed?

    ➤ Have you identified the needs of these customer groups and segments correctly?

2. The products and services you provide:

    ➤ Do the products and services meet the needs of the major customer groups and segments?

    ➤ Are new or additional products and services required?

3. The value that you add:

- Is your value proposition viable in the market – does it really address the intangible needs of the customers?

- Do you really make a difference in the market? Would anyone notice if you went out of business?

It is a valuable exercise to get groups of management and staff together to review the current and desired business definition. Although only a short exercise, it enables you to capture the essence of the organisation's strategy in a very succinct way.

Competitive focus: Once you have reviewed the business definition, it is time to review the competitive focus of the organisation.

As we discussed in Chapter 4, competitive advantage is achieved by having a clear focus in business strategy. We can use the PADI model to identify the different focus areas for the organisation. This can also illustrates the trade-offs that are made to achieve the chosen focus.

Remember, the strategic focus should match the needs of the customer group.

The competitive focus should be defined as "P", "A", "D" or "I", or combinations of these. Remember that, in most cases, diagonal combinations are not very viable, particularly in the implementation of the strategy.

Finally, we also need to ensure that the business definition is consistent with the competitive focus. For example, if we have a business definition that emphasises strategic partnership and collaborative processes with customers, the competitive focus should have an emphasis on "I".

Focus in strategy

Objective focus

Rapid response and sharp focus	**Low cost of supply**
New product & solution development	**Customer franchise & intimacy**

External emphasis — Internal emphasis

Subjective focus

Culture/organisation design

When the culture or organisation design is misaligned with the strategy, it is likely that there will be difficulty implementing the strategy – the internal behaviours will be out of synch with those of the strategy.

In these cases, there are a few factors that will drive the shifts required in the culture and organisation design.

> **Autonomy, control and performance rewards:** These are three of the culture factors discussed in Chapter 5 – they are also linked to the psychology of change outlined earlier in this chapter.
>
> I regard these as the leverage points for shifting the culture. This does not mean that you don't have to do much about the other factors – it's just that the culture will be hard to shift without addressing these!

Strategic Alignment

AUTONOMY — What people are allowed to do

P (External, Objective): Autonomy is determined by the need to perform to set objectives

A (Internal, Objective): Autonomy is task specific and limited by the need to make decisions according to tried and tested formulae

D (External, Subjective): Autonomy is limited only by the individual's creative response to organisational ideas

I (Internal, Subjective): Autonomy is limited by the need to obtain consensus about the way things should be done

In general, the three factors are linked to the culture as follows:

CONTROL — What is *inspected*

P (External, Objective): Control is achieved by individually agreed performance standards

A (Internal, Objective): Control is achieved through conforming to explicit rules and procedures

D (External, Subjective): Control is achieved by the individual's commitment to a shared vision of the future

I (Internal, Subjective): Control is achieved by collective adherence to a set of common values and beliefs

PERFORMANCE REWARDS — What is *expected* of people

```
                        Objective
    P                       |                        A
                            |
      Value is placed on the | Value is placed on the
      individual's ability to | ability to maintain
      meet shorter term      | productivity and
      operational goals      | efficiency
                            |
External ───────────────────┼─────────────────── Internal
                            |
      Value is placed on the | Value is placed on
      individual's ability to| group harmony and
      be flexible and        | human interaction skills
      creative               |
                            |
    D                        |                        I
                        Subjective
```

> ➤ Autonomy — the job and role designs used in the organisation. How much latitude are staff given?

> ➤ Control — the performance measures that are used to monitor and control what people do. What do we inspect and measure to evaluate the job?

> ➤ Performance rewards — those behaviours that are valued in the organisation and how they are rewarded. What do we expect people to do within the organisation?

Depending on the nature of the shift required, these factors should be adjusted to reflect the appropriate culture. So, we need to review the way we design the roles in the organisation, the nature of the measures used and the way we reward the desired behaviours.

PADI organisational forms: When we discussed strategy in Chapter 5, we spoke of the need to develop focus. Indeed, as we have seen, the nature of the focus is an important part of the alignment process.

It is possible to identify specific organisation designs and structures that drive particular cultures within the organisation:

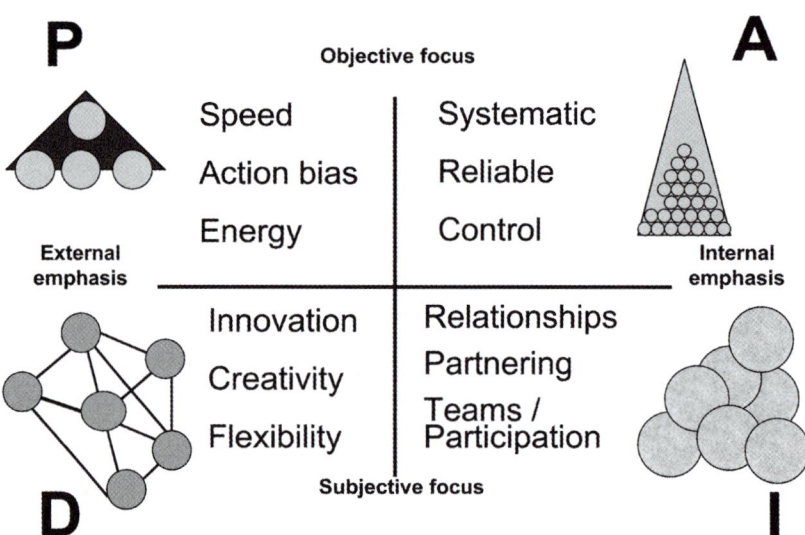

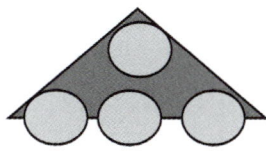

"P" cultures are driven by organisation designs with the following features:
- flat organisations – few levels between the top and bottom of the organisation
- broad spans of control
- broad job descriptions – individuals allowed latitude in the way they achieve the outcomes
- high levels of individual accountability

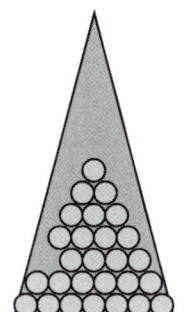

"A" cultures are characterised by the following features in the organisation design:
- taller organisations with narrower spans of control for each management level
- specific and highly prescribed job descriptions – individuals given explicit directions about the processes to be used
- many checks and balances so that decisions are all subject to detailed process
- high level of control and tight measurement of key indicators

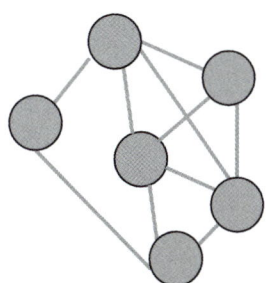

"D" cultures are induced by the following organisation designs:
- fluid organisation structures – people play the role that is needed at the time
- job descriptions shaped by the individual's skills and preferences
- high level of personal accountability – individuals have separate "agreements" regarding their responsibilities
- very informal patters of communication – no real "chain of command"

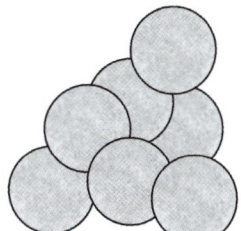

"I" cultures are shaped by the following organisation structures:
- team-oriented structures that organise responsibilities to teams
- job descriptions that emphasise collaboration and contributions to the team
- consultation and partnering
- participative decision-making structures

Strategic Alignment

Leadership

As you know, I believe leadership is a key influence in shaping and realigning the organisation. Accordingly, the leverage points for shifting the leadership focus are vital leverage points for the organisation as a whole.

How you spend your time: How leaders spend their time is a visible indicator of the things they value in the organisation. It means much more than the homilies they give or the memorandums they write.

These visible behaviours send messages to the staff about:

- What is important in the organisation;
- How to "get ahead" in the organisation – the behaviours to emulate in order to succeed;
- What is the "real" culture and strategy.

As a guide, the following leadership behaviours are associated with the different PADI cultures:

How leaders spend their time

Objective

P
- Emphasising goal achievement
- Visiting customers and selling the organisation
- Planning and setting objectives

A
- Emphasising systems, controls and cost cutting
- Focus on financial reports and profitability
- Developing processes and procedures for reporting and management control

External ─────────── **Internal**

D
- Wandering through the organisation suggesting changes and improvements
- Involved in new product development activities
- Networking within the industry and amongst opinion leaders to keep novel

I
- Promoting training and development of staff
- Promoting collaboration and team work - initiating liaison between different parts of the organisation
- Emphasising the values and culture – building commitment to the organisation

Subjective

So, spend your time according to the outcomes you need to achieve!

What information you seek: The information you call for and seek out not only signals what issues you are interested in, it also influences the types of decisions you make.

As a guide, we can relate the following information to the different types of PADI strategies and cultures:

What information leaders seek

Objective

P (External)
- Sales, market share and competitor activity
- results of customer satisfaction and production levels
- Progress on projects and business plans

A (Internal)
- Accounting, financial budgets and profitability
- Minutes of meetings from across the organisation
- Customer and product profitability

D (External)
- Levels of new product development & innovation
- Staff suggestions for changes and improvement
- Future trends and possibilities in the industry

I (Internal)
- Employee satisfaction and opinion surveys
- Training and development activity
- Reports on major customers, their needs, their complaints

Subjective

Although only a rough guide, it does highlight the types of information and decisions that leaders focus on in different types of organisations. My experience is that you can begin to shift the orientation of leadership by shifting the kind of information on which your staff focus. So, including new types of appropriate information for them to process is a good way to start the transition.

Phase D: Set up the program for change

As I mentioned earlier, change management is an entire discipline and many authors have made contributions to this field. I don't pretend to offer a comprehensive insight into this complex area.

However, I have learned a few key principles that appear to be associated with change programs that work. My understanding is best captured by the following diagram:

A Framework for Organisational Change

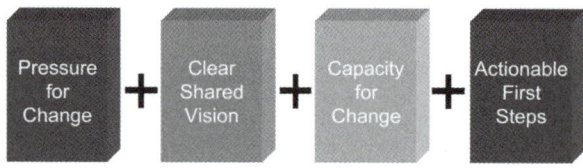

=

It suggests that there are four key steps to managing change/re-alignment in your organisation:

1. Make sure that the organisation and people understand the pressure for change – *why do we need to change*?

2. Develop and share a clear vision about where the organisation is headed – *where are we going*?

3. Put in place the organisational and people capabilities for change – *what do we need to make the change*?

4. Have a plan of action that outlines what has to be done to get it all started – *what do we have to do tomorrow when we come to work*?

Whenever any of these are missing, I have found the change often fails!

1. Build pressure for change

Pressure for change is essential for the effectiveness of a change program. Without it, the initiative seems to sink to the bottom of the 'in-tray'. Other priorities take precedence and organisational behaviour does not change.

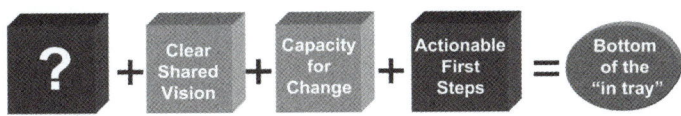

> *A doctor tells her patient that she should give up smoking. She sets him a clear goal, a program with actionable steps outlined; access to support services and nicotine patches to help him cope with withdrawal difficulties.*
>
> *The patient says, 'That's great. It looks like it would work. But I feel fine. I exercise for an hour four times per week. I eat well, I'm fit, I have no health problems and I enjoy smoking. I can't see the need to give up.'*
>
> *The patient understands the vision, knows what they need to do and has the resources to do it but feels no pressure for change. He is unmotivated to change his behaviour.*

So, how does pressure for change come about?

Re-alignment and change programs often arise after an analysis of the organisation's position and the competitive realities. Management and staff may realise that that they face threats and opportunities – this often creates a sense of urgency.

A number of my clients have faced major shifts in their operating environment, such as deregulation or new competitors entering the market. Industry deregulation – for example, in utilities, banking and air travel – has been a major driver of change in many Australian organisations.

These changes often create a sense of urgency. Leadership can create powerful pressure for change by clearly spelling out the reasons for change – and then communicating this to the rest of the organisation.

2. Establish a clear, shared vision

If there is no clear, shared vision, the change begins quickly but then dies out because people don't know what they are aiming for.

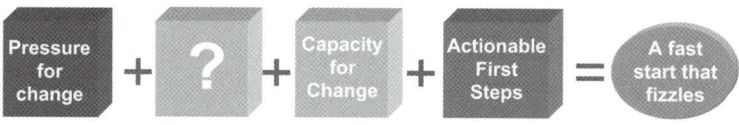

I find that a clear, shared vision acts as a compass that provides ongoing direction to the change journey. But, the vision needs to be clear and widely shared throughout the organisation.

For example, organisations that want to become more 'customer-focused' must ensure that this vision is widely held and understood. What does it mean to be more customer-focused? The actual behaviours required to become 'customer-focused' must be spelled out to members of the organisation in explicit ways.

Over the years, I have been a vocal critic of "generic" style vision statements that organisations write for themselves. Unless the vision statement really captures the "spirit" and intent of the organisation, it is rarely effective in mobilising support for change. I have learned a number of useful guidelines to developing effective vision statements. They include:

➤ A vision statement embodies a long-term view of what the organisation is or is striving to become

➤ Vision statements should have at least four major components:

- A description of who we are and how we fit into the industry/market

- Our business definition (as per the Abell model earlier in this chapter) – particularly the value we add

- Our distinctive competencies as an organisation

- Major strategic thrusts for the future

➤ Vision statements should define what we stand for. My former business partner, John Gattorna, always said that if you don't stand for something, you will end up falling for anything!

➤ Vision statements should not be so generic that you are able to replace your organisation's name with your competitor's name – and still have it make sense!

➤ The vision statement should give clues to the people in the organisation about the behaviours they should display.

Finally, if you have to mention profit (or meeting shareholder's returns), try to keep it to the end and not very prominent. I have not met many people who are motivated to get up in the morning because they are going to earn profits for the shareholders! (I believe that earning a profit is a given in vision statements and does not have to be emphasised).

3. Ensure the organisation has the capacity for change

If the organisation and the people do not have the necessary capacity for the change, you will generate much anxiety and frustration. People often want to change and know where to go, but don't have the wherewithal to do so.

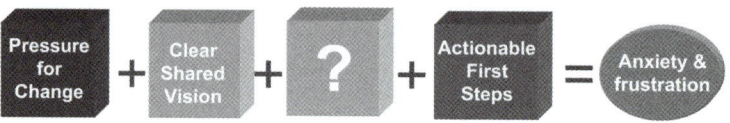

Providing the capacity to change in an organisation must be achieved at both the individual and group level.

For individuals, we need to recognise the "ladder" that produces results:

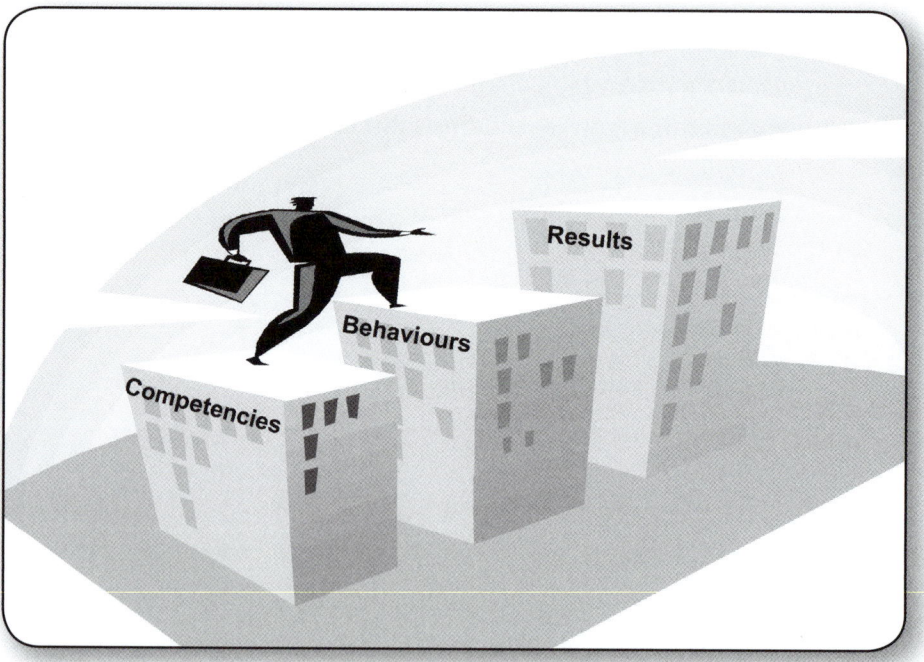

This means that the desired results must be clearly understood before we can specify what behaviours are required. Once the behaviours are identified, the T&D process can address the development of the required competencies.

At the organisational level, we need to create the appropriate capabilities for the organisation to change. This means two things:

(a) Ensure that you have designed the appropriate culture and organisation structure.

In particular, remember to make the changes in:

- Autonomy/job designs – to allow the people to do what needs to be done

- Control – to inspect and control the appropriate behaviours

- Performance rewards – to expect and reward the appropriate behaviours

- Structure – to reflect the outcomes you want to achieve

(b) Allow the organisation and people some *slack* during the "changeover period". Generally, it is difficult to maintain the same levels of efficiency when making changes to one's routine.

People need room to experiment with new behaviours – they will make mistakes and this has to be legitimised by management. If they are punished for their initial errors, they will become very anxious and frustrated – and change will not occur!

4. Determine actionable first steps

We need to provide explicit guidelines for people to make the important first steps. Without these actionable first steps, the change will be haphazard and suffer many false starts:

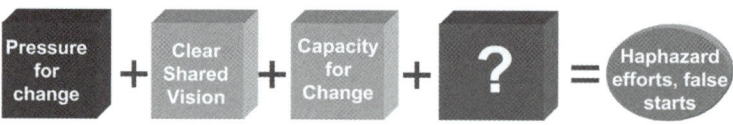

This may seem like an obvious point. But change attempts can fail because no one knows where to start.

Having articulated a vision, you will need to break down the vision into its separate parts. Specific, measurable, achievable, realistic, time-bound objectives need to be set. Then list the actions (strategies) needed to bring about your objectives.

Finally, set performance measures that are appropriate for your desired culture with specific time frames. Ensure that you plan for early, even small, "wins" by setting achievable goals. Celebrate these wins to help the change initiative develop momentum.

And now what?

I have found that this four-phase process can provide an effective way to bring about re-alignment of the organisation. But, as I said earlier, alignment is an elusive state. You cannot sit back and relax once you have completed the process.

The market shifts, the organisation drifts and issues change. Organisations are living things – they do not stand still. Indeed, organisations have a natural momentum and they move anyway – whether you are driving the changes or not.

So, the task of strategic alignment is an ongoing one. It requires constant vigilance and preparedness to experiment and make changes. Strategy needs refining, culture needs re-aligning and leadership needs to continuously be thinking a few steps ahead.

But, as I experienced in some of my earliest work roles as a restaurant waiter and shop assistant, there is nothing that quite gives me a buzz like an organisation that is functioning well. The customers are happy, the staff are happy, and the results just keep getting better.

At the start of the book, I had hoped to provide organisations and managers a way of improving their overall effectiveness. By analysing your organisation in terms of the concepts I have outlined, I believe there are useful insights that can be discussed and communicated in PADI terms. This should allow you to look at where you are now and where you want to be. Also at the outset, we started with the premise of relevance to the market place. Ask yourselves what do our customers want and then ask yourselves do we meet these needs? If there are large gaps, then change your structures and behaviours to make yourself relevant and aligned. I hope the preceding chapters give you some insight into how to do it.

In the final chapter, we turn our attention to some of the challenges brought on by the post GFC (global financial crisis) conditions. While presenting organisations with unprecedented level of volatility and uncertainty, they demonstrate once again the importance of remaining strategically aligned."

Chapter 8

Strategic Alignment

Chapter 9
Aligning with the new normal

The new normal

The unusually challenging conditions brought about by the post-GFC situation has prompted some observers to coin the term "New Normal"[1] to describe the fact that these conditions – usually thought of as abnormal shocks and discontinuity in otherwise orderly conditions – have now become the norm. Organisations have to find new approaches and develop new capabilities to deal with a range of challenges, including:

- Regulators and states playing a more prominent role in financial and capital markets – a factor that will reduce the likelihood of high levels of debt-leveraged growth

- Customers well informed through the internet – making asymmetrical value-adding (and high margins) harder to achieve

- A rapid reduction of transaction costs through EDI and related internet applications – ensuring that the middleman is squeezed out of many value chains

- The entry of ultra low cost competitors from emerging markets – threatening the position of many established industry leaders

- An apparent conflict between the needs of shareholders (profits) and the demands from communities (survival and job security)

---

1 See Ian Davies in McKinsy Quarterly xx of 2009 foreword "The New Normal"

➤ Changing industry structures that continue to place more and more market power in the hands of fewer competitors.

These conditions are having a significant impact on the shape of operating environments in which organisations operate. The new environmental, social, cultural and economic conditions have, in a sense, re-shaped the very landscape in which organisations play (see figure 1 below):

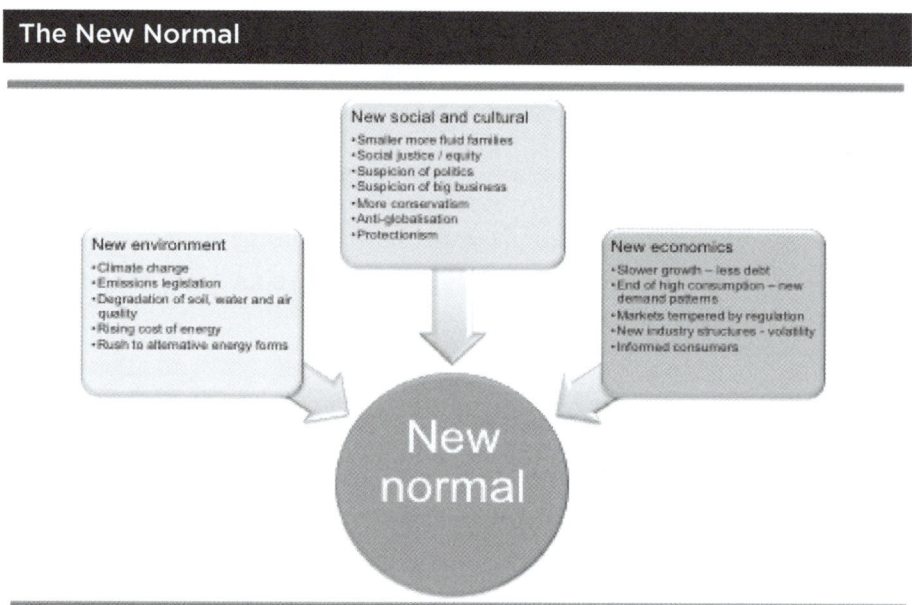

This means that the task of strategic alignment becomes all the more important and challenging. There are four key issues we can examine as we address the alignment of organisations in this environment:

1. The traditional building blocks of organisation design may be questioned in the light of the (perhaps different) capabilities required by organisations as they move into the future

2. The role played by leaders in innovation is also worth consideration. In particular, we note the role of "management innovation" as the special focus of leaders who are focused on the alignment of their organisations with the New Normal

3. How to manage the future poses a particular challenge as leaders seek to build appropriate capabilities for the future. The use of scenario planning can be considered a useful tool in this regard

4. Finally, it is worth considering a key, but often overlooked, distinction between *strategy* and *planning* as leaders seek to become more proactive in their alignment efforts.

Approaches to organisation design

A number of principles have tended to dominate our thinking in the design of organisations. These have become the very pillars upon which we have built our modern organisations. But, as Hamel[1] and other have noted, the use of these pillars have created a number of unwanted consequences in organisations. Some of these principles include:

➤ Standardisation as a means of reducing variation in processes - thereby improving efficiencies

➤ Specialisation as a technique for reducing complexity, particularly in production or process-oriented environments

➤ Aligning the goals and objectives of divisions, departments and individuals as a means of creating synergy within organisations

---

2 Hamel Gary, The Future of Management, Harvard Business Press, 2007.

- ➤ Hierarchy as a strategy for creating a pyramid of authority and a clear chain of command

- ➤ Strict regimes of planning and control so as to improve the ability of the organisation to forecast demand and supply requirements

- ➤ Extrinsic rewards as a means of achieving motivation and compliance.

These principles have almost become the standards of modern organisation design. They have enabled us to achieve many of the gains made in organisational efficiency and effectiveness. However, these gains have often come at a cost to the organisation in the form of reduced levels of adaptability. And given the increased and almost continual change in operating environments, a reduced level of adaptability will almost certainly contribute to an erosion of strategic alignment.

Now it may be that this is a natural consequence of "organisation", since the very concept of "organising" is focused on reducing complexity and uncertainty. And a key element of this is arranging things in an almost habitual manner to discourage change and experimentation. And so, these key building blocks of organisations – their very DNA – are set up to reduce levels of flexibility. Unintended or not, these principles of organisation design reduce the level of adaptability of the organisation to the changing conditions in the environment.

So, are there other principles that offer an alternative perspective for designing organisations – preferably organisations that are better suited to the demands of the New Normal? Some alternative principles may be considered if we relax the metaphor of the "machine" (inherent in the building blocks described above) and consider some of the following metaphors[3]:

---

3. The ideas in this section are influenced by the work of:
   — Joshua Cooper Ramo, *The age of the unthinkable,* Little Brown, 2009
   — Gary Hamel, The Future of Management, Harvard Business Press, 2007.

➤ **Life:** A key factor in determining the survival and adaptation of the human species is the diversity in the gene pool. Introducing diversity into organisations is likely to assist greatly in enhancing the capacity of survival under challenging conditions

➤ **Markets:** Markets offer the ability to allocate scarce resources in an optimum way. Despite some of the obvious limitations that markets have (at their limits), they offer a more flexible and responsive approach to resource allocation. Some obvious areas of application include the setting up of "market' conditions for the allocation of investment funds to new projects or the allocation of talent within the organisation

➤ **Democracy:** A key feature of modern democracies is the activism and "ownership" of issues by individuals. Giving people a stake in decision-making and the outcomes of these decisions offers real benefits to organisations with respect to people taking ownership in their roles

➤ **Religion:** Through its ability to appeal to a significant cause and the use of relevant symbols, religion has the ability to provide meaning to individuals. While we need to steer well away from any fundamentalist principles, religion has some lessons for organisations who seek to develop the commitment of staff

➤ **Well designed cities:** A feature of well designed cities is their potential for "planned serendipity". Because they offer many alternative routes to the same destination, and many possible meeting points along the way, the likelihood of "chance" encounters is increased. This enhances the potential for new ideas and insights as people mingle in the crowds. Building and office layouts could benefit from these designs.

Clearly, there is much further work to be done to develop these ideas into workable organisation designs, but the new metaphors offer welcome alternatives to the traditional "machine" approach that has dominated our thinking.

Leadership and innovation

That innovation is important to organisations in these uncertain and changing times is not up for debate here. Our focus is to examine the role that leadership can play in fostering and leading this effort in organisations.

Again, the work of Hamel is helpful in assisting our understanding. He points out that one of the roles played by leadership is to aggregate and amplify the effort of people in the organisation. They use the tools of structure, systems, incentives and the like to do so. But they also play an important role in the so-called 'innovation pyramid':

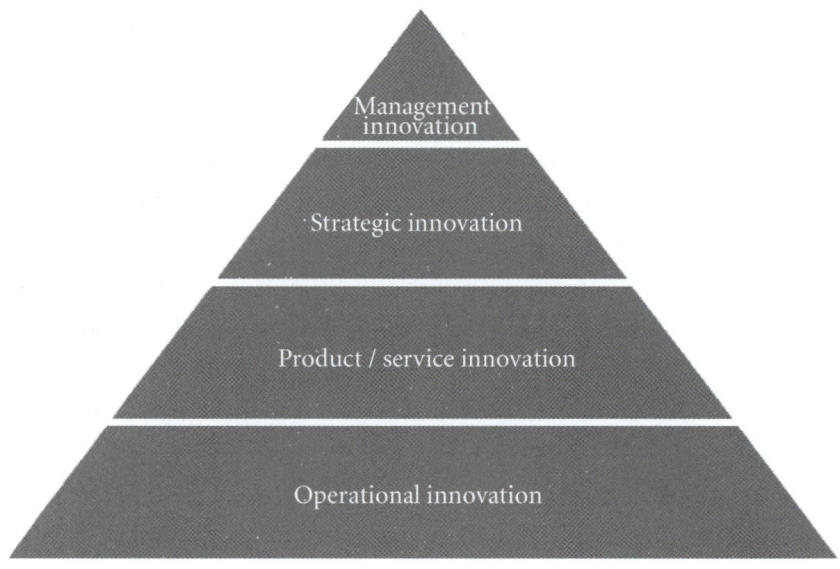

---

4. Hamel Gary, The Future of Managements, Harvard Business Press, 2007.

Imagine the pyramid to represent the various layers of innovation as follows:

- ➤ Operational innovation describes the various initiatives around process and quality improvement that are driven as part of many continuous improvement programs

- ➤ Product and service innovation deals with the new product and service development that takes place as part of the growth and improvement strategies within organisations

- ➤ Strategic innovation encompasses the development of new business models and ways of defining the business of the organisation

- ➤ Management innovation addresses the overall management system and approach used by the organisation in the conduct of its business. As such, it encompasses the culture, organisation design and the very manner in which the organisation goes about its business.

Importantly, the impact and potential leverage on the organisation increases as we make our way up through the layers of the pyramid. Consequently, it suggests that management innovation – innovating with the way we design and conceive of the organisation – holds the greatest potential for improving the organisation and adapting to new demands from the environment. And given that this form of innovation is almost the exclusive domain of leadership, it makes sense that leaders should concentrate a good proportion of their effort here.

Based on the earlier discussion of organisation design, leaders have a key role to play in exploring opportunities to introduce greater levels of diversity, flexibility and commitment into their organisations – because of the impact this has on improving the organisation's adaptability to the New Normal. Innovating through organisation design, therefore, will become a powerful tool for leaders as they guide their organisations into the future.

Managing the future

But how do we manage the future? How do we prepare ourselves and our organisations for a future that is increasingly uncertain and changing? And how do we go about strategic planning when the future is so hard to predict?

Some answers to these questions may be provided by considering the following three principles:

The future does not exist a priori:

Many people assume that the future has been pre-determined and is "waiting" for us to come along and experience it. However, another way of thinking about this is to imagine that the future is simply a set of possibilities that can be influenced by purposeful behaviour. Consider the following account:

From an early age my daughter had a fascination with the traffic that would rush past us on a busy highway. She would often exclaim "daddy, that's the traffic" as she pointed to cars and trucks travelling past.

One morning, as I was driving her to pre-school along this same part of the highway, she said to me "daddy, we are the traffic". I was astounded that she had realised that one could observe a phenomenon as an objective observer in one time period, and then actually be part of that phenomenon in another.

If I had had a problem with my car that morning and required roadside assistance to get started again, I would have created a sizeable hold up and delay in traffic conditions. Imagine then some 30 minutes later when I had dropped her off and turned on the radio to listen to the traffic report – I would have been advised to avoid the intersection at which I had broken down earlier, in order to avoid the disrupted traffic flow!

Chapter 9

This is a useful analogy for the future and our relationship with it.

The future does not exist *a priori* – it is influenced by the way we act and react. In a given time period we take an action that affects the environment in which we operate, and in the second time period we "discover" this environment and plan a response to it.

So, while we may be unable to completely control our environment, we can influence and study it.

Planning for the future by embracing uncertainty

Because of the uncertainties inherent in the future, there is little point in attempting to predict it. And yet, that is what traditional strategic planning does. Most planning exercises usually begin with a set of assumptions about the environment, interest rates and the like. And when these assumptions are proved wrong (this often occurs soon after the start of the planning period), the resultant plan has little validity.

Instead of trying to predict the future, we can study the trends, drivers and uncertainties that shape the various possibilities for the future. We can then construct "alternative futures" – or scenarios – that describe the different ways the future can unfold.

Our planning is then focused on developing the capabilities to cope with these alternative scenarios. Competitive advantage is achieved by learning and adapting to these futures as they unfold. Of course, the better our scenario planning, the better we are able to understand how the future is unfolding and what capabilities are required to achieve ultimate strategic alignment.

So, the key implication is that our approach to strategy should embrace the inherent uncertainty and recognise that competitive advantage is gained by studying the future (through scenarios) and adapting to the change as it unfolds. This way we focus on achieving strategic alignment into the future.

No monarchy has ever fomented it's own overthrow

Because potential change can often threaten the status quo, the future is best envisaged by those with contrary views. Moreover, those in positions of seniority and power within the organisation are often simply unable to recognise the drivers of change due to their vested interests.

We recommend the use of "Pathfinder" groups – people who are close to the customer and technology, who are unencumbered with senior management positions. These groups are useful for generating the alternative scenarios for the future and the possible responses by the organisation. But they must receive "air-cover" from the leadership –they have to be protected from the vested interests and the tendency for convergent thinking by those in management.

Once these alternative scenarios have been developed, the organisation can focus on developing capabilities for coping and adapting to future operating conditions. The goal is to achieve strategic alignment into the future.

Planning is not strategy

One of the insights to emerge from the previous discussion on strategy for the future is that there is a clear distinction between planning and strategy. The simple distinction is:

Planning	*Strategy*
Setting objectives and actions to achieve a set goal	Positioning and equipping the organisation for the future

Chapter 9

A better understanding may be achieved by examining some aspects of military history.

Napoleon's exploits offer good examples of how effective strategy is used to achieve competitive advantage. And the work of Von Clausewitz, in his classic treatise on the practice of military warfare[1], provides valuable insights into Napoleon's work.

Von Clausewitz outlines the four key elements that constituted Napoleon's approach and contributed to his many of his greatest victories[2]:

1. Study everything you can about the history of the situation. Combine your own experience with the research and insights of others

2. Immerse yourself in the battle (competitive situation) and empty your mind of all your pre-conceived notions (the so-called "beginners mind"). Thoroughly absorb what is taking place around you

3. Wait for the flash of insight to occur – **the combination of selected elements of past examples that combine in a unique way to identify the "decisive" point in the battle**

4. Follow through with resolution and enact your plan.

A few points are worth commenting upon:

➤ It is important to do your homework, to study the research and previous history

---

5. Von Clausewitz, *On war*, 1832
6. Duggan, 2007

> When immersing yourself in the situation, you need lose your preconceived notions and your "favourite" management techniques

> Your focus should be on the "decisive point" as opposed to the "objective point". The decisive point is the element that can shift the game in your favour, while the objective point is the goal that was set before the competition began. Importantly, the decisive point usually emerges after you have immersed yourself in the situation and understood the true nature of the situation

> The process whereby the insight emerges may be described as "strategic intuition"[7] and is the process that describes major innovations and breakthroughs. Importantly, it is not a "break" from the past – but rather a "bend" in the road. Studies into scientific breakthroughs[8,9] describe this bend as a new combination of past events / examples in order to produce a different result.

A more complete comparison between planning and strategy may be presented in the table below. Strategy, as we are now defining it, is a more appropriate approach when managing the organisation's future in an uncertain environment.

This is not to say that planning does not have its place. Indeed, there are many instances where projects are undertaken in a relatively steady state. In these cases, particularly where the completion of the project is required on time and within budget, the use of the planning approach is essential.

However, where the organisation is seeking to navigate through conditions of uncertainty and is required to be adaptable and flexible, management need to

---

7. Duggan, 2007
8. Kuhn, *The structure of scientific revolution*, 1962
9. Tang, *Competition and innovation behaviour*, 2006

embrace the concept of strategic intuition in their definition of strategy.

	Planning	Strategy
Approach	o Define your starting point o Determine your objective o Identify key actions and initiatives to achieve your objective	o Learn from history and own experience o Clear your mind and immerse yourself in the situation o Seek the flash of insight from strategic intuition o Act with resolution and commitment
How to win	By focusing your efforts and resources at the objective	By identifying the decisive point and focusing resources at that point
Objectives	Chosen beforehand	Emerges as you learn and adapt
Key element	Objective point	Decisive point

What does all this mean for strategic alignment?

We have argued that parts of the current model of organisation, management and strategy have not kept pace with the changes in the environment. Our organisations are unable to adapt quickly enough and our strategy processes can't cope with the high levels of uncertainty.

It seems as if the new order emerging at this time may well be an opportunity to re-examine the way we do things.

Clearly, we need to inject greater levels of diversity, activism and meaning into our organisations. Some of the new metaphors such as life, markets and democracy provide examples of how this might be done. Happily, we don't have to throw the baby out with the bathwater. Depending on the organisation and its context, we can introduce these new elements in a progressive way, learning our way into the new approaches.

In so doing, we have to remember that a key role of leadership is to innovate in the pursuit of competitive advantage and strategic alignment. And not just any innovation – management innovation seems to offer the most leverage and the best long-term gains.

Developing strategy in conditions of complexity and uncertainty represents a further challenge. However, if we begin to conceive of our organisations in terms of some of the new metaphors described in the paper, we will recognise that strategy is a learning process and we will begin to construct scenarios to help us study and understand the future.

We will realise that the only truly sustainable competitive advantage is to learn and adapt more quickly than one's competitors. In so doing, we will distinguish between planning and strategy and use them both appropriately.

These are challenging times, but the survival and future prosperity of our organisations depends on us rising to the challenge and re-examining the way we design and manage our organisations.

Appendix 1
Theoretical basis of strategic alignment

The Concept of Strategic Alignment is based on three major premises.

1. That there is a relationship between the nature of the operating environment and the form of the organisation. Moreover, certain combinations of operating environment and organisational types produce superior performance. This is the concept of Strategic Fit.

2. That the attributes of organisations are not randomly distributed through the population of organisations. Instead, these attributes cluster together in a number of different patterns. These patterns, or archetypes, are found repeatedly when researching and describing organisations.

3. That competitive advantage is an outcome of the activities of the organisation and how these activities interact with the environment.

We will consider each of these premises in turn.

The notion of strategic fit

The concept of strategic fit has its origins in the "Strategy-structure" debate. Alfred Chandler (1962) made a major contribution to this debate in his longitudinal study of 20 major US corporations. His basic premise was that the form of the organisation should shift in response to the changes in environmental conditions. Indeed, he found that certain organisational forms appeared to be better suited to certain environmental conditions.

Chandler argued that the strategy of the organisation (in response to the environmental conditions) would give rise to a specific organisational form. When this organisational form produced a "fit" with the strategy, the organisation enjoyed superior economic returns.

Chandler's work gave rise to a number of doctoral theses at the Harvard Business School. Rumelt[1] showed how various organisational structures were associated with different approaches to diversification. Channon[2] validated the basic strategic fit thesis in his study of British corporations. In addition to these authors, who adopted a "strategy-structure" perspective, Lawrence and Lorsch[3] have researched the relationship between the nature of the environment and the organisation structure that appeared most effective. These contingency theorists (so-called because they assert that the shape of the successful organisation is contingent upon the nature of the environment) relied much on the work of Emory and Trist[4] who provided ways of describing and classifying environments.

The conclusions that may be drawn from these and more recent work are:

➤ There is no universally desirable strategy.

➤ There is no universally desirable structure and organisational form.

➤ The appropriate strategy is contingent on the operating environment.

➤ The appropriate structure is contingent on the strategy being implemented.

---

1 RP Rumelt, "Strategy, structure and economic performance", Doctoral Dissertation, Harvard Business School, 1972.
2 DF Channon, *The strategy and structure of British enterprise*, MacMillan, London, 1973.
3 PR Lawrence and JW Lorsch, *Organisation and environment*, Harvard University Press, Boston, 1967.
4 FE Emory and EL Trist, "The causal texture of organisational environments", *Human Relations*, February, 1965.

> Strategic fit is the condition that exists when the strategy, structure and environment are all compatible, that is, when there is "fit" between the elements.

> Performance of the organisation is enhanced under conditions of sustained strategic fit.

The concept of organisational archetypes

The work of Carl Jung[5] is perhaps the best known in the field of archetypes. As opposed to stereotypes, archetypes describe the different patterns made up of the clusters of individual tendencies.

Miles and Snow[6,7] have identified a number of organisational archetypes that they have found to be robust and enduring. The "defender", "analyser", "reactor", and "prospector" types are all described in detail in their work. Subsequent research has found that these models of organisational type are useful for the development of various functional strategies, including human resources and IT.

Mitroff[8] draws on Jungian constructs to develop an archetype of organisational forms that may be applied to researching organisations.

Finally, archetypes are often used to describe organisations and strategies in our planning efforts. The large number of "two-by-two" matrices that are used to classify markets and competitive strategies are other good examples of the archetypes in action models by other bodies. These include the "product-

---

5   CJ Jung, *Archetypes and the collective unconscious*, Pantheon, New York, 1959.
6   RE Miles and CC Snow, *Organisation strategy structure and process*, McGraw-Hill, New York, 1978.
7   RE Miles and CC Snow, "Fit, failure and the hall of fame", *California Management Review*, 26, 3, 1984.
8   II Mitroff, *Stakeholders of the organisational mind*, Jossey-Bass, San Francisco, 1983.

market" matrix and the business portfolio matrix devolved by General Electric and the Boston Consulting Group.

The major conclusions that can be drawn from this body of work include:

➤ Attributes of organisations and strategy cluster together to form patterns.

➤ These patterns can be called archetypes. Archetypes are generally arranged into a classification system which attempts to describe the individual types, as well as the relationships between them.

In developing the Strategic Alignment model we have named the archetypes Forces or Logics.

Although there may be some variation in the actual attributes within a particular type, it is the overall relationship between the attributes, and the resultant pattern, that provides most of the insight into a particular archetype.

Archetypes are robust over time. Change to the archetype may occur over a period of time. This change will either be incremental (a fine-tuning or refinement of the basic archetype) or quantum (where the change results in the emergence of a different archetypal form).

Competitive advantage as an outcome of organisational activity

The modern concepts of competitive advantage emerge from the work of Aaker,[9] Andrews,[10] Ansoff[11] and Abell.[12] Abell demonstrates that the starting

---

9   DA Aaker, "How to select a business strategy", *California Management Review*, 26, 3, 1984.
10 KR Andrews, *The concept of corporate strategy* Dow Jones-Irwin, Homewood, Illinios, 1971.
11 HHI Ansoff, *Corporate strategy,* McGraw-Hill, New York, 1965.
12 DF Abell, *Defining the business: The starting point of strategic planning,* Prentice Hall, New Jersey, 1980.

point of planning for competitive advantage is the definition of the business. In this argument, he shows that the manner in which the business is defined sets up the preconditions for the development of future competitive advantage. John Child[13] demonstrates that the strategic choices made in the resource allocation process will determine the definition of the business.

Competitive advantage comes about where an organisation has positioned itself within an operating environment in such a way that it is better placed to meet the expectations of stakeholders that its competitors. Michael Porter[14] argues that the sustainability of the position achieved is the key to this competitive advantage.

Since competitive advantage is an outcome of the organisation's activities, it follows that these activities have to be performed in a superior manner to those of the competitors. In his recent research on the origins of competitive advantage, Porter[15] argues that this superiority comes about as a result of the trade-offs made in the resource allocation of the organisation.

The key conclusions to emerge from this body of work include:

- There are different pathways to the achievement of competitive advantage.

- Each pathway involves a systematic process of trade-offs and focus in the allocation of resource and effort within the organisation.

- The systematic trade-offs and focus of effort result in the development of distinctive competences within the organisation.

13　J Child, "Organisation structure, environment and performance. The role of strategic choice", *Sociology*, 6, 1972.
14　ME Porter, *Competitive advantage: Creating and sustaining superior performance,* Free Press, New York, 1985.
15　ME Porter, "What is strategy?" *Harvard Business Review,* November-December, 1996.

> The nature of these distinctive competencies reflects the nature of the trade-offs and focus of effort.

> The interaction of these distinctive competencies and the operating environment produces the outcome known as competitive advantage.

Conclusions

By combining the insights from the above research, the concept of Strategic Alignment was developed.

First, Strategic Alignment asserts that there is a natural relationship between the environment and the organisation. When the elements of environment, strategy, culture and leadership are aligned in a strategic fit, the overall performance of the organisation is enhanced. Evidence for this comes from the strategy-structure debate, the Australian research[16] as well as our own research.

Secondly, Strategic Alignment argues that environments, strategies, cultures and leadership approaches can be described by using an archetypal model based on Jungian constructs. The "PADI" framework is derived from the Organisation Effectiveness research, Jungian concepts of archetypes and our own research into environments and organisational forms. Further, our research has derived the particular patterns of behaviour that occur under the "PADI" types for the levels of environment (market), strategy, culture and leadership.

Finally, Strategic Alignment asserts that the organisation can achieve a competitive advantage by achieving a superior response to the needs of stakeholders within the environment. This, in turn, is achieved as an outcome of two pre-conditions:

---

16 D Limerick, B Cunningham and B Trevor-Roberts, *Frontiers of excellence: A study of strategy, structure and culture in fifty Australian organisations,* Australian Institute of Management, QLD division, Brisbane, 1984.

➤ The organisation has achieved an alignment between the needs of the environment (market) and its strategy, culture and leadership; and

➤ The organisation has developed distinctive competencies in an area(s) valued by the market, by allocating resources in a sustained and focused manner.

Strategic Alignment

Appendix 2
PADI ideal types

The PADI framework is useful for conceptualising differences and similarities in organisation types. However it is not always easy to recognise exemplar organisations in "real life". First, organisations rarely manifest a "pure" PADI logic – they are usually some combination of two. Secondly, many organisations are made up of a number of cross-cutting cultures.

Despite these difficulties, it is still possible to identify examples of different organisational combinations. Below are some common combination types.

The "A" organisation

These organisations are dominated by a concern for efficiency and attention to detail. They are characterised by a high reliance on systems, procedures and detailed processes. Two combinations are common:

"Ai" organisations

These are organisations that combine their systems and efficiency emphasis with a partnering focus towards their clients. Examples include auditing and legal firms.

In these cases, the organisations work collaboratively with their clients to ensure a tight relationship. Often the joint focus of the partnership is to ensure trouble-free, efficient dealing between the supplier and client. In an attempt to achieve the "seamless" relationship, these organisations can make use of EDI and other "just in time" approaches to ensure a low-cost solution for the client.

"Ap" organisations

These organisations use their systems and efficiency emphasis to achieve a rapid response to client needs and market demands. It is important to note however, that the fast response is limited somewhat by self-imposed boundaries. These boundaries are set by the systems and processes of the organisation and their desire to limit the repertoire of responses in the interest of efficiency.

Examples include fast food operations that have a well-defined menu and a list of options that are delivered immediately.

In these cases, the organisation can effect a rapid response to the needs of customers provided they order from the menu. In other words, by strictly limiting the repertoire of responses, the organisation gives the appearance of being highly responsive. However, it is only the high level of pre-preparation and dedicated systems that allow this. Any attempt to deviate from the "menu" will incur significant time and cost penalties.

The "P" organisation

These organisations are dominated by a concern for action and rapid response. They are characterised by high levels of individual autonomy and empowerment among staff, plus a desire to meet the needs of their clients by whatever means are available. Two combinations are common:

"Pd" organisations

These organisations use their empowered staff and bias for action to generate creative and innovative solutions for clients. Examples include contractors and sales-driven organisations. Certain retailers may also fall into this category.

"Pd" organisations place a premium on speed and streamlined operations. They continually seek ways of eliminating unnecessary steps in their operations and are driven by pragmatism rather than a desire for the "perfect solution". In most cases, they will "bend" the prevailing system and/or rules in order to achieve the desired outcome for the client.

The organisational form can be somewhat unstable in the longer term, as it is prone to a loss of focus. Because it's primary concern is fast response and meeting customer needs, it can move beyond its core competencies and lose coherence. While each individual "move" appears logical and pragmatic, the combination of several such moves may take the organisation off course in the longer term.

"Pa" organisations

These organisations combine their bias for action and customer-responsiveness with a well-developed set of systems and procedures. Although not as explicit and dominating as the "A" organisation, the level of pre-determined systems and processes in the "Pa" organisation is relatively high.

Importantly though, these organisations regard the system and process as the *means* whereby customer needs are met. They do not suffer the "means-end" inversion that can occur in "Ap" organisations and are more willing to modify the systems when customer needs are not being met.

Examples of "Pa" organisations are similar to "Pd" organisations - in that it is not the *type* of organisation that determines its logic, but rather the *manner* in which it operates. For example, the "Pa" contractor or retailer will also be very customer-focused and responsive but this will be tempered by recognition that the system must be able to accommodate whatever solution is developed. Whereas the "Pd" organisation is happy to treat the system as only a guideline and therefore bend it frequently, the "Pa" organisation will do whatever it can *within the system*. Here the *system* has a higher level of importance than in the "Pd" organisation.

The "D" organisation

"D" organisations are characterised by a desire to continuously seek new and better ways of doing things. The primary drivers are individuality, innovation, and the willingness to introduce quantum change into the organisation and the solutions offered to clients. Again, two combinations are common:

"Di" organisations

"Di" organisations combine their drive for innovation and unique solutions with a focus on partnering and collaboration with the client. Whereas the pure "D" organisation is highly individualistic (both internally with respect to its members, and externally with respect to its tendency to leave its customers behind) the "Di" organisation operates creatively by taking its customers along. Examples would be strategy and change consultants who use their relationships with clients in order to introduce new and unique thinking.

The "Di" organisation is driven by visions of the future and a sense of idealism about the way things could be. They have high levels of technical expertise and a clear vision of how the market will unfold. They spend most time developing the vision and the expertise but are also adept at keeping their clients well-informed and up-to-date. As with all "D" organisations, the level of operating risk is somewhat high as they position themselves at the cutting edge of their market and industry. The "Di" organisation can alleviate some of this risk by keeping their customers informed and themselves customer relevant. In the final analysis, however, these organisations are usually niche players who operate in a small segment of the total industry.

"Dp" organisations

These organisations combine their uniqueness and innovation with a level of pragmatism and concern for commerciality. Less idealistic than the "Di" organisation, "Dp" organisations respond rapidly to the needs of customers and the changing market. Good examples here are the commercially-focused design studios or architects, consulting firms and R&D organisations that are focused on the development *and* application end of new technologies.

Effective "Dp" organisations have a good blend of the innovative and the practical. Although they are always on the leading edge of their fields and have a strong desire to develop unique solutions, they have a sense of pragmatism that allows them to understand the realities of the market. In a sense they are not quite as captive to their own ideas as some "D" organisations can be.

The "I" organisation

"I" organisations are characterised by a sense of harmony, collaboration and team effort. Their primary drivers are consultation, partnerships and long-term relationships. More than other types, it is rare to find a pure "I" organisation in commercial settings. However, two combinations are relatively common:

"Ia" organisations

These organisations combine their sense of harmony and belonging with systems and processes designed to increase efficiency. Examples include sports and social clubs, training organisations that focus on personal development, and other "membership-oriented" organisations such as frequent flyer/executive clubs for airlines. Importantly, these attributes characterise both the internal workings of the organisation as well as their dealings with clients and members.

The primary driver of these organisations is to create a close bond between their members/clients and themselves. The systems and processes are used to ensure that clients' needs are dealt with in an efficient and equitable way. In all instances the needs for harmony and good relationships are paramount. Hence the systems and processes will not be allowed to get in the way of empathetic and fair treatment of the organisation's members and clients. Some bending of the systems to suit individual clients is common.

"Id" organisations

These organisations combine their sense of team and relationships with the desire to introduce innovative solutions. They will never be as radical as other "D" organisations. The desire to retain rapport with members and clients is a constraining factor but these organisations will use group processes and consultation to explore the limits of change and innovation. Some examples include policy and research units, process consultants, and community advocacy organisations.

"Id" organisations can develop very successful *participative revolutions* among members and clients. By focusing on process and consultation they will gradually develop leading edge solutions and approaches. The disadvantage is that these processes are time consuming and resource intensive and the organisations are often somewhat slow in responding to changes in the market. Their sense of idealism is both a distinguishing characteristic and one that can render their approach somewhat impractical.

Appendix 3
Strategic alignment diagnostic

This short questionnaire is designed to be used as a *quick guide* to determining your organisation's alignment in terms of its Operating Environment, Strategy, Culture and Leadership.

It is *not* intended as a definitive research instrument. Results are indicative and should only be used as a guide.

The diagnostic consists of four sections:

- ➤ Operating Environment (customers)
- ➤ Strategy
- ➤ Culture
- ➤ Leadership

Each section has four questions. For each question, you should select one of the options, (a), (b), (c) or (d).

You should choose the answer that *best* describes your situation (many organisations will be combinations of answers but choose the best or strongest descriptor). Remember you are trying to determine your *dominant* logic as this will be the most helpful in determining your degree of alignment and/or best ways to move forward. So, in each case, choose the answers that best describe your situation.

See the end of the questionnaire for how to score your diagnosis.

NOTE: This is a useful exercise to do along with your team or colleagues Debate each option thoroughly, and be clear why you are selecting a particular answer.

Strategic Alignment

Section 1 – Operating environment

Select one of your customers, or a group of customers, that receive or purchase a product or service from you. Answer the questions in relation to them. Remember to choose only *ONE* answer per question.

1. Clients/Customers prefer, expect or value …

| (a) Empathy | (b) Innovation | (c) Energy | (d) Accuracy |

2. The phrase that best describes what clients/customers want is …

| (a) Show me you care | (b) Show me what's new | (c) Show me your previous results | (d) Show me the most economical option |

3. Clients/customers make decisions based on …

| (a) How they feel about you/your people | (b) What they think of your ideas | (c) Whether you can deliver the results they want | (d) Whether you are reliable with them |

4. To your clients/customers, quality means …

| (a) Personal attention | (b) Creative response to unique needs | (c) Responsiveness and commercialism | (d) Efficiency and value for money |

Section 2 — Strategy

Select a *business unit* within your organisation – preferably the one that serves the customers you described in Section 1 of this diagnostic. Answer the questions in relation to this business unit. Remember to choose only ONE answer per question.

1. My business unit mainly focuses on …

(a) Developing long-term relationships with customers	(b) Providing unique services/products	(c) Responding rapidly to customer demands	(d) Providing low cost products/services

2. The image my business unit tries to portray is …

(a) They really care about customer needs	(b) They are always first with a product/service	(c) They get the job done no matter what	(d) They are reliable and consistent

3. Our focus in the market is …

(a) Defend market share by fostering customer loyalty	(b) Build market share by being first with a product/service	(c) Increase market share in each niche by getting it right	(d) Consolidate market share through low cost and efficiency

4. My business unit's orientation is focused on …

(a) Good implementation and commitment to customers	(b) Innovation and creativity	(c) Outputs and operations	(d) Systems, processes and controls

Section 3 — Culture

Select a business unit in the organisation (preferably the same one you described in sections 1 and 2 of this diagnostic). Consider how things *currently* happen in the business unit, not how they should be or how you would like them to be. Answer in relation to what the business unit actually does. Remember to choose only *ONE* answer per question.

1. In my business unit …

(a) It is necessary to reach consensus on how things are to be done	(b) People can do what is needed to achieve results that are in line with the vision	(c) People are allowed to do whatever is necessary to get the job done	(d) People have to follow defined procedures and methods when undertaking most tasks

2. Management is mainly interested in …

(a) Whether people work together as an effective team	(b) Whether people are working towards the overall vision	(c) *What* people actually achieve not how they got there	(d) *How* people do their jobs and whether procedures are followed

3. People are valued and rewarded for …

(a) Showing team spirit, loyalty and working together	(b) Being flexible, inventive and having new ideas	(c) Achieving challenging targets and overcoming adversity	(d) Having sound experience and knowledge

4. In my business unit …

(a) There is always someone you can go to about work or personal problems	(b) People are expected to speak up openly for themselves when there is a disagreement	(c) People often argue with each other but conflict is resolved quickly in order to get the job done	(d) People use the appropriate channels and follow formal procedures to resolve conflict

Section 4 — Leadership

Consider the approach of management in your business unit. Do not consider one individual manager – look instead at the management team. Answer the questions in relation to what management does as an entity. Remember to choose only *ONE* answer per question.

1. The dominant focus of management is …

(a) Integrating the parts to form a coherent whole	(b) Creating the business	(c) Building the business	(d) Ensuring people are productive

2. Management places a high value on …

(a) Maintaining long term customer relationships	(b) Being the leader in its field	(c) Beating the competition	(d) Reducing costs

3. Managements' communication contains …

(a) Personal appreciation and personal views	(b) Broad perspectives, future challenges	(c) The pros and cons, objective reasoning	(d) Facts, details, examples

4. Management motivates people by providing …

(a) Collaborative and supportive environment	(b) Opportunities to try new things	(c) Challenging goals and targets	(d) Promotion and security

Scoring the diagnostic

For each section count the number of times you chose (a), (b), (c), or (d answers.

(a) answers correspond to Integration ("I") logics in PADI terminology

(b) answers correspond to Divergence ("D") logics in PADI terminology.

(c) answers correspond to Pragmatism ("P") logics in PADI terminology.

(d) answers correspond to Administration ("A") logics in PADI terminology.

> *For example:*
>
> *3 x (d) answers in section 1 mean you have an operating environment that is dominated by Administration ("A") logics. Your environment expects you to be reliable, procedural and deliver at low cost.*
>
> *When analysing your Strategy and Culture sections you answered mostly (c)s (Pragmatism "P" focus) then you have a strategy and culture that support speed, results and outputs with minimal procedures and a focus on getting a result rather than reliability.*
>
> *This would show your organisation is out of alignment with its environment and you would need to take steps to change your strategy and culture to be more Administration ("A") focused.*

You should now be able to understand your organisation in PADI terms for each of the four areas. From this you can see your level of alignment or misalignment. This should help you in determining your next steps in achieving alignment and effectiveness.

Remember this diagnostic provides a guide only and should not be taken as a definitive analysis.

References

Abell DF, 1980, *Defining the Business: The Starting Point of Strategic Planning*, Prentice-Hall.

Baghai M, Coley S & White D, 1999, *The Alchemy of Growth: Kickstaring and Sustaining Growth in your Company* Orion Business Books.

Balogun J & Hope Hailey V, 1999, *Exploring Strategic Change* Prentice-Hall.

Belbin RM, 1981, *Management Teams: Why they succeed or fail?* Butterworth-Heinemann.

Burns T & Stalker G, 1961, *The Management of Innovation* Tavistock.

Cattell RB, 1946, *The Description and Measurement of Personality,* World Book.

Cattell RB, 1973, *Personality and Mood by Questionnaire*, Jossey Bass.

Chandler AD, 1962, Strategy and Structure: Chapters in the History of American Industrial Enterprise Cambridge, Mass: MIT Press.

Channon DF, 1973, *The Strategy and Structure of British Enterprise*, MacMillan

Chorn NH, 1991, "Total Quality Management: Panacea or Pitfall", *International Journal of Physical Distributions and Logistics Management* 21(8) 31-35.

Chorn NH, 1986, *The Relationship Between Business Level Strategy and Organisational Culture* unpublished Doctoral dissertation, University of Witwatersrand.

Costa PT & McCrae RR, 1993, "Ego Development and Trait Models of Personality", *Psychological Inquiry*, Vol 4, pp 20-23.

Costa PT & McCrae RR, 1988, "Personality in Adulthood: A Six Year Longitudinal Study of Self-Reports and Spouse Ratings on the NEO Personality Inventory", *Journal of Personality and Social Psychology*, Vol 55, pp 258-265.

Davis I, 2009 "The New normal" *Mckinsey Quarterly*, Mckinsey and Company, Chicago

Duggan W, 2007 *Strategic Intuition*, Columbia Business School.

De Geus A, 1988, "Planning as Learning", *Harvard Business Review* 66(2) 70-74.

Dyas GP, 1972, *The Strategy and Structure if French Industrial Enterprise* unpublished Doctoral dissertation, Harvard Business School.

Emery FE & Twist EL, 1965, "The Causal Texture of Organizational Environments", *Human Relations*, February 1965.

Gale BT, 1994, *Managing Customer Value Creating Quality and Service That Customers Can See*, The Free Press

Greiner LE, 1972, "Evolution and Revolution as Organisations Grow", *Harvard Business Review* July-August.

Greiner LE, 1967, "Patterns of Organisations Change", *Harvard Business Review* May-June.

Grove AS, 1996, *Only the Paranoid Survive: How to Exploit the Crisis Points that Challenge Every Company*, Doubleday.

Hall RH, 1982, *Organisations: Structure & Process*, 3rd edn, Prentice-Hall.

Hamel G & Prahalad CK, 1994, *Competing for the Future*, Harvard Business School Press.

Hamel G, 2007, *Futures of Management*, Harvard Business Press.

Handy C, 1965, *The Gods of Management*, Pan.

Handy C, 1994, *The Empty Raincoat: Making Sense of the Future*, Arrow Business Books.

Handy C, 1997, *Understanding Organisations*, Penguin.

Harrison R, 1972, "Understanding Your Organization's Character", *Harvard Business Review* May-June.

Hunter TA, 1998, A *Behavioural Validation of Belbin's Team Roles and Model Derived From the 16PF5 and OPQ Personality Questionnaires*, Doctoral thesis, University Of Strathclyde Glasgow, Scotland.

Jacques E & Clement SD, 1994, *Executive Leadership; A Practical Guide to Managing Complexity*, Cason Hall & Company.

Jaworski J, 1996, *Synchronicity: The Inner Path of Leadership*, Berrett-Koehler Publishers Inc.

Johnson G & Scholes K, 2002, *Exploring Corporate Strategy*, Prentice Hall

Johnson G, 1992, "Strategic Change and the Management Process", *Long Range Planning*, vol 25, p 1.

Jung CG, 1959, *Archetypes and the Collective Unconscious*, Pantheon.

Jung CG, 1968, *Analytical Psychology*, Vintage.

Jung CG, 1971, *Psychological Types*, trans RFC Hall, Princeton.

Kay J, 1993, *Foundations of Corporate Success: How Business Strategies Add Value*, Oxford University Press.

Kono T, 1984, *Strategy and Structure of Japanese Enterprises*, MacMillan.

Kuhn, T, 1962 *The Structure of Scientific Revolution*, University of Chicago Press, Chicago

Lawrence PR & Lorsch JW, 1967, *Organisation and Environment Boston*, Harvard University Press.

Lawrence PR & Dyer D, 1983, *Renewing American Industry*, Free Press.

Limerick D, Cunnington B, & Trevor-Roberts B, 1984, *Frontiers of Excellence: A Study of Strategy, Structure and Culture in Fifty Australian Organisations*, Australian Institute of Management, Queensland Division.

Miles RE & Snow CC, 1978, *Organisational Strategy, Structure and Process*, McGraw-Hill.

Miles RE & Snow CC, 1984, "Designing Strategic Human Resource Systems", *Organisational Dynamics* 13(1) 1984.

Miles RE & Snow CC, 1984, "Fit, Failure and the Hall of Fame", *California Management Review* 26(3) 1984.

Miller D, 1990, *The Icarus Paradox*, Harper Business.

Miller LM, 1984, *American Spirit: Visions of a New Corporate Culture*, William Morrow.

Mintzberg H, 1978, "Patterns in Strategy Formation", *Management Science*, 24(9) 1978.

Mintzberg H, 1979, *The Structuring of Organisations*, Prentice Hall.

Mintzberg H, 1981, "Organisation Design: Fashion or Fit?" *Harvard Business Review*, Jan-Feb.

Mintzberg H, 1984, "Who Should Control the Corporation?", *California Management Review* 28(1) 1884.

Mintzberg H, 1989, *Inside our Strange World of Organizations*, Free Press.

Mintzberg H & Quinn JB, 1995, *The Strategy Process: Concepts & Cases*, Prentice Hall.

Myers IB & Briggs KC, 1962, *Myers-Briggs Type Indicator*, Consulting Psychologists Press.

Nadler DA, Gerstein MS, Shaw RB & Associates, 1992, *Organisational Architecture: Designs for Changing Organizations,* Jossey-Bass.

Parry K, 1996, *Transformational Leadership: Developing an Enterprising Management Structure*, Pitman Publishing.

Ramo JC, 2009 *The Age of the Unthinkable*, Little Brown, London

Perrow C, 1967, "A Framework for the Competitive Analysis of Organisations", *American Sociological Review*, April.

Porter ME, 1985, *Competitive Advantage: Creating and Sustaining Superior Performance*, Free Press.

Porter ME, 1980, *Competitive Strategy: Techniques for Analysing Industries and Competitors*, Free Press.

Peters TJ & Waterman RH, 1982, *In Search of Excellence: Lessons from America's Best Run Companies*, Harper & Row.

Pfeffer J & Sutton RI, 2000, *The Knowing-Doing Gap: How Smart Companies Turn Knowledge into Action*, Harvard Business School Press.

Quin JB, Mintzberg H & James RM, 1988, *The Strategy Process: Concepts, Contexts and Cases* Prentice-Hall.

Rumelt RP, 1972, *Strategy, Structure and Economic Performance*, unpublished Doctoral dissertation, Harvard Business School.

Rumelt, RP, 1979, "Evaluation of Strategy: Theory and Models", in Schendel DE & Hofer CW (eds), *Strategic Management: A New View of Business Policy and Planning*, Little Brown, pp 196-212.

Saville P & Holdsworth RH, 1978, Occupational Personality Questionnaire, SHL Group.

Saville P & Holdsworth RH, 1993, Occupational Personality Questionnaire, Concept 52, SHL Group.

Schein EH, 1997, *Organizational Culture and Leadership*, Jossey-Bass.

Schein EH, 1986, "What You Need to Know About Organisational Culture", *Training and Development Journal*, January.

Schwartz H & Davis SM, 1981, "Matching Corporate Culture and Business Strategy", *Organizational Dynamics*, Summer.

Simon HA, 1957, *Administrative Behaviour*, MacMillan.

Smircich L, 1983, "Concepts of Culture and Organisational Analysis" *Administrative Science Quarterly*, 28, 1983.

Tang J, 2006, *Competition and innovation behaviour*, Research Policy, volume 35, issue 1.

Van Clausewitz C, 1968, *On War*, Penguin, New York.

Van Der Heijden K, 1996, *Scenarios: The Art of Strategic Conversation*, Wiley & Sons.

Van Der Heijden K, Bradfield R, Burt G Cairns G & Wright G, 2002, *The Sixth Sense; Accelerating Organizational Learning with Scenarios*, Wiley & Sons.

Welch J, with Byrne JA, 2001, *Jack: What I've Learned Leading a Great Company and Great People*, Warner Books.

Wilkins AL & Ouchi WG, 1983, "Efficient Cultures: Exploring the Relationship Between Culture and Organizational Performance", *Administrative Science Quarterly*, 28, 1983.

Woodward J, 1965, *Industrial Organisation: Theory and Practice*, Oxford University Press.

INDEX

A

administration logic......................................22-23
    "Ai" organisations 243
    "Ap" organisations 244
    cultural factors 105, 209
    cultural misalignment 123
    leadership 146
    reinforcement of culture 118
    strategic platform...................................... 78, 81
    trade-offs in strategic capability..................... 85
analyser organisation 164, 237
archetypes..............................21, 51-52, 62, 237-238
attitude, role of 160
"attribute" theory 1-4
autonomy 2-3, 113, 128, 205-207, 217

B

behaviour patterns 49, 19-20
    logics... 22
    organisation and 155-159
    visible... 97
bounded rationality 178-179
business definition 84-85
business strategy..72-73
    responsibility for change 183-184, 192
    building pressure for...............................213-214
    capacity for..214-217
    clarity and comprehensibility.................214-215
    determination of actionable steps................. 218
    identification of elements.......................200-201
    levers for 127, 131, 202-211
    motivation.. 199
    opportunities 198-199
    program for...212-217
    psychology of 198
    skills and competencies 199-200

C

climate 100
    culture, distinguished 100-101

communication...............................11, 118, 119, 160
    customer needs 62, 56-57
community groups....................................8-9, 37, 63
competition 8, 37, 63
    competitive advantage strategy..82-83, 89, 238-240
    competitive focus complexity 204-205
    organisation design................. 183, 192, 170-171
    risk and... 155-156, 160
    size, and 174-177, 192
competitive advantage 231
contingency theory 4-5
continuous production 173
control 2-3, 129, 205-207, 217
    direct/objective.. 168
    indirect/subjective... 169
    technology and...171-174
core activities... -2-3
corporate strategy 72-73
    responsibility for.............................. 183-184, 192
crafts 173
culture..7, 10-13, 15, 19, 91-93
    alignment, developing 108-109
    capacity for change 217
    changing...126-131
    climate, distinguished 100-101
    development of 20, 110-115
    diagnostic 252
    dominant logic.. 24, 29
    elements..92-93
    "good" and "bad" 93, 130
    lever for change......................................205-209
    misalignment 121-125, 131, 200-201
    multiple concept, as 130-131, 94-95
    PADI combinations 25-28
    reinforcing existing................................116-120
    seen and unseen 97-99, 130
    strategic alignment 93-94, 102
customer 38-39
    context..48-49
    describing needs of 51-62
    environmental factors...............................63-70
    expectations 3, 8, 48

focus 2-3, 32, 44, 73-74
identification of 38-45, 203
interface.. 154, 189
internal business unit, distinguished, ... 42-44, 191
stakeholder, distinguished, ...41-42
"trade-offs", importance of.... 50-51, 54-55, 74-75
understanding needs of, ...35-38, 45-51, 143, 20

D

decentralisation...2-3
decision-making... 11
    consultative 2-3
defender organisation 164, 237
delegation 11
design
    alternative forms 180
    clarity and comprehensibility ...182, 193, 214-215
    complexity and fragmentation..170-171, 183, 192
    importance of.................................. 159-160, 192
    influences on 165
    lever for change...205-209
    misconceptions 161-164
    organisational..153-154
    principles..................................... 180-190, 193
    size, importance of................. 166, 174-177, 192
    strategic choice............... 178-179, 182-183, 192
    technology, and 171-174
    uncertainty 192, 166-170
divergence logic...22-23
    cultural factors 106, 209
    cultural misalignment 124
    "Di" organisations 246
    "Dp" organisations 246-247
    leadership 146
    reinforcement of culture 119
    strategic platform...................................... 79, 81
    trade-offs in strategic capability...................... 84

E

effective management .... xiii-xiv, 1, 240
    holistic approach... 6
    measuring... 17

strategic alignment and 16-17
engineering... 173
environmental factors..4-5
    complexity of 165, 170-171, 183, 192
    customer needs and 63-70
    identification of 64-65
    responding to 11, 143, 219
environmental issues.................................8, 37, 63
excellence, searching for....................................1-4

F

federal structures.................................. 185-186, 193
flexibility
    change, for... 218
    structure and................................... 163-164, 218
focus 2-3, 73-74, 89
    resource and capability...................... 85, 204-205
    strategy 82-83
fragmentation
    organisation design.................................170-171
    risk and.. 155-156, 160
Freud, Sigmund.. 19
functional strategy 72-73
functional structure and design 180
future capabilities... 223
future, managing the......................................228-230

G

GFC 221
geographic structure and design 180
government regulations................................8, 37, 63

H

hardware market 11-13, 16, 36, 56, 68-69
human resources strategies.............................73-74

I

initiatives .... xi-xii
innovation ....
    operational 227
    product and service 227

Index

strategic 227
    management 227
integration logic 22-23, 171
    cultural factors 107, 209
    cultural misalignment 125
    "Ia" organisations 247-248
    "Id" organisations 248
    leadership 147
    reinforcement of culture 120
    size, importance of 175-176
    strategic platform 80, 81
    trade-offs in strategic capability 84
internal business units
    customer, distinguished 42-44, 191
    shared services 189-191, 193
    similar strategic logics 191

J

Jung, Carl 19-20

L

leadership 7, 14-15, 19, 111-112, 131, 150-151, 210
    dangers 149-150, 151, 201
    definition 133-134
    diagnostic 253
    elitism 135-136, 150
    "followership" 138
    function and process 134, 150-151
    innovation, and 226-227
    lever for change 210-211
    management and 139, 151
    multiple concept 137, 151
    PADI logics and 144-149, 151
    qualities 134
    research 211
    self-awareness 140-141, 151
    strategic alignment, producing 143, 147
    strategic context, understanding 142
    visible behaviours 210
learning and development strategies .. xiv-xv, 199-200
levers for change 127, 131, 202-211
logics 22, 26
    dominant 24, 29
    PADI combinations 25-28, 85-86, 243-248

M

management innovation 223, 227
managing the future 228-230
market-based structure and design 180
market conditions 3
market foresight 65
market segmentation 57-62, 94-95
    distribution 60
marketing strategies 73-74
mass production 173
Myers-Briggs Type Indicator (MBTI) 21, 141

N

Napoleon 231
new normal 221-223
    regulation, and 221
    internet, and 221
    transaction costs, and 221
    low cost entry, and 221
    conflicts, and 221
    structures, and 221
    strategic alignment, and 233

O

operating environment 7-9, 15, 19
    diagnostic 250
    understanding 35-38, 143
operational innovation 227
organisation
    culture *see* culture
    design 153-154, 222-226
    differentiation 171
    flexibility 163-164
    framework for change 212
    history of 115, 131
    integration 171
    risk, managing 155-156, 160
    size, importance of 166, 174-177, 192
    structure 2-3, 154, 156-158

organisation design 222-226
    questioning 222
    approaches to 223
    standardisation 223
    specialisation 223
    aligning 223
    hierarchy of 224
    planning and control 224
    rewards 224
    principles of 224-225
outsourcing 188, 193

P

PADI model 23-29, 195, 207-209
    combinations 25-28, 85-86, 243-248
    communication of customer needs 56-57, 62
    cultural misalignment 121-125
    culture, defining 102-107
    customer archetypes 52-55, 62
    ideal types 243-248
    leadership and 144-149, 151
    strategy and 76-81
    uncertainty in design and 168-170
partner 39-40, 44
performance management and reward .. 11-13, 113,
                128-130, 160, 205, 207, 217
policy implementation 11
positioning strategies .... xiv-xv
pragmatism logic 22-23, 30-31
    cultural factors 104, 209
    cultural misalignment 122
    leadership 145
    "Pa" organisations 245
    "Pd" organisations 244-245
    reinforcement of culture 117
    strategic platform 77, 81
    trade-offs in strategic capability 84
process
    structure and 161-163, 180, 192
    view of leadership 134-135, 150-151
product and service innovation 227
product-based structure and design 180

prospector organisation 164, 237
psychology 5-6
    change of 198

Q

quality
    outsourcing and 188, 193

R

reactor organisation 164, 237
research
    leaders, by 211
    role of 9, 54-55
resource
    configuration 154, 158
    focus 85
risk, managing 155-156, 160

S

scenario planning xiv
self-awareness 140-141, 151
Service Level Agreements (SLAs) 42-44
shared services 189-191, 193
shareholder 39
    expectations 8, 37, 63
size, organisational 166, 174-177, 192
staff 114
    autonomy and empowerment 2-3, 113,
                128, 205-207, 217
    climate 100
    control 129, 205-207, 217
    needs and capabilities 3, 113, 198
    performance and reward 11-13, 113, 128-130,
                160, 205, 207, 217
    training 12-13, 112-113, 131, 199-200
stakeholder 39
    customer, distinguished 41-42
strategic alignment 218-219
    creating 196-197
    culture, and 93-94, 102
    designing 153-154
    diagnostic 249-254

effective management and 16-17, 195
leadership producing 143, 147
misalignment, potential for 200-201
new normal, and 233
strategic fit 235-237
theory 235-241
strategic innovation 227
strategy 7, 9-11, 15, 19, 89
    balance or focus 73-74
    business 72-73, 183-184, 193
    change, setting 218
    choice 71-72, 165, 178-179, 182-183, 192
    competitive advantage 82-83, 89, 238-240
    corporate 72-73, 183-184, 193
    culture, alignment with 93-94, 102
    diagnostic 251
    effective 88-89
    functional 72-73
    intended 9
    lever for change 202-205
    PADI logics 76-81
    realised 9
    types 76-77
subsidiarity 185-186, 192
supplier, role of 188

T

team structures 2, 22-23, 80-81, 84, 107, 120, 125, 156-158
technology 3, 8, 37, 63, 131, 166, 171-174, 192
Total Quality Management
    processes (TQM) 161-163
trade-off ....
    importance of 50-51, 54-55, 74-75
    strategy and 82-89
training and development 12-13, 112-113, 131, 199-200
"trait" theory 1-4
"twin citizenship" 185-186, 193

U

uncertainty 166-170, 192, 229
    technology 171-173, 192
underlying assumptions 98
"uniqueness paradox" 20
unit production 173

V

value-adding 187-188, 193, 204
values and beliefs 97-98
vision statements 214-215
Von Clausewitz 231

About the Authors

Dr Norman Chorn is a strategy and organisation development practitioner with experience in Australia, UK, New Zealand and South Africa. After leaving a leading consulting firm, Norman founded the Centre for Strategy Development, a strategy and research firm with affiliations in UK and North America.

He works in the areas of growth and resilience; organisation design and change; and the development of strategic leadership.

Norman has particular skills in the alignment of organisations with their markets and environments. He has developed a range of proprietary techniques and approaches to achieve this improvement in performance.

Norman has published widely in his field and has contributed to a range of journals and international conferences. His recent book, **Strategic Alignment**, has received wide acclaim in the management and business press. He is finalising a new book on **Growth and Resilience** in organisations and this is due for publication shortly.

He holds visiting and adjunct appointments at a number of leading Graduate Schools of Management, including Macquarie University Graduate School of Management (Australia), the University of Witwatersrand (South Africa) and the Gordon Institute of Business Science, University of Pretoria (South Africa).

Prior to his consulting career, Norman held a variety of senior management positions in the services and manufacturing sectors.

He has a BA (Economics and Sociology) from the University of Cape Town, a Postgraduate Diploma in Management, an MBA, and PhD from the University of Witwatersrand. He serves on the Advisory Board of the Australian Institute of Management (AIM) and is a member of the Australian Human Resources Institute.

norman.chorn@centstrat.com
www.centstrat.com

About the Author

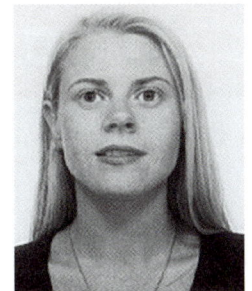

Dr Terri Hunter is a highly experienced facilitator and consultant in the areas of team and leadership development. Her major consultancy experience, both in Europe and Australia, was gained as a managing consultant for organisational psychology firms, SHL (UK) Ltd and Oxford Psychology Press.

She works in the areas of leadership and team development. She coaches senior executives and assists them in improving their personal effectiveness. She also has a major interest and research focus in the impact of personality on the performance of teams and groups.

She is both qualified and experienced in the use of a wide range of psychometric instruments, and has successfully run a large number of assessment and development centres.

Terri has lectured in organisational psychology and organisational behaviour at the universities of Glasgow, Strathclyde and Heriot Watt in Scotland, the University of Wollongong in Australia; and the University of Witwatersrand in South Africa. She has published widely on the subject of team effectiveness, and has presented papers at international conferences, including a keynote address for Meredith Belbin at a recent conference. She is currently researching in the area of strategic team development.

Terri has broad commercial experience, including the setting up and running of a successful chain of small pet shops on the west coast of Scotland.

Terri has a Masters degree in Psychology from Glasgow University (Scotland) and a PhD in Organisational Psychology from Strathclyde University (Scotland)

terri.hunter@centstrat.com
www.centstrat.com

Other Business Titles by Woodslane Press

Making Contracts Work
Author: Beverley Honig

Until now, there has been no book that sets out structures and strategies for sound supply contract management. This book does just this – and more: it aligns the science of sourcing supplies/suppliers with the art of smart contract management. And it does so based on the author's sound knowledge of global markets and keen understanding of commercial deal-making. Supply contract management is explained, using examples and case studies for illustration, as a 4-stage process so that all the layers of contract management can be peeled away to shape the best-fit supply chain.

RRP: $34.95 • **ISBN:** 9781921606885

Persuasion & Influence
Author: Bruce Hilliard

Moving away from the traditional hit-and-miss methods of persuasion, this book applies real science to fundamental business and life skills. From a business perspective, the very practical process described in this book allows anyone to rapidly create a truly persuasive message, that is very easy to understand, and highly influential. Additionally, the techniques can be used for almost any endeavour where you need to clearly convey an important message. This is the power of the universal principles described in this book.

RRP: $49.95 • **ISBN:** 9781921606663

Woodslane Press can be contacted by:
Email: info@woodslane.com.au • www.woodslaneonline.com.au
Phone: (02) 9970 5111 • Fax: (02) 9970 5002

Other Business Titles by Woodslane Press

Anatomy of a Business Plan

Author: Linda Pinson

What does it take to succeed in starting and running a small business? For expert guidance to take advantage of powerful business-building opportunities, the Australian edition of the bestselling *Anatomy of a Business Plan* offers step-by-step, proven advice. Updated with the latest changes affecting small business, this edition also includes a new resource section to help businesses research financial and marketing information. Three complete sample business plans, along with the blank forms to create a plan, make this a hands-on, user-friendly guide.

RRP: $29.99 • **ISBN:** 9781875889952

Get That Government Job

Author: Dawn Richards

Are you feeling overwhelmed with the whole process of applying for a government or private sector job? Here's an easy way to understand the requirements of the position and write your own powerful application using proven marketing strategies that 'sell' your skills to the employer. Answering the selection criteria is easy when you know how. This book takes you through the application process step by step and provides dozens of examples from a wide range of occupations and industries.

RRP: $29.95 • **ISBN:** 9781921606120

Woodslane Press can be contacted by:

Email: info@woodslane.com.au • www.woodslaneonline.com.au
Phone: (02) 9970 5111 • Fax: (02) 9970 5002

Strategic Alignment

Other Business Titles by Woodslane Press

Mastering Incoming Sales Calls
Author: Nigel Allan

Every time someone calls a business they have chosen that organisation as a possible supplier of something they want. Each incoming call is not just a possible customer, but a probable customer. Converting them into sales can be easy, but only if you manage the calls properly! This book focuses exclusively on the hitherto largely ignored area of dealing with incoming calls, and dealing with them in a way that will allow business owners, managers and sales staff to get face-to-face opportunities to sell their products. It includes step-by-step examples and case studies to show exactly how to become a `Phone Master'. The reader will be able to create and follow presentations, and see why up to 96% of the top salespeople in the world use a planned presentation when using the telephone.

RRP: $29.99 • **ISBN:** 9781921203800

Hiring & Firing
Author: John Grant

This book deals with the complex issues of Australian employment law in a straightforward and matter of fact way. All the issues that come up in the daily process of running a business are presented in the language of the business owner. Supported by templates for letters and contracts ready to download and use on the accompanying CD, this book will keep owners and managers out of the employment tribunal and focused on running their businesses. John Grant, cut his teeth in the Arbitration and Conciliation commission on behalf of the Australian Workers Union. Combining his legal practice with journalism he has focused on the issues he understands best.

RRP: $39.95 • **ISBN:** 9781875889846

Woodslane Press can be contacted by:
Email: info@woodslane.com.au • www.woodslaneonline.com.au
Phone: (02) 9970 5111 • Fax: (02) 9970 5002

Other Business Titles by Woodslane Press

How to be a Successful Consultant

Author: Don Matlock

Written in an easy-to-read style, this book is suitable for anyone who operates as a consultant. It contains strategies and techniques for increased success by focusing on key topics such as: self-promotion, communication, building credibility and building and maintaining relationships. If you have decided to become an independent consultant, you face two challenges: being good at what you do, and being good at bringing in the business. In the latter case you may need a very different set of skills: knowing how to seek, obtain and serve clients. That's where this book comes in.

RRP: $29.99 • **ISBN:** 9781921203909

How to Sell Your Business

Author: Don Matlock

How To Sell Your Business is tailored primarily for the owners of small to medium sized businesses. It contains a route map of the main factors you need to be both aware of and to consider in contemplating the sale process. It offers clear vision and methodology through what can be a very complicated and stressful process. Drawing on twenty plus years of personal experience selling and consulting on the selling of businesses big and small, Don Matlock is the perfect guide to anyone entering this potential minefield. His book shows you how to value your business, present for sale, maximise the price, find a potential buyer, handle due diligence and sign a contract for sale among other aspects.

RRP: $29.95 • **ISBN:** 9781921203916

Woodslane Press can be contacted by:
Email: info@woodslane.com.au • www.woodslaneonline.com.au
Phone: (02) 9970 5111 • Fax: (02) 9970 5002

Strategic Alignment

Feedback and Registration

We do hope that you have found this book useful, but we know that nothing in this world is perfect and your suggestions for improving future editions would be much appreciated.

Even if you have no comment on this current edition but would like to register, you will be sent occasional information on pertinent new books (both printed and those new to e-format) and will also be sent free pdf update notes as and when they become necessary for this edition.

Your name: _____

Your address or email address: _____
_____

Your contact phone (optional): _____

What you most liked about Strategic Alignment: _____
_____
_____

What you least liked about the book: _____
_____
_____

Please tick below and return this form (or simply email us the salient details) if you would like to be kept informed of Woodslane's products and services:

☐ pdf update notes for this book
☐ notifications of new editions of this book
☐ details of other business books published by Woodslane Press
☐ details of other business books distributed by Woodslane
☐ details of other computer-user books distributed by Woodslane

Woodslane Press can be contacted by:
Email: info@woodslane.com.au • www.woodslaneonline.com.au
Phone: (02) 9970 5111 • Fax: (02) 9970 5002